# Air Fryer Cookbook UK

**365**

Delicious Recipes for Beginners and Advanced Users.
Crunchy Meals for Your Family and Friends.
Family Meals for Fry, Bake, Grill and Roast.

**Julia Ross**

## All Rights Reserved:

The content contained within this book may not be reproduced, duplicated, or transmitted without direct written permission from the author or the publisher. Under no circumstances will any blame or legal responsibility be held against the publisher, or author, for any damages, reparation, or monetary loss due to the information contained within this book, either directly or indirectly.

Legal Notice: This book is copyright protected. It is only for personal use. You cannot amend, distribute, sell, use, quote or paraphrase any part, or the content within this book, without the consent of the author or publisher.

## Disclaimer Notice:

Please note the information contained within this document is for educational and entertainment purposes only. All effort has been executed to present accurate, up to date, reliable, complete information. No warranties of any kind are declared or implied. Readers acknowledge that the author is not engaged in the rendering of legal, financial, medical, or professional advice. The content within this book has been derived from various sources. Please consult a licensed professional before attempting any techniques outlined in this book. By reading this document, the reader agrees that under no circumstances is the author responsible for any losses, direct or indirect, that are incurred as a result of the use of the information contained within this document, including, but not limited to, errors, omissions, or inaccuracies.

# Table of Contents

**Table of Contents** ..................................................... 3

**Introduction** ............................................................. 7
- How air frying works ............................................. 7
- Using Your Air Fryer ............................................. 7
- 9 Benefits of Air Fryer Machine ........................... 7
- Caring for Your Air Fryer ...................................... 8
- Cleaning your air fryer .......................................... 8
- Storing your air fryer ............................................. 8
- Know Your Appliance ........................................... 8

**Desserts And Sweets** ............................................. 9
- Cheesecake Wontons ........................................... 9
- Giant Oatmeal–peanut Butter Cookie ................. 9
- Annie's Chocolate Chunk Hazelnut Cookies .... 10
- Date Oat Cookies ................................................ 10
- Oreo-coated Peanut Butter Cups ...................... 10
- White Chocolate Cranberry Blondies ................ 11
- Carrot-oat Cake Muffins ..................................... 11
- Lemon Iced Donut Balls ..................................... 11
- Giant Buttery Chocolate Chip Cookie ............... 11
- Rustic Berry Layer Cake ..................................... 12
- S'mores Pockets ................................................. 12
- Magic Giant Chocolate Cookies ........................ 12
- Dark Chocolate Peanut Butter S'mores ............ 13
- Orange Gooey Butter Cake ............................... 13
- Chocolate Cake ................................................... 14
- Baked Apple Crisp .............................................. 14
- Struffoli ................................................................. 14
- Gingerbread ........................................................ 15
- Apple Crisp ......................................................... 15
- Brownies After Dark ........................................... 15
- Cinnamon Tortilla Crisps .................................... 16
- Orange-chocolate Cake ..................................... 16
- Fried Oreos ......................................................... 16
- Fudgy Brownie Cake .......................................... 16
- Peanut Butter S'mores ....................................... 17
- Coconut Cream Roll-ups .................................... 17
- Pumpkin Brownies .............................................. 17
- Giant Buttery Oatmeal Cookie ........................... 18
- Pecan-oat Filled Apples ..................................... 18
- Strawberry Donut Bites ...................................... 18

**Sandwiches And Burgers Recipes** ..................... 19
- Chicken Gyros .................................................... 19
- Lamb Burgers ..................................................... 19
- Perfect Burgers .................................................. 19
- Thanksgiving Turkey Sandwiches ..................... 20
- Dijon Thyme Burgers ......................................... 20
- Sausage And Pepper Heros .............................. 21
- Inside Out Cheeseburgers ................................. 21
- Inside-out Cheeseburgers ................................. 21
- Reuben Sandwiches ........................................... 22
- Chili Cheese Dogs .............................................. 22
- Chicken Club Sandwiches ................................. 22
- Eggplant Parmesan Subs ................................... 23
- Asian Glazed Meatballs ..................................... 23
- Best-ever Roast Beef Sandwiches ................... 24
- Crunchy Falafel Balls ......................................... 24

**Appetizers And Snacks** ........................................ 25
- Cheesy Green Pitas ........................................... 25
- Pork Pot Stickers With Yum Yum Sauce ......... 25
- Beet Chips With Guacamole ............................. 26
- Kale Chips ........................................................... 26
- Country Wings .................................................... 26
- Crunchy Parmesan Edamame ........................... 26
- Curly Kale Chips With Greek Sauce ................ 27
- Hot Nachos With Chile Salsa ............................ 27
- Mozzarella En Carrozza With Puttanesca Sauce ........ 27
- Eggs In Avocado Halves .................................... 28
- Curried Pickle Chips ........................................... 28
- Russian Pierogi With Cheese Dip ..................... 28
- Onion Puffs ......................................................... 28
- Fried Green Tomatoes ....................................... 29
- Cauliflower "tater" Tots ...................................... 29
- Enchilada Chicken Dip ....................................... 30
- Chili Corn On The Cob ...................................... 30
- Buffalo Wings ..................................................... 30
- No-guilty Spring Rolls ........................................ 30
- Corn Tortilla Chips .............................................. 31
- Crunchy Lobster Bites ....................................... 31
- Buffalo Cauliflower ............................................. 31
- Baba Ghanouj ..................................................... 32
- Skinny Fries ........................................................ 32
- Roasted Red Pepper Dip ................................... 32
- Canadian-inspired Waffle Poutine .................... 32
- Cheeseburger Slider Pockets ............................ 33
- Charred Shishito Peppers .................................. 33
- Sausage And Cheese Rolls ............................... 33
- Mustard Greens Chips With Curried Sauce .... 34

Piri Piri Chicken Wings ........................................... 34
Cherry Chipotle Bbq Chicken Wings ..................... 34
Sweet And Salty Snack Mix ................................... 34
Homemade Pretzel Bites ........................................ 35
Crispy Wontons ...................................................... 35

## Bread And Breakfast ........................................................................................................................ 36

Cheesy Egg Bites ................................................... 36
Carrot Muffins ........................................................ 36
Pumpkin Loaf ......................................................... 36
Smoked Salmon Croissant Sandwich ..................... 36
Walnut Pancake ..................................................... 37
Parsley Egg Scramble With Cottage Cheese ......... 37
Green Strata .......................................................... 37
Apple-cinnamon-walnut Muffins ............................. 37
Spiced Apple Roll-ups ........................................... 38
Lemon-blueberry Morning Bread ........................... 38
Spring Vegetable Omelet ....................................... 38
Peppered Maple Bacon Knots ............................... 39
White Wheat Walnut Bread .................................... 39
Hashbrown Potatoes Lyonnaise ............................ 39
Egg & Bacon Toasts .............................................. 39
Almond Cranberry Granola .................................... 40
Chorizo Sausage & Cheese Balls .......................... 40
Chocolate Chip Banana Muffins ............................. 40
Maple-peach And Apple Oatmeal .......................... 40
Viking Toast ........................................................... 41
Morning Loaded Potato Skins ................................ 41
Vegetarian Quinoa Cups ........................................ 41
Eggless Mung Bean Tart ........................................ 41
Coconut Mini Tarts ................................................. 42
Tri-color Frittata ..................................................... 42
Blueberry French Toast Sticks ............................... 42
Egg & Bacon Pockets ............................................ 42
Matcha Granola ..................................................... 43
Easy Caprese Flatbread ........................................ 43
Farmers Market Quiche ......................................... 43

## Poultry Recipes ................................................................................................................................. 44

Spicy Black Bean Turkey Burgers With Cumin-avocado Spread ........................................................... 44
Chicken & Fruit Biryani .......................................... 44
Chicken Fried Steak With Gravy ............................ 44
Gluten-free Nutty Chicken Fingers ......................... 45
Yummy Maple-mustard Chicken Kabobs ............... 45
Saucy Chicken Thighs ........................................... 46
Chicken Nuggets ................................................... 46
Chicken Cutlets With Broccoli Rabe And Roasted Peppers ............................................ 46
Sticky Drumsticks .................................................. 47
Chicken Breasts Wrapped In Bacon ...................... 47
Kale & Rice Chicken Rolls ..................................... 47
Fancy Chicken Piccata .......................................... 47
Japanese-style Turkey Meatballs .......................... 48
Jerk Turkey Meatballs ............................................ 48
Cornflake Chicken Nuggets ................................... 48
Chicken Cordon Bleu Patties ................................. 48
Simple Buttermilk Fried Chicken ............................ 49
Indian-inspired Chicken Skewers ........................... 49
Buttery Chicken Legs ............................................. 49
Easy Turkey Meatballs ........................................... 50
Sesame Orange Chicken ....................................... 50
Fiesta Chicken Plate .............................................. 50
Indian Chicken Tandoori ........................................ 51
Spinach & Turkey Meatballs .................................. 51
Spiced Mexican Stir-fried Chicken ......................... 51
Enchilada Chicken Quesadillas ............................. 51
Mustardy Chicken Bites ......................................... 52
Bacon & Chicken Flatbread ................................... 52
Creole Chicken Drumettes ..................................... 52
Thai Chicken Drumsticks ....................................... 52
Chicken Burgers With Blue Cheese Sauce ........... 53
Southwest Gluten-free Turkey Meatloaf ................ 53
Satay Chicken Skewers ......................................... 53
Teriyaki Chicken Bites ........................................... 54
Moroccan-style Chicken Strips .............................. 54
Italian-inspired Chicken Pizzadillas ....................... 54
Spinach And Feta Stuffed Chicken Breasts ........... 54
Farmer´s Fried Chicken ......................................... 55
Harissa Chicken Wings .......................................... 55
Greek Chicken Wings ............................................ 55
Chicken Skewers ................................................... 56
Tortilla Crusted Chicken Breast ............................. 56
Fantasy Sweet Chili Chicken Strips ....................... 56
Simple Salsa Chicken Thighs ................................ 56
Guajillo Chile Chicken Meatballs ........................... 57
Parmesan Crusted Chicken Cordon Bleu ............. 57
Crispy Chicken Tenders ........................................ 57
Chicken Wellington ................................................ 58
Ranch Chicken Tortillas ......................................... 58
Chicken Salad With White Dressing ...................... 58

## Fish And Seafood Recipes ............................................................................................................... 59

Crispy Sweet-and-sour Cod Fillets ........................ 59
Miso-rubbed Salmon Fillets ................................... 59
Herb-crusted Sole .................................................. 60
Sweet & Spicy Swordfish Kebabs .......................... 60
Stuffed Shrimp ....................................................... 60
Almond-crusted Fish .............................................. 60
Tex-mex Fish Tacos ............................................... 61
Easy Asian-style Tuna ........................................... 61

| | |
|---|---|
| Fish Sticks For Grown-ups .................................... 61 | Feta & Shrimp Pita ........................................... 68 |
| Crunchy And Buttery Cod With Ritz® Cracker Crust ... 62 | Catfish Nuggets ................................................ 68 |
| Lightened-up Breaded Fish Filets ........................... 62 | Restaurant-style Breaded Shrimp ....................... 68 |
| Mediterranean Sea Scallops .................................. 62 | Crab Stuffed Salmon Roast ................................ 69 |
| Hot Calamari Rings ............................................. 62 | Shrimp Al Pesto ................................................ 69 |
| Piña Colada Shrimp ............................................. 63 | Korean-style Fried Calamari ............................... 69 |
| Tuna Patties With Dill Sauce ................................. 63 | Family Fish Nuggets With Tartar Sauce .............. 69 |
| Shrimp ................................................................ 63 | Lime Flaming Halibut ........................................ 70 |
| Halibut Quesadillas .............................................. 64 | Maple Balsamic Glazed Salmon ......................... 70 |
| Honey Pecan Shrimp ........................................... 64 | Pecan-crusted Tilapia ........................................ 70 |
| Saucy Shrimp ...................................................... 64 | Curried Sweet-and-spicy Scallops ...................... 70 |
| Mom´s Tuna Melt Toastie ..................................... 65 | Home-style Fish Sticks ...................................... 71 |
| Mahi-mahi "burrito" Fillets .................................... 65 | Chinese Firecracker Shrimp ............................... 71 |
| Yummy Salmon Burgers With Salsa Rosa ............. 65 | Coconut Jerk Shrimp ......................................... 71 |
| Mediterranean Salmon Burgers ............................ 66 | Garlic-butter Lobster Tails ................................. 71 |
| The Best Oysters Rockefeller ............................... 66 | Mojito Fish Tacos .............................................. 72 |
| Baltimore Crab Cakes .......................................... 66 | Rich Salmon Burgers With Broccoli Slaw ........... 72 |
| Fish Cakes .......................................................... 67 | Tuna Nuggets In Hoisin Sauce ........................... 72 |
| Breaded Parmesan Perch ..................................... 67 | Peppery Tilapia Roulade .................................... 72 |
| Fish-in-chips ....................................................... 67 | Cheesy Tuna Tower .......................................... 73 |
| Teriyaki Salmon .................................................. 68 | Coconut Shrimp With Plum Sauce ..................... 73 |

## Beef, pork & Lamb Recipes ..................................................................................................................... 73

| | |
|---|---|
| Pork Cutlets With Almond-lemon Crust ................ 73 | Santorini Steak Bowls ....................................... 82 |
| Boneless Ribeyes ................................................ 74 | Meatloaf With Tangy Tomato Glaze ................... 83 |
| Kielbasa Sausage With Pierogies And Caramelized Onions 74 | Grilled Pork & Bell Pepper Salad ....................... 83 |
| Almond And Sun-dried Tomato Crusted Pork Chops ........ 74 | Cheesy Mushroom-stuffed Pork Loins ............... 83 |
| Premium Steakhouse Salad .................................. 75 | Kawaii Pork Roast ............................................. 84 |
| Mongolian Beef ................................................... 75 | Lamb Chops ..................................................... 84 |
| Cinnamon-stick Kofta Skewers ............................. 76 | Honey Mesquite Pork Chops ............................. 84 |
| Indian Fry Bread Tacos ........................................ 76 | Crispy Lamb Shoulder Chops ............................ 84 |
| Pork & Beef Egg Rolls ......................................... 76 | Horseradish Mustard Pork Chops ...................... 85 |
| Aromatic Pork Tenderloin .................................... 77 | Citrus Pork Lettuce Wraps ................................. 85 |
| Corned Beef Hash ............................................... 77 | Easy Tex-mex Chimichangas ............................. 85 |
| Paprika Fried Beef ............................................... 77 | Lollipop Lamb Chops With Mint Pesto ............... 85 |
| Beef & Barley Stuffed Bell Peppers ...................... 78 | Homemade Pork Gyoza .................................... 86 |
| Herby Lamb Chops ............................................. 78 | Fried Spam ....................................................... 86 |
| Red Curry Flank Steak ........................................ 78 | Peppered Steak Bites ........................................ 86 |
| Lamb Chops In Currant Sauce ............................. 78 | Crunchy Fried Pork Loin Chops ......................... 87 |
| Italian Meatballs .................................................. 79 | German-style Pork Patties ................................. 87 |
| Stuffed Pork Chops ............................................. 79 | Chile Con Carne Galette .................................... 87 |
| Calzones South Of The Border ............................. 79 | Fusion Tender Flank Steak ................................ 88 |
| Indonesian Pork Satay ......................................... 80 | Mustard-crusted Rib-eye ................................... 88 |
| Tonkatsu ............................................................. 80 | Stuffed Cabbage Rolls ....................................... 88 |
| Traditional Moo Shu Pork Lettuce Wraps .............. 80 | Meat Loaves ..................................................... 88 |
| Pepper Steak ...................................................... 81 | Pork Tenderloin With Apples & Celery ............... 89 |
| Blackberry Bbq Glazed Country-style Ribs ........... 81 | Bbq Back Ribs .................................................. 89 |
| Exotic Pork Skewers ........................................... 81 | Mini Meatloaves With Pancetta .......................... 89 |
| Kochukaru Pork Lettuce Cups ............................. 82 | Suwon Pork Meatballs ...................................... 89 |
| Skirt Steak With Horseradish Cream .................... 82 | Minted Lamb Chops .......................................... 90 |
| Greek Pork Chops ............................................... 82 | |

## Vegetarians Recipes ................................................................................................................................. 90

| | |
|---|---|
| Egg Rolls ............................................................ 90 | Cheddar Stuffed Portobellos With Salsa ............ 90 |

| | |
|---|---|
| Crunchy Rice Paper Samosas | 91 |
| Grilled Cheese Sandwich | 91 |
| Quinoa Green Pizza | 91 |
| Sweet Corn Bread | 91 |
| Cheesy Eggplant Lasagna | 92 |
| Tex-mex Potatoes With Avocado Dressing | 92 |
| Vegetable Couscous | 92 |
| Easy Cheese & Spinach Lasagna | 93 |
| Mushroom, Zucchini And Black Bean Burgers | 93 |
| Balsamic Caprese Hasselback | 93 |
| Creamy Broccoli & Mushroom Casserole | 94 |
| Pineapple & Veggie Souvlaki | 94 |
| Cheddar Bean Taquitos | 94 |
| Kale & Lentils With Crispy Onions | 94 |
| Colorful Vegetable Medley | 94 |
| Stuffed Portobellos | 95 |
| Mushroom Bolognese Casserole | 95 |
| Fake Shepherd´s Pie | 95 |
| Tortilla Pizza Margherita | 96 |
| Lentil Fritters | 96 |
| Two-cheese Grilled Sandwiches | 96 |
| Roasted Vegetable Thai Green Curry | 96 |
| Tofu & Spinach Lasagna | 97 |
| Chive Potato Pierogi | 97 |
| Spicy Vegetable And Tofu Shake Fry | 97 |
| Spaghetti Squash And Kale Fritters With Pomodoro Sauce | 98 |
| Thyme Meatless Patties | 98 |
| Parmesan Portobello Mushroom Caps | 99 |
| Effortless Mac `n´ Cheese | 99 |
| Thyme Lentil Patties | 99 |
| Charred Cauliflower Tacos | 99 |
| Gorgeous Jalapeño Poppers | 100 |
| Italian Stuffed Bell Peppers | 100 |
| Basic Fried Tofu | 100 |
| Falafel | 100 |
| Rainbow Quinoa Patties | 101 |
| Smoked Paprika Sweet Potato Fries | 101 |
| Mushroom Lasagna | 101 |
| Cheddar-bean Flautas | 102 |
| Vietnamese Gingered Tofu | 102 |
| Garlicky Roasted Mushrooms | 102 |
| Vegetarian Eggplant "pizzas" | 102 |
| Meatless Kimchi Bowls | 103 |

**Vegetable Side Dishes Recipes ...... 103**

| | |
|---|---|
| Fried Eggplant Slices | 103 |
| Street Corn | 104 |
| Roasted Broccoli And Red Bean Salad | 104 |
| Spiced Pumpkin Wedges | 104 |
| Buttery Stuffed Tomatoes | 104 |
| Air-fried Potato Salad | 105 |
| Smashed Fried Baby Potatoes | 105 |
| Veggie Fritters | 105 |
| Hot Okra Wedges | 106 |
| Mushrooms | 106 |
| Fried Eggplant Balls | 106 |
| Double Cheese-broccoli Tots | 107 |
| Sweet Potato Fries | 107 |
| Green Peas With Mint | 107 |
| Home Fries | 107 |
| Sweet Potato Puffs | 107 |
| Basic Corn On The Cob | 108 |
| Gorgonzola Stuffed Mushrooms | 108 |
| Rosemary New Potatoes | 108 |
| Hawaiian Brown Rice | 108 |
| Roasted Fennel Salad | 108 |
| Perfect Broccolini | 109 |
| Classic Stuffed Shells | 109 |
| Asparagus Wrapped In Pancetta | 109 |
| Fried Green Tomatoes With Sriracha Mayo | 109 |
| Crispy Cauliflower Puffs | 110 |
| Pancetta Mushroom & Onion Sautée | 110 |
| Almond Green Beans | 110 |
| Summer Vegetables With Balsamic Drizzle, Goat Cheese And Basil | 111 |
| Simple Peppered Carrot Chips | 111 |
| Roasted Baby Carrots | 111 |
| Crispy Noodle Salad | 111 |
| Cheesy Potato Skins | 112 |
| Parmesan Asparagus | 112 |
| Blistered Shishito Peppers | 112 |
| Buttery Rolls | 113 |
| Corn On The Cob | 113 |
| Brown Rice And Goat Cheese Croquettes | 113 |
| Easy Parmesan Asparagus | 114 |
| Dijon Artichoke Hearts | 114 |
| Succulent Roasted Peppers | 114 |
| Homemade Potato Puffs | 114 |
| Rosemary Roasted Potatoes With Lemon | 115 |
| Beet Fries | 115 |
| Pecorino Dill Muffins | 115 |
| Lemony Fried Fennel Slices | 115 |
| Herbed Baby Red Potato Hasselback | 115 |
| Layered Mixed Vegetables | 116 |
| Spicy Bean Stuffed Potatoes | 116 |
| Roasted Brussels Sprouts With Bacon | 116 |
| Sicilian Arancini | 116 |
| Teriyaki Tofu With Spicy Mayo | 117 |
| Broccoli Au Gratin | 117 |
| Buttered Brussels Sprouts | 117 |
| Savory Brussels Sprouts | 117 |

**RECIPE INDEX ...... 118**

# Introduction

## How air frying works

Have you ever seen one of those money machines, where someone steps inside a cylinder, closes the door, and air starts flowing up from the bottom with money flying through the air?

An air fryer is kind of like one of those money machines. When you put your food into the air fryer and close it, hot air circulates around the food and begins to cook it. The temperature of the air fryer and the type of food you're cooking will help determine the amount of time you need to cook your recipe.

## Using Your Air Fryer

Each make and model of air fryer has its own instructions, but air fryers don't require extensive knowledge to operate. We recommend that you start by reading the manual that came with your air fryer and getting to know your particular machine. With that said, here are a few basic steps that work for all machines:

1. Clean the air fryer basket and accessories (if they came with your air fryer) with hot soapy water and dry with a dish towel before use.
2. Plug in your air fryer and preheat it.
3. This allows the machine time to get to temperature before you actually put the recipe inside.
4. If applicable, select Air Fry as the function.
5. Some models have a variety of selections to choose from such as Dehydrate, Roast, and so on.
6. Place your food on the wire rack or trivet, securely seal or close the drawer, and begin to air fry.
7. Check the food as applicable, following the recipe instructions.
8. When cooking completes, press Cancel and unplug the air fryer.

## 9 Benefits of Air Fryer Machine

### 1) It makes delicious food.

When you bake food in regular ovens (especially not convention ovens), you are often left with uneven results, with some parts burnt and other parts undercooked. The mechanism of Air Fryers described above allows hot air to circulate all around the food, maximizing surface area-to-heat ratio and allowing for perfectly even crispiness and crunchiness. While an Air Fryer won't taste exactly like if you used a traditional deep fryer, we really love the end result of each recipe we've tried so far.

### 2) It is a healthier option

Love the taste of fried food but not the way it makes you feel afterwards (for instance Zoe tends to get heartburn with fried food)? Are you disappointed with the end result when you try the oven-roasted version of the same recipe? If yes to these questions, then an Air Fryer might be the solution!

You can usually get away with using little-to-no oil when cooking with an Air Fryer, which can cut calories. Furthermore, one study showed that compared to traditional frying methods, using an air fryer reduces acrylamide (a compound associated with certain types of cancer) by up to 90%.

### 3) It is time and energy efficient

With their compact size and efficient circulation of hot air, Air Fryers out-compete your oven. With most recipes only needing 8-20 minutes of cooking, Air Fryers reduce cooking time by up to 25% (they also only need a fraction of the time to preheat, unlike your oven), saving you both time and energy.

### 4) They are easy to clean

With removable parts, nonstick materials, and most being dishwasher-safe, cleaning your air fryer is no hassle at all! And compared to the grease that coats your kitchen walls after deep frying foods, an Air Fryer produces no mess.

### 5) They are versatile and can make all kinds of recipes

See below for a sample of all of the different types of food you can make using an Air Fryer. From meat to vegetables to even pizza, we've been able to incorporate air frying into a ton of our meal preparations.

### 6) Many have different modes, allowing different types of cooking

Not only used for frying foods, an Air Fryer can also be used for reheating leftovers, thawing frozen food, and much, much more. Ours lets you change the settings to "air fry", "roast", "dehydrate", and "reheat". It's up to you to experiment!

### 7) They come in all different shapes and sizes

It's true that they take up some counter space. But there's an Air Fryer of every size to fit your needs. If you mostly cook for one or two people, you can get away with 2 to 3 quart sized Air Fryers. If you usually cook for a family of 3-5, consider 5 to 6 quart ones. But generally, air fryers between 3 to 5 quarts are versatile enough for most types and quantities of cooking.

### 8) They make for a great gift

What a perfect gift for the budding home chef?! I got ours for Zoe for Christmas. But whether its for a birthday, wedding registry, or any other special occasion, an Air Fryer makes for an ideal long-lasting and useful present.

### 9) They let you join the Air Fryer community

With niche Air Fryer blogs to Air Fryer recipe books, buying one of these lets you drastically expand your culinary repertoire and connect with a whole new community of home chefs.

## Caring for Your Air Fryer

You don't have to invest in any specific detergent or cleanser to keep your air fryer smelling like new. Use this section as your guide to keep your new kitchen appliance in tip-top shape so you can use it for years to come.

## Cleaning your air fryer

Cleaning your air fryer is actually a really simple task. With a little elbow grease, some regular dish detergent, and hot water, your air fryer will come back to life, even with the toughest of buildup.

We've experimented with various makes and models and had our fair share of epic disasters in our air fryers (think: cream cheese melted with panko all over the baking tray), but guess what? After letting the basket and/or tray cool, we were easily able to get the buildup off with a regular kitchen sponge and hot soapy water.

Plus, even when switching between seafood and a decadent dessert, the air fryer doesn't require a deep clean.

Wipe down the outside of your fryer after each use. A hot, soapy towel is all that's necessary. This helps get off any grease or food particles that may have latched on during cooking.

## Storing your air fryer

You can purchase a snazzy air fryer cover online, but this isn't necessary. We store our air fryers on the countertop because, well, we're writing a cookbook and we use them more frequently! Unfortunately, many models are too bulky for under-the-counter storage. Wherever you choose to store your air fryer, just be sure to put it in an area of your kitchen that isn't near your stovetop or oven so you don't get the residual grease from your day-to-day cooking building up on the outside of it.

## Know Your Appliance

First, and most important, read your appliance manual. All air fryers are not created equal. Features differ among models. Even timers work differently. Parts of some air fryers may be dishwasher safe, but you may have to hand-wash others. Any misuse of your air fryer or its parts could void the warranty. Read all safety information, and never use the machine in any way that violates the manufacturer's instructions for safe use. In addition to keeping you safe, your manual should provide details about your model's features and functions. Most of us hate reading instructions or manuals, but it's worth taking the time to understand how to use it. Sometimes that can make all the difference between frustration and success.

# Desserts And Sweets

## Cheesecake Wontons

Servings: 16
Cooking Time: 6 Minutes

**Ingredients:**
- ¼ cup Regular or low-fat cream cheese (not fat-free)
- 2 tablespoons Granulated white sugar
- 1½ tablespoons Egg yolk
- ¼ teaspoon Vanilla extract
- ⅛ teaspoon Table salt
- 1½ tablespoons All-purpose flour
- 16 Wonton wrappers (vegetarian, if a concern)
- Vegetable oil spray

**Directions:**
1. Preheat the air fryer to 400°F (205°C).
2. Using a flatware fork, mash the cream cheese, sugar, egg yolk, and vanilla in a small bowl until smooth. Add the salt and flour and continue mashing until evenly combined.
3. Set a wonton wrapper on a clean, dry work surface so that one corner faces you (so that it looks like a diamond on your work surface). Set 1 teaspoon of the cream cheese mixture in the middle of the wrapper but just above a horizontal line that would divide the wrapper in half. Dip your clean finger in water and run it along the edges of the wrapper. Fold the corner closest to you up and over the filling, lining it up with the corner farthest from you, thereby making a stuffed triangle. Press gently to seal. Wet the two triangle tips nearest you, then fold them up and together over the filling. Gently press together to seal and fuse. Set aside and continue making more stuffed wontons, 11 more for the small batch, 15 more for the medium batch, or 23 more for the large one.
4. Lightly coat the stuffed wrappers on all sides with vegetable oil spray. Set them with the fused corners up in the basket with as much air space between them as possible. Air-fry undisturbed for 6 minutes, or until golden brown and crisp.
5. Gently dump the contents of the basket onto a wire rack. Cool for at least 5 minutes before serving.

## Giant Oatmeal–peanut Butter Cookie

Servings: 4
Cooking Time: 18 Minutes

**Ingredients:**
- 1 cup Rolled oats (not quick-cooking or steel-cut oats)
- ½ cup All-purpose flour
- ½ teaspoon Ground cinnamon
- ½ teaspoon Baking soda
- ⅓ cup Packed light brown sugar
- ¼ cup Solid vegetable shortening
- 2 tablespoons Natural-style creamy peanut butter
- 3 tablespoons Granulated white sugar
- 2 tablespoons (or 1 small egg, well beaten) Pasteurized egg substitute, such as Egg Beaters
- ⅓ cup Roasted, salted peanuts, chopped
- Baking spray

**Directions:**
1. Preheat the air fryer to 350°F (175°C).
2. Stir the oats, flour, cinnamon, and baking soda in a bowl until well combined.
3. Using an electric hand mixer at medium speed, beat the brown sugar, shortening, peanut butter, granulated white sugar, and egg substitute or egg (as applicable) until smooth and creamy, about 3 minutes, scraping down the inside of the bowl occasionally.
4. Scrape down and remove the beaters. Fold in the flour mixture and peanuts with a rubber spatula just until all the flour is moistened and the peanut bits are evenly distributed in the dough.
5. For a small air fryer, coat the inside of a 6-inch round cake pan with baking spray. For a medium air fryer, coat the inside of a 7-inch round cake pan with baking spray. And for a large air fryer, coat the inside of an 8-inch round cake pan with baking spray. Scrape and gently press the dough into the prepared pan, spreading it into an even layer to the perimeter.
6. Set the pan in the basket and air-fry undisturbed for 18 minutes, or until well browned.
7. Transfer the pan to a wire rack and cool for 15 minutes. Loosen the cookie from the perimeter with a spatula, then invert the pan onto a cutting board and let the cookie come free. Remove the pan and reinvert the cookie onto the wire rack. Cool for 5 minutes more before slicing into wedges to serve.

# Annie's Chocolate Chunk Hazelnut Cookies

Servings: 24
Cooking Time: 12 Minutes
**Ingredients:**
- 1 cup butter, softened
- 1 cup brown sugar
- ½ cup granulated sugar
- 2 eggs, lightly beaten
- 1½ teaspoons vanilla extract
- 1½ cups all-purpose flour
- ½ cup rolled oats
- 1 teaspoon baking soda
- ½ teaspoon salt
- 2 cups chocolate chunks
- ½ cup toasted chopped hazelnuts

**Directions:**
1. Cream the butter and sugars together until light and fluffy using a stand mixer or electric hand mixer. Add the eggs and vanilla, and beat until well combined.
2. Combine the flour, rolled oats, baking soda and salt in a second bowl. Gradually add the dry ingredients to the wet ingredients with a wooden spoon or spatula. Stir in the chocolate chunks and hazelnuts until distributed throughout the dough.
3. Shape the cookies into small balls about the size of golf balls and place them on a baking sheet. Freeze the cookie balls for at least 30 minutes, or package them in as airtight a package as you can and keep them in your freezer.
4. When you're ready for a delicious snack or dessert, Preheat the air fryer to 350°F (175°C). Cut a piece of parchment paper to fit the number of cookies you are baking. Place the parchment down in the air fryer basket and place the frozen cookie ball or balls on top (remember to leave room for them to expand).
5. Air-fry the cookies at 350°F (175°C) for 12 minutes, or until they are done to your liking. Let them cool for a few minutes before enjoying your freshly baked cookie.

# Date Oat Cookies

Servings: 6
Cooking Time: 20 Minutes
**Ingredients:**
- ¼ cup butter, softened
- 2 ½ tbsp milk
- ½ cup sugar
- ½ tsp vanilla extract
- ½ tsp lemon zest
- ½ tsp ground cinnamon
- 3/4 cup flour
- ¼ tsp salt
- ¾ cup rolled oats
- ¼ tsp baking soda
- ¼ tsp baking powder
- 2 tbsp dates, chopped

**Directions:**
1. Use an electric beater to whip the butter until fluffy. Add the milk, sugar, lemon zest, and vanilla. Stir until well combined. Add the cinnamon, flour, salt, oats, baking soda, and baking powder in a separate bowl and stir. Add the dry mix to the wet mix and stir with a wooden spoon. Pour in the dates.
2. Preheat air fryer to 350°F (175°C). Drop tablespoonfuls of the batter onto a greased baking pan, leaving room in between each. Bake for 6 minutes or until light brown. Make all the cookies at once, or save the batter in the fridge for later. Let them cool and enjoy!

# Oreo-coated Peanut Butter Cups

Servings:8
Cooking Time: 4 Minutes
**Ingredients:**
- 8 Standard ¾-ounce peanut butter cups, frozen
- ⅓ cup All-purpose flour
- 2 Large egg white(s), beaten until foamy
- 16 Oreos or other creme-filled chocolate sandwich cookies, ground to crumbs in a food processor
- Vegetable oil spray

**Directions:**
1. Set up and fill three shallow soup plates or small pie plates on your counter: one for the flour, one for the beaten egg white(s), and one for the cookie crumbs.
2. Dip a frozen peanut butter cup in the flour, turning it to coat all sides. Shake off any excess, then set it in the beaten egg white(s). Turn it to coat all sides, then let any excess egg white slip back into the rest. Set the candy bar in the cookie crumbs. Turn to coat on all parts, even the sides. Dip the peanut butter cup back in the egg white(s) as before, then into the cookie crumbs as before, making sure you have a solid, even coating all around the cup. Set aside while you dip and coat the remaining cups.
3. When all the peanut butter cups are dipped and coated, lightly coat them on all sides with the vegetable oil spray. Set them on a plate and freeze while the air fryer heats.
4. Preheat the air fryer to 400°F (205°C).
5. Set the dipped cups wider side up in the basket with as much air space between them as possible. Air-fry undisturbed for 4 minutes, or until they feel soft but the coating is set.
6. Turn off the machine and remove the basket from it. Set aside the basket with the fried cups for 10 minutes. Use a nonstick-safe spatula to transfer the fried cups to a wire rack. Cool for at least another 5 minutes before serving.

## White Chocolate Cranberry Blondies

Servings: 6
Cooking Time: 18 Minutes
**Ingredients:**
- ⅓ cup butter
- ½ cup sugar
- 1 teaspoon vanilla extract
- 1 large egg
- 1 cup all-purpose flour
- ½ teaspoon baking powder
- ⅛ teaspoon salt
- ¼ cup dried cranberries
- ¼ cup white chocolate chips

**Directions:**
1. Preheat the air fryer to 320°F (160°C).
2. In a large bowl, cream the butter with the sugar and vanilla extract. Whisk in the egg and set aside.
3. In a separate bowl, mix the flour with the baking powder and salt. Then gently mix the dry ingredients into the wet. Fold in the cranberries and chocolate chips.
4. Liberally spray an oven-safe 7-inch springform pan with olive oil and pour the batter into the pan.
5. Cook for 17 minutes or until a toothpick inserted in the center comes out clean.
6. Remove and let cool 5 minutes before serving.

## Carrot-oat Cake Muffins

Servings: 4
Cooking Time: 20 Minutes
**Ingredients:**
- 3 tbsp butter, softened
- ¼ cup brown sugar
- 1 tbsp maple syrup
- 1 egg white
- ½ tsp vanilla extract
- 1/3 cup finely grated carrots
- ½ cup oatmeal
- 1/3 cup flour
- ½ tsp baking soda
- ¼ cup raisins

**Directions:**
1. Preheat air fryer to 350°F (175°C). Mix the butter, brown sugar, and maple syrup until smooth, then toss in the egg white, vanilla, and carrots. Whisk well and add the oatmeal, flour, baking soda, and raisins. Divide the mixture between muffin cups. Bake in the fryer for 8-10 minutes.

## Lemon Iced Donut Balls

Servings: 6
Cooking Time: 25 Minutes
**Ingredients:**
- 1 can jumbo biscuit dough
- 2 tsp lemon juice
- ½ cup icing sugar, sifted

**Directions:**
1. Preheat air fryer to 360°F (180°C). Divide the biscuit dough into 16 equal portions. Roll the dough into balls of 1½ inches thickness. Place the donut holes in the greased frying basket and Air Fry for 8 minutes, flipping once. Mix the icing sugar and lemon juice until smooth. Spread the icing over the top of the donuts. Leave to set a bit. Serve.

## Giant Buttery Chocolate Chip Cookie

Servings: 4
Cooking Time: 16 Minutes
**Ingredients:**
- ⅔ cup plus 1 tablespoon All-purpose flour
- ¼ teaspoon Baking soda
- ¼ teaspoon Table salt
- Baking spray (see the headnote)
- 4 tablespoons (¼ cup/½ stick) plus 1 teaspoon Butter, at room temperature
- ¼ cup plus 1 teaspoon Packed dark brown sugar
- 3 tablespoons plus 1 teaspoon Granulated white sugar
- 2½ tablespoons Pasteurized egg substitute, such as Egg Beaters
- ½ teaspoon Vanilla extract
- ¾ cup plus 1 tablespoon Semisweet or bittersweet chocolate chips

**Directions:**
1. Preheat the air fryer to 350°F (175°C) .
2. Whisk the flour, baking soda, and salt in a bowl until well combined.
3. For a small air fryer, coat the inside of a 6-inch round cake pan with baking spray. For a medium air fryer, coat the inside of a 7-inch round cake pan with baking spray. And for a large air fryer, coat the inside of an 8-inch round cake pan with baking spray.
4. Using a hand electric mixer at medium speed, beat the butter, brown sugar, and granulated white sugar in a bowl until smooth and thick, about 3 minutes, scraping down the inside of the bowl several times.
5. Beat in the pasteurized egg substitute or egg (as applicable) and vanilla until uniform. Scrape down and

remove the beaters. Fold in the flour mixture and chocolate chips with a rubber spatula, just until combined. Scrape and gently press this dough into the prepared pan, getting it even across the pan to the perimeter.

6. Set the pan in the basket and air-fry undisturbed for 16 minutes, or until the cookie is puffed, browned, and feels set to the touch.

7. Transfer the pan to a wire rack and cool for 10 minutes. Loosen the cookie from the perimeter with a spatula, then invert the pan onto a cutting board and let the cookie come free. Remove the pan and reinvert the cookie onto the wire rack. Cool for 5 minutes more before slicing into wedges to serve.

## Rustic Berry Layer Cake

Servings: 6
Cooking Time: 45 Minutes
**Ingredients:**
- 2 eggs, beaten
- ½ cup milk
- 2 tbsp Greek yogurt
- ¼ cup maple syrup
- 1 tbsp apple cider vinegar
- 1 tbsp vanilla extract
- ¾ cup all-purpose flour
- 1 tsp baking powder
- ½ tsp baking soda
- ¼ cup dark chocolate chips
- 1/3 cup raspberry jam

**Directions:**
1. Preheat air fryer to 350°F (175°C). Combine the eggs, milk, Greek yogurt, maple syrup, apple vinegar, and vanilla extract in a bowl. Toss in flour, baking powder, and baking soda until combined. Pour the batter into a 6-inch round cake pan, distributing well, and Bake for 20-25 minutes until a toothpick comes out clean. Let cool completely.

2. Turn the cake onto a plate, cut lengthwise to make 2 equal layers. Set aside. Add chocolate chips to a heat-proof bowl and Bake for 3 minutes until fully melted. In the meantime, spread raspberry jam on top of the bottom layer, distributing well, and top with the remaining layer. Once the chocolate is ready, stir in 1 tbsp of milk. Pour over the layer cake and spread well. Cut into 6 wedges and serve immediately.

## S'mores Pockets

Servings: 6
Cooking Time: 5 Minutes
**Ingredients:**
- 12 sheets phyllo dough, thawed
- 1½ cups butter, melted
- ¾ cup graham cracker crumbs
- 1 (7-ounce) Giant Hershey's® milk chocolate bar
- 12 marshmallows, cut in half

**Directions:**
1. Place one sheet of the phyllo on a large cutting board. Keep the rest of the phyllo sheets covered with a slightly damp, clean kitchen towel. Brush the phyllo sheet generously with some melted butter. Place a second phyllo sheet on top of the first and brush it with more butter. Repeat with one more phyllo sheet until you have a stack of 3 phyllo sheets with butter brushed between the layers. Cover the phyllo sheets with one quarter of the graham cracker crumbs leaving a 1-inch border on one of the short ends of the rectangle. Cut the phyllo sheets lengthwise into 3 strips.

2. Take 2 of the strips and crisscross them to form a cross with the empty borders at the top and to the left. Place 2 of the chocolate rectangles in the center of the cross. Place 4 of the marshmallow halves on top of the chocolate. Now fold the pocket together by folding the bottom phyllo strip up over the chocolate and marshmallows. Then fold the right side over, then the top strip down and finally the left side over. Brush all the edges generously with melted butter to seal shut. Repeat with the next three sheets of phyllo, until all the sheets have been used. You will be able to make 2 pockets with every second batch because you will have an extra graham cracker crumb strip from the previous set of sheets.

3. Preheat the air fryer to 350°F (175°C).

4. Transfer 3 pockets at a time to the air fryer basket. Air-fry at 350°F (175°C) for 4 to 5 minutes, until the phyllo dough is light brown in color. Flip the pockets over halfway through the cooking process. Repeat with the remaining 3 pockets.

5. Serve warm.

## Magic Giant Chocolate Cookies

Servings: 2
Cooking Time: 30 Minutes
**Ingredients:**
- 2 tbsp white chocolate chips
- ½ cup flour
- 1/8 tsp baking soda
- ¼ cup butter, melted
- ¼ cup light brown sugar
- 2 tbsp granulated sugar
- 2 eggs
- 2 tbsp milk chocolate chips

- ¼ cup chopped pecans
- ¼ cup chopped hazelnuts
- ½ tsp vanilla extract
- Salt to taste

**Directions:**

1. Preheat air fryer at 350°F. In a bowl, combine the flour, baking soda, butter, brown sugar, granulated sugar, eggs, milk chocolate chips, white chocolate chips, pecans, hazelnuts, vanilla extract, and salt. Press cookie mixture onto a greased pizza pan. Place pizza pan in the frying basket and Bake for 10 minutes. Let cool completely for 10 minutes. Turn over on a plate and serve.

## Dark Chocolate Peanut Butter S'mores

Servings: 4
Cooking Time: 6 Minutes

**Ingredients:**

- 4 graham cracker sheets
- 4 marshmallows
- 4 teaspoons chunky peanut butter
- 4 ounces dark chocolate
- ½ teaspoon ground cinnamon

**Directions:**

1. Preheat the air fryer to 390°F (200°C). Break the graham crackers in half so you have 8 pieces.
2. Place 4 pieces of graham cracker on the bottom of the air fryer. Top each with one of the marshmallows and bake for 6 or 7 minutes, or until the marshmallows have a golden brown center.
3. While cooking, slather each of the remaining graham crackers with 1 teaspoon peanut butter.
4. When baking completes, carefully remove each of the graham crackers, add 1 ounce of dark chocolate on top of the marshmallow, and lightly sprinkle with cinnamon. Top with the remaining peanut butter graham cracker to make the sandwich. Serve immediately.

## Orange Gooey Butter Cake

Servings: 6
Cooking Time: 85 Minutes

**Ingredients:**

- Crust Layer:
- ½ cup flour
- ¼ cup sugar
- ½ teaspoon baking powder
- ⅛ teaspoon salt
- 2 ounces (½ stick) unsalted European style butter, melted
- 1 egg
- 1 teaspoon orange extract
- 2 tablespoons orange zest
- Gooey Butter Layer:
- 8 ounces cream cheese, softened
- 4 ounces (1 stick) unsalted European style butter, melted
- 2 eggs
- 2 teaspoons orange extract
- 2 tablespoons orange zest
- 4 cups powdered sugar
- Garnish:
- powdered sugar
- orange slices

**Directions:**

1. Preheat the air fryer to 350°F (175°C).
2. Grease a 7-inch cake pan and line the bottom with parchment paper. Combine the flour, sugar, baking powder and salt in a bowl. Add the melted butter, egg, orange extract and orange zest. Mix well and press this mixture into the bottom of the greased cake pan. Lower the pan into the basket using an aluminum foil sling (fold a piece of aluminum foil into a strip about 2-inches wide by 24-inches long). Fold the ends of the aluminum foil over the top of the dish before returning the basket to the air fryer. Air-fry uncovered for 8 minutes.
3. To make the gooey butter layer, beat the cream cheese, melted butter, eggs, orange extract and orange zest in a large bowl using an electric hand mixer. Add the powdered sugar in stages, beat until smooth with each addition. Pour this mixture on top of the baked crust in the cake pan. Wrap the pan with a piece of greased aluminum foil, tenting the top of the foil to leave a little room for the cake to rise.
4. Air-fry for 60 minutes at 350°F (175°C). Remove the aluminum foil and air-fry for an additional 17 minutes.
5. Let the cake cool inside the pan for at least 10 minutes. Then, run a butter knife around the cake and let the cake cool completely in the pan. When cooled, run the butter knife around the edges of the cake again and invert it onto a plate and then back onto a serving platter. Sprinkle the powdered sugar over the top of the cake and garnish with orange slices.

# Chocolate Cake

Servings: 8
Cooking Time: 20 Minutes
**Ingredients:**
- ½ cup sugar
- ¼ cup flour, plus 3 tablespoons
- 3 tablespoons cocoa
- ½ teaspoon baking powder
- ½ teaspoon baking soda
- ¼ teaspoon salt
- 1 egg
- 2 tablespoons oil
- ½ cup milk
- ½ teaspoon vanilla extract

**Directions:**
1. Preheat air fryer to 330°F (165°C).
2. Grease and flour a 6 x 6-inch baking pan.
3. In a medium bowl, stir together the sugar, flour, cocoa, baking powder, baking soda, and salt.
4. Add all other ingredients and beat with a wire whisk until smooth.
5. Pour batter into prepared pan and bake at 330°F (165°C) for 20 minutes, until toothpick inserted in center comes out clean or with crumbs clinging to it.

# Baked Apple Crisp

Servings: 4
Cooking Time: 23 Minutes
**Ingredients:**
- 2 large Granny Smith apples, peeled, cored, and chopped
- ¼ cup granulated sugar
- ¼ cup plus 2 teaspoons flour, divided
- 2 teaspoons milk
- ¼ teaspoon cinnamon
- ¼ cup oats
- ¼ cup brown sugar
- 2 tablespoons unsalted butter
- ⅛ teaspoon baking powder
- ⅛ teaspoon salt

**Directions:**
1. Preheat the air fryer to 350°F (175°C).
2. In a medium bowl, mix the apples, the granulated sugar, 2 teaspoons of the flour, the milk, and the cinnamon.
3. Spray 4 oven-safe ramekins with cooking spray. Divide the filling among the four ramekins.
4. In a small bowl, mix the oats, the brown sugar, the remaining ¼ cup of flour, the butter, the baking powder, and the salt. Use your fingers or a pastry blender to crumble the butter into pea-size pieces. Divide the topping over the top of the apple filling. Cover the apple crisps with foil.
5. Place the covered apple crisps in the air fryer basket and cook for 20 minutes. Uncover and continue cooking for 3 minutes or until the surface is golden and crunchy.

# Struffoli

Servings: X
Cooking Time: 20 Minutes
**Ingredients:**
- ¼ cup butter, softened
- ⅔ cup sugar
- 5 eggs
- 2 teaspoons vanilla extract
- zest of 1 lemon
- 4 cups all-purpose flour
- 2 teaspoons baking soda
- ¼ teaspoon salt
- 16 ounces honey
- 1 teaspoon ground cinnamon
- zest of 1 orange
- 2 tablespoons water
- nonpareils candy sprinkles

**Directions:**
1. Cream the butter and sugar together in a bowl until light and fluffy using a hand mixer (or a stand mixer). Add the eggs, vanilla and lemon zest and mix. In a separate bowl, combine the flour, baking soda and salt. Add the dry ingredients to the wet ingredients and mix until you have a soft dough. Shape the dough into a ball, wrap it in plastic and let it rest for 30 minutes.
2. Divide the dough ball into four pieces. Roll each piece into a long rope. Cut each rope into about 25 (½-inch) pieces. Roll each piece into a tight ball. You should have 100 little balls when finished.
3. Preheat the air fryer to 370°F (185°C).
4. In batches of about 20, transfer the dough balls to the air fryer basket, leaving a small space in between them. Air-fry the dough balls at 370°F (185°C) for 3 to 4 minutes, shaking the basket when one minute of cooking time remains.
5. After all the dough balls are air-fried, make the honey topping. Melt the honey in a small saucepan on the stovetop. Add the cinnamon, orange zest, and water. Simmer for one minute. Place the air-fried dough balls in a large bowl and drizzle the honey mixture over top. Gently toss to coat all the dough balls evenly. Transfer the coated struffoli to a platter and sprinkle the nonpareil candy sprinkles over top. You can dress the presentation up by piling the balls into the shape of a wreath or pile them high in a cone shape to resemble a Christmas tree.
6. Struffoli can be made ahead. Store covered tightly.

# Gingerbread

Servings: 6
Cooking Time: 20 Minutes
**Ingredients:**
- cooking spray
- 1 cup flour
- 2 tablespoons sugar
- ¾ teaspoon ground ginger
- ¼ teaspoon cinnamon
- 1 teaspoon baking powder
- ½ teaspoon baking soda
- ⅛ teaspoon salt
- 1 egg
- ¼ cup molasses
- ½ cup buttermilk
- 2 tablespoons oil
- 1 teaspoon pure vanilla extract

**Directions:**
1. Preheat air fryer to 330°F (165°C).
2. Spray 6 x 6-inch baking dish lightly with cooking spray.
3. In a medium bowl, mix together all the dry ingredients.
4. In a separate bowl, beat the egg. Add molasses, buttermilk, oil, and vanilla and stir until well mixed.
5. Pour liquid mixture into dry ingredients and stir until well blended.
6. Pour batter into baking dish and cook at 330°F (165°C) for 20minutes or until toothpick inserted in center of loaf comes out clean.

# Apple Crisp

Servings: 4
Cooking Time: 16 Minutes
**Ingredients:**
- Filling
- 3 Granny Smith apples, thinly sliced (about 4 cups)
- ¼ teaspoon ground cinnamon
- ⅛ teaspoon salt
- 1½ teaspoons lemon juice
- 2 tablespoons honey
- 1 tablespoon brown sugar
- cooking spray
- Crumb Topping
- 2 tablespoons oats
- 2 tablespoons oat bran
- 2 tablespoons cooked quinoa
- 2 tablespoons chopped walnuts
- 2 tablespoons brown sugar
- 2 teaspoons coconut oil

**Directions:**
1. Combine all filling ingredients and stir well so that apples are evenly coated.
2. Spray air fryer baking pan with nonstick cooking spray and spoon in the apple mixture.
3. Cook at 360°F (180°C) for 5minutes. Stir well, scooping up from the bottom to mix apples and sauce.
4. At this point, the apples should be crisp-tender. Continue cooking in 3-minute intervals until apples are as soft as you like.
5. While apples are cooking, combine all topping ingredients in a small bowl. Stir until coconut oil mixes in well and distributes evenly. If your coconut oil is cold, it may be easier to mix in by hand.
6. When apples are cooked to your liking, sprinkle crumb mixture on top. Cook at 360°F (180°C) for 8 minutes or until crumb topping is golden brown and crispy.

# Brownies After Dark

Servings: 4
Cooking Time: 13 Minutes
**Ingredients:**
- 1 egg
- ½ cup granulated sugar
- ¼ teaspoon salt
- ½ teaspoon vanilla
- ¼ cup butter, melted
- ¼ cup flour, plus 2 tablespoons
- ¼ cup cocoa
- cooking spray
- Optional
- vanilla ice cream
- caramel sauce
- whipped cream

**Directions:**
1. Beat together egg, sugar, salt, and vanilla until light.
2. Add melted butter and mix well.
3. Stir in flour and cocoa.
4. Spray 6 x 6-inch baking pan lightly with cooking spray.
5. Spread batter in pan and cook at 330°F (165°C) for 13 minutes. Cool and cut into 4 large squares or 16 small brownie bites.

## Cinnamon Tortilla Crisps

Servings: 4
Cooking Time: 8 Minutes
**Ingredients:**
- 1 tortilla
- 2 tsp muscovado sugar
- ½ tsp cinnamon

**Directions:**
1. Preheat air fryer to 350°F (175°C). Slice the tortilla into 8 triangles like a pizza. Put the slices on a plate and spray both sides with oil. Sprinkle muscovado sugar and cinnamon on top, then lightly spray the tops with oil. Place in the frying basket in a single layer. Air Fry for 5-6 minutes or until they are light brown. Enjoy warm.

## Orange-chocolate Cake

Servings: 6
Cooking Time: 35 Minutes
**Ingredients:**
- ¾ cup flour
- ½ cup sugar
- 7 tbsp cocoa powder
- ½ tsp baking soda
- ½ cup milk
- 2 ½ tbsp sunflower oil
- ½ tbsp orange juice
- 2 tsp vanilla
- 2 tsp orange zest
- 3 tbsp butter, softened
- 1 ¼ cups powdered sugar

**Directions:**
1. Use a whisk to combine the flour, sugar, 2 tbsp of cocoa powder, baking soda, and a pinch of salt in a bowl. Once combined, add milk, sunflower oil, orange juice, and orange zest. Stir until combined. Preheat the air fryer to 350°F (175°C). Pour the batter into a greased cake pan and Bake for 25 minutes or until a knife inserted in the center comes out clean.
2. Use an electric beater to beat the butter and powdered sugar together in a bowl. Add the remaining cocoa powder and vanilla and whip until fluffy. Scrape the sides occasionally. Refrigerate until ready to use. Allow the cake to cool completely, then run a knife around the edges of the baking pan. Turn it upside-down on a plate so it can be frosted on the sides and top. When the frosting is no longer cold, use a butter knife or small spatula to frost the sides and top. Cut into slices and enjoy!

## Fried Oreos

Servings: 12
Cooking Time: 6 Minutes Per Batch
**Ingredients:**
- oil for misting or nonstick spray
- 1 cup complete pancake and waffle mix
- 1 teaspoon vanilla extract
- ½ cup water, plus 2 tablespoons
- 12 Oreos or other chocolate sandwich cookies
- 1 tablespoon confectioners' sugar

**Directions:**
1. Spray baking pan with oil or nonstick spray and place in basket.
2. Preheat air fryer to 390°F (200°C).
3. In a medium bowl, mix together the pancake mix, vanilla, and water.
4. Dip 4 cookies in batter and place in baking pan.
5. Cook for 6minutes, until browned.
6. Repeat steps 4 and 5 for the remaining cookies.
7. Sift sugar over warm cookies.

## Fudgy Brownie Cake

Servings: 6
Cooking Time: 25-35 Minutes
**Ingredients:**
- 6½ tablespoons All-purpose flour
- ¼ cup plus 1 teaspoon Unsweetened cocoa powder
- ½ teaspoon Baking powder
- ¼ teaspoon Table salt
- 6½ tablespoons Butter, at room temperature
- 9½ tablespoons Granulated white sugar
- 1 egg plus 1 large egg white Large egg(s)
- ¾ teaspoon Vanilla extract
- Baking spray (see here)

**Directions:**
1. Preheat the air fryer to 325°F (160°C) (or 330°F (165°C), if that's the closest setting).
2. Mix the flour, cocoa powder, baking powder, and salt in a small bowl until well combined.
3. Using an electric hand mixer at medium speed, beat the butter and sugar in a medium bowl until creamy and smooth, about 3 minutes, occasionally scraping down the inside of the bowl.
4. Beat in the egg(s) and the white or yolk (as necessary), as well as the vanilla, until smooth. Turn off the beaters and add the flour mixture. Beat at low speed until thick and smooth.

5. Use the baking spray to generously coat the inside of a 6-inch round cake pan for a small batch, a 7-inch round cake pan for a medium batch, or an 8-inch round cake pan for a large batch. Scrape and spread the batter into the pan, smoothing the batter out to an even layer.
6. Set the pan in the basket and air-fry for 25 minutes for a 6-inch layer, 30 minutes for a 7-inch layer, or 35 minutes for an 8-inch layer, or until the cake is set but soft to the touch. Start checking it at the 20-minute mark to know where you are.
7. Use hot pads or silicone baking mitts to transfer the cake pan to a wire rack. Cool for at least 1 hour or up to 4 hours. Using a nonstick-safe knife, slice the cake into wedges right in the pan and lift them out one by one.

## Peanut Butter S'mores

Servings: 10
Cooking Time: 1 Minute
**Ingredients:**
- 10 Graham crackers (full, double-square cookies as they come out of the package)
- 5 tablespoons Natural-style creamy or crunchy peanut butter
- ½ cup Milk chocolate chips
- 10 Standard-size marshmallows (not minis and not jumbo campfire ones)

**Directions:**
1. Preheat the air fryer to 350°F (175°C).
2. Break the graham crackers in half widthwise at the marked place, so the rectangle is now in two squares. Set half of the squares flat side up on your work surface. Spread each with about 1½ teaspoons peanut butter, then set 10 to 12 chocolate chips point side up into the peanut butter on each, pressing gently so the chips stick.
3. Flatten a marshmallow between your clean, dry hands and set it atop the chips. Do the same with the remaining marshmallows on the other coated graham crackers. Do not set the other half of the graham crackers on top of these coated graham crackers.
4. When the machine is at temperature, set the treats graham cracker side down in a single layer in the basket. They may touch, but even a fraction of an inch between them will provide better air flow. Air-fry undisturbed for 45 seconds.
5. Use a nonstick-safe spatula to transfer the topped graham crackers to a wire rack. Set the other graham cracker squares flat side down over the marshmallows. Cool for a couple of minutes before serving.

## Coconut Cream Roll-ups

Servings: 4
Cooking Time: 20 Minutes
**Ingredients:**
- ½ cup cream cheese, softened
- 1 cup fresh raspberries
- ¼ cup brown sugar
- ¼ cup coconut cream
- 1 egg
- 1 tsp corn starch
- 6 spring roll wrappers

**Directions:**
1. Preheat air fryer to 350°F (175°C). Add the cream cheese, brown sugar, coconut cream, cornstarch, and egg to a bowl and whisk until all ingredients are completely mixed and fluffy, thick and stiff. Spoon even amounts of the creamy filling into each spring roll wrapper, then top each dollop of filling with several raspberries. Roll up the wraps around the creamy raspberry filling, and seal the seams with a few dabs of water.
2. Place each roll on the foil-lined frying basket, seams facing down. Bake for 10 minutes, flipping them once until golden brown and perfect on the outside, while the raspberries and cream filling will have cooked together in a glorious fusion. Remove with tongs and serve hot or cold. Serve and enjoy!

## Pumpkin Brownies

Servings: 4
Cooking Time: 30 Minutes
**Ingredients:**
- ¼ cup canned pumpkin
- ½ cup maple syrup
- 2 eggs, beaten
- 1 tbsp vanilla extract
- ¼ cup tapioca flour
- ¼ cup flour
- ½ tsp baking powder

**Directions:**
1. Preheat air fryer to 320°F (160°C). Mix the pumpkin, maple syrup, eggs, and vanilla extract in a bowl. Toss in tapioca flour, flour, and baking powder until smooth. Pour the batter into a small round cake pan and Bake for 20 minutes until a toothpick comes out clean. Let cool completely before slicing into 4 brownies. Serve and enjoy!

## Giant Buttery Oatmeal Cookie

Servings: 4
Cooking Time: 16 Minutes
**Ingredients:**
- 1 cup Rolled oats (not quick-cooking or steel-cut oats)
- ½ cup All-purpose flour
- ½ teaspoon Baking soda
- ½ teaspoon Ground cinnamon
- ½ teaspoon Table salt
- 3½ tablespoons Butter, at room temperature
- ⅓ cup Packed dark brown sugar
- 1½ tablespoons Granulated white sugar
- 3 tablespoons (or 1 medium egg, well beaten) Pasteurized egg substitute, such as Egg Beaters
- ¾ teaspoon Vanilla extract
- ⅓ cup Chopped pecans
- Baking spray

**Directions:**
1. Preheat the air fryer to 350°F (175°C) .
2. Stir the oats, flour, baking soda, cinnamon, and salt in a bowl until well combined.
3. Using an electric hand mixer at medium speed , beat the butter, brown sugar, and granulated white sugar until creamy and thick, about 3 minutes, scraping down the inside of the bowl occasionally. Beat in the egg substitute or egg (as applicable) and vanilla until uniform.
4. Scrape down and remove the beaters. Fold in the flour mixture and pecans with a rubber spatula just until all the flour is moistened and the nuts are even throughout the dough.
5. For a small air fryer, coat the inside of a 6-inch round cake pan with baking spray. For a medium air fryer, coat the inside of a 7-inch round cake pan with baking spray. And for a large air fryer, coat the inside of an 8-inch round cake pan with baking spray. Scrape and gently press the dough into the prepared pan, spreading it into an even layer to the perimeter.
6. Set the pan in the basket and air-fry undisturbed for 16 minutes, or until puffed and browned.
7. Transfer the pan to a wire rack and cool for 10 minutes. Loosen the cookie from the perimeter with a spatula, then invert the pan onto a cutting board and let the cookie come free. Remove the pan and reinvert the cookie onto the wire rack. Cool for 5 minutes more before slicing into wedges to serve.

## Pecan-oat Filled Apples

Servings: 4
Cooking Time: 20 Minutes
**Ingredients:**
- 2 cored Granny Smith apples, halved
- ¼ cup rolled oats
- 2 tbsp honey
- ½ tsp ground cinnamon
- ½ tsp ground ginger
- 2 tbsp chopped pecans
- A pinch of salt
- 1 tbsp olive oil

**Directions:**
1. Preheat air fryer to 380°F (195°C). Combine together the oats, honey, cinnamon, ginger, pecans, salt, and olive oil in a bowl. Scoop a quarter of the oat mixture onto the top of each half apple. Put the apples in the frying basket and Roast for 12-15 minutes until the apples are fork-tender.

## Strawberry Donut Bites

Servings: 6
Cooking Time: 25 Minutes
**Ingredients:**
- 2/3 cup flour
- A pinch of salt
- ½ tsp baking powder
- 1 tsp vanilla extract
- 2 tbsp light brown sugar
- 1 tbsp honey
- ½ cup diced strawberries
- 1 tbsp butter, melted
- 2 tbsp powdered sugar
- 2 tsp sour cream
- ¼ cup crushed pretzels

**Directions:**
1. Preheat air fryer at 325ºF. In a bowl, sift flour, baking powder, and salt. Add in vanilla, brown sugar, honey, 2 tbsp of water, butter, and strawberries and whisk until combined. Form dough into balls. Place the balls on a lightly greased pizza pan, place them in the frying basket, and Air Fry for 10-12 minutes. Let cool onto a cooling rack for 5 minutes. Mix the powdered sugar and sour cream in a small bowl, 1 tsp of sour cream at a time until you reach your desired consistency. Gently pour over the donut bites. Scatter with crushed pretzels and serve.

# Sandwiches And Burgers Recipes

## Chicken Gyros

Servings: 4
Cooking Time: 14 Minutes
**Ingredients:**
- 4 4- to 5-ounce boneless skinless chicken thighs, trimmed of any fat blobs
- 2 tablespoons Lemon juice
- 2 tablespoons Red wine vinegar
- 2 tablespoons Olive oil
- 2 teaspoons Dried oregano
- 2 teaspoons Minced garlic
- 1 teaspoon Table salt
- 1 teaspoon Ground black pepper
- 4 Pita pockets (gluten-free, if a concern)
- ½ cup Chopped tomatoes
- ½ cup Bottled regular, low-fat, or fat-free ranch dressing (gluten-free, if a concern)

**Directions:**
1. Mix the thighs, lemon juice, vinegar, oil, oregano, garlic, salt, and pepper in a zip-closed bag. Seal, gently massage the marinade into the meat through the plastic, and refrigerate for at least 2 hours or up to 6 hours. (Longer than that and the meat can turn rubbery.)
2. Set the plastic bag out on the counter (to make the contents a little less frigid). Preheat the air fryer to 375°F (190°C).
3. When the machine is at temperature, use kitchen tongs to place the thighs in the basket in one layer. Discard the marinade. Air-fry the chicken thighs undisturbed for 12 minutes, or until browned and an instant-read meat thermometer inserted into the thickest part of one thigh registers 165°F (75°C). You may need to air-fry the chicken 2 minutes longer if the machine's temperature is 360°F (180°C).
4. Use kitchen tongs to transfer the thighs to a cutting board. Cool for 5 minutes, then set one thigh in each of the pita pockets. Top each with 2 tablespoons chopped tomatoes and 2 tablespoons dressing. Serve warm.

## Lamb Burgers

Servings: 3
Cooking Time: 17 Minutes
**Ingredients:**
- 1 pound 2 ounces Ground lamb
- 3 tablespoons Crumbled feta
- 1 teaspoon Minced garlic
- 1 teaspoon Tomato paste
- ¾ teaspoon Ground coriander
- ¾ teaspoon Ground dried ginger
- Up to ⅛ teaspoon Cayenne
- Up to a ⅛ teaspoon Table salt (optional)
- 3 Kaiser rolls or hamburger buns (gluten-free, if a concern), split open

**Directions:**
1. Preheat the air fryer to 375°F (190°C).
2. Gently mix the ground lamb, feta, garlic, tomato paste, coriander, ginger, cayenne, and salt (if using) in a bowl until well combined, trying to keep the bits of cheese intact. Form this mixture into two 5-inch patties for the small batch, three 5-inch patties for the medium, or four 5-inch patties for the large.
3. Set the patties in the basket in one layer and air-fry undisturbed for 16 minutes, or until an instant-read meat thermometer inserted into one burger registers 160°F (70°C). (The cheese is not an issue with the temperature probe in this recipe as it was for the Inside-Out Cheeseburgers, because the feta is so well mixed into the ground meat.)
4. Use a nonstick-safe spatula, and perhaps a flatware fork for balance, to transfer the burgers to a cutting board. Set the buns cut side down in the basket in one layer (working in batches as necessary) and air-fry undisturbed for 1 minute, to toast a bit and warm up. Serve the burgers warm in the buns.

## Perfect Burgers

Servings: 3
Cooking Time: 13 Minutes
**Ingredients:**
- 1 pound 2 ounces 90% lean ground beef
- 1½ tablespoons Worcestershire sauce (gluten-free, if a concern)
- ½ teaspoon Ground black pepper
- 3 Hamburger buns (gluten-free if a concern), split open

**Directions:**
1. Preheat the air fryer to 375°F (190°C).
2. Gently mix the ground beef, Worcestershire sauce, and pepper in a bowl until well combined but preserving as much of the meat's fibers as possible. Divide this mixture into two 5-inch patties for the small batch, three 5-inch patties for the medium, or four 5-inch patties for the large. Make a thumbprint indentation in the center of each patty, about halfway through the meat.

3. Set the patties in the basket in one layer with some space between them. Air-fry undisturbed for 10 minutes, or until an instant-read meat thermometer inserted into the center of a burger registers 160°F (705°C) (a medium-well burger). You may need to add 2 minutes cooking time if the air fryer is at 360°F (180°C).

4. Use a nonstick-safe spatula, and perhaps a flatware fork for balance, to transfer the burgers to a cutting board. Set the buns cut side down in the basket in one layer (working in batches as necessary) and air-fry undisturbed for 1 minute, to toast a bit and warm up. Serve the burgers in the warm buns.

## **Thanksgiving Turkey Sandwiches**

Servings: 3
Cooking Time: 10 Minutes
**Ingredients:**
- 1½ cups Herb-seasoned stuffing mix (not cornbread-style; gluten-free, if a concern)
- 1 Large egg white(s)
- 2 tablespoons Water
- 3 5- to 6-ounce turkey breast cutlets
- Vegetable oil spray
- 4½ tablespoons Purchased cranberry sauce, preferably whole berry
- ⅛ teaspoon Ground cinnamon
- ⅛ teaspoon Ground dried ginger
- 4½ tablespoons Regular, low-fat, or fat-free mayonnaise (gluten-free, if a concern)
- 6 tablespoons Shredded Brussels sprouts
- 3 Kaiser rolls (gluten-free, if a concern), split open

**Directions:**
1. Preheat the air fryer to 375°F (190°C).
2. Put the stuffing mix in a heavy zip-closed bag, seal it, lay it flat on your counter, and roll a rolling pin over the bag to crush the stuffing mix to the consistency of rough sand. (Or you can pulse the stuffing mix to the desired consistency in a food processor.)
3. Set up and fill two shallow soup plates or small pie plates on your counter: one for the egg white(s), whisked with the water until foamy; and one for the ground stuffing mix.
4. Dip a cutlet in the egg white mixture, coating both sides and letting any excess egg white slip back into the rest. Set the cutlet in the ground stuffing mix and coat it evenly on both sides, pressing gently to coat well on both sides. Lightly coat the cutlet on both sides with vegetable oil spray, set it aside, and continue dipping and coating the remaining cutlets in the same way.

5. Set the cutlets in the basket and air-fry undisturbed for 10 minutes, or until crisp and brown. Use kitchen tongs to transfer the cutlets to a wire rack to cool for a few minutes.

6. Meanwhile, stir the cranberry sauce with the cinnamon and ginger in a small bowl. Mix the shredded Brussels sprouts and mayonnaise in a second bowl until the vegetable is evenly coated.

7. Build the sandwiches by spreading about 1½ tablespoons of the cranberry mixture on the cut side of the bottom half of each roll. Set a cutlet on top, then spread about 3 tablespoons of the Brussels sprouts mixture evenly over the cutlet. Set the other half of the roll on top and serve warm.

## **Dijon Thyme Burgers**

Servings: 3
Cooking Time: 18 Minutes
**Ingredients:**
- 1 pound lean ground beef
- ⅓ cup panko breadcrumbs
- ¼ cup finely chopped onion
- 3 tablespoons Dijon mustard
- 1 tablespoon chopped fresh thyme
- 4 teaspoons Worcestershire sauce
- 1 teaspoon salt
- freshly ground black pepper
- Topping (optional):
- 2 tablespoons Dijon mustard
- 1 tablespoon dark brown sugar
- 1 teaspoon Worcestershire sauce
- 4 ounces sliced Swiss cheese, optional

**Directions:**
1. Combine all the burger ingredients together in a large bowl and mix well. Divide the meat into 4 equal portions and then form the burgers, being careful not to over-handle the meat. One good way to do this is to throw the meat back and forth from one hand to another, packing the meat each time you catch it. Flatten the balls into patties, making an indentation in the center of each patty with your thumb (this will help it stay flat as it cooks) and flattening the sides of the burgers so that they will fit nicely into the air fryer basket.

2. Preheat the air fryer to 370°F (185°C).

3. If you don't have room for all four burgers, air-fry two or three burgers at a time for 8 minutes. Flip the burgers over and air-fry for another 6 minutes.

4. While the burgers are cooking combine the Dijon mustard, dark brown sugar, and Worcestershire sauce in a small bowl and mix well. This optional topping to the

burgers really adds a boost of flavor at the end. Spread the Dijon topping evenly on each burger. If you cooked the burgers in batches, return the first batch to the cooker at this time – it's ok to place the fourth burger on top of the others in the center of the basket. Air-fry the burgers for another 3 minutes.

5. Finally, if desired, top each burger with a slice of Swiss cheese. Lower the air fryer temperature to 330°F (165°C) and air-fry for another minute to melt the cheese. Serve the burgers on toasted brioche buns, dressed the way you like them.

## Sausage And Pepper Heros

Servings: 3
Cooking Time: 11 Minutes
**Ingredients:**
- 3 links (about 9 ounces total) Sweet Italian sausages (gluten-free, if a concern)
- 1½ Medium red or green bell pepper(s), stemmed, cored, and cut into ½-inch-wide strips
- 1 medium Yellow or white onion(s), peeled, halved, and sliced into thin half-moons
- 3 Long soft rolls, such as hero, hoagie, or Italian sub rolls (gluten-free, if a concern), split open lengthwise
- For garnishing Balsamic vinegar
- For garnishing Fresh basil leaves

**Directions:**
1. Preheat the air fryer to 400°F (205°C).
2. When the machine is at temperature, set the sausage links in the basket in one layer and air-fry undisturbed for 5 minutes.
3. Add the pepper strips and onions. Continue air-frying, tossing and rearranging everything about once every minute, for 5 minutes, or until the sausages are browned and an instant-read meat thermometer inserted into one of the links registers 160°F (70°C).
4. Use a nonstick-safe spatula and kitchen tongs to transfer the sausages and vegetables to a cutting board. Set the rolls cut side down in the basket in one layer (working in batches as necessary) and air-fry undisturbed for 1 minute, to toast the rolls a bit and warm them up. Set 1 sausage with some pepper strips and onions in each warm roll, sprinkle balsamic vinegar over the sandwich fillings, and garnish with basil leaves.

## Inside Out Cheeseburgers

Servings: 2
Cooking Time: 20 Minutes
**Ingredients:**
- ¾ pound lean ground beef
- 3 tablespoons minced onion
- 4 teaspoons ketchup
- 2 teaspoons yellow mustard
- salt and freshly ground black pepper
- 4 slices of Cheddar cheese, broken into smaller pieces
- 8 hamburger dill pickle chips

**Directions:**
1. Combine the ground beef, minced onion, ketchup, mustard, salt and pepper in a large bowl. Mix well to thoroughly combine the ingredients. Divide the meat into four equal portions.
2. To make the stuffed burgers, flatten each portion of meat into a thin patty. Place 4 pickle chips and half of the cheese onto the center of two of the patties, leaving a rim around the edge of the patty exposed. Place the remaining two patties on top of the first and press the meat together firmly, sealing the edges tightly. With the burgers on a flat surface, press the sides of the burger with the palm of your hand to create a straight edge. This will help keep the stuffing inside the burger while it cooks.
3. Preheat the air fryer to 370°F (185°C).
4. Place the burgers inside the air fryer basket and air-fry for 20 minutes, flipping the burgers over halfway through the cooking time.
5. Serve the cheeseburgers on buns with lettuce and tomato.

## Inside-out Cheeseburgers

Servings: 3
Cooking Time: 9-11 Minutes
**Ingredients:**
- 1 pound 2 ounces 90% lean ground beef
- ¾ teaspoon Dried oregano
- ¾ teaspoon Table salt
- ¾ teaspoon Ground black pepper
- ¼ teaspoon Garlic powder
- 6 tablespoons (about 1½ ounces) Shredded Cheddar, Swiss, or other semi-firm cheese, or a purchased blend of shredded cheeses
- 3 Hamburger buns (gluten-free, if a concern), split open

**Directions:**
1. Preheat the air fryer to 375°F (190°C).
2. Gently mix the ground beef, oregano, salt, pepper, and garlic powder in a bowl until well combined without turning the mixture to mush. Form it into two 6-inch patties for the small batch, three for the medium, or four for the large.
3. Place 2 tablespoons of the shredded cheese in the center of each patty. With clean hands, fold the sides of the patty

up to cover the cheese, then pick it up and roll it gently into a ball to seal the cheese inside. Gently press it back into a 5-inch burger without letting any cheese squish out. Continue filling and preparing more burgers, as needed.

4. Place the burgers in the basket in one layer and air-fry undisturbed for 8 minutes for medium or 10 minutes for well-done. (An instant-read meat thermometer won't work for these burgers because it will hit the mostly melted cheese inside and offer a hotter temperature than the surrounding meat.)

5. Use a nonstick-safe spatula, and perhaps a flatware fork for balance, to transfer the burgers to a cutting board. Set the buns cut side down in the basket in one layer (working in batches as necessary) and air-fry undisturbed for 1 minute, to toast a bit and warm up. Cool the burgers a few minutes more, then serve them warm in the buns.

## Reuben Sandwiches

Servings: 2
Cooking Time: 11 Minutes
**Ingredients:**
- ½ pound Sliced deli corned beef
- 4 teaspoons Regular or low-fat mayonnaise (not fat-free)
- 4 Rye bread slices
- 2 tablespoons plus 2 teaspoons Russian dressing
- ½ cup Purchased sauerkraut, squeezed by the handful over the sink to get rid of excess moisture
- 2 ounces (2 to 4 slices) Swiss cheese slices (optional)

**Directions:**
1. Set the corned beef in the basket, slip the basket into the machine, and heat the air fryer to 400°F (205°C). Air-fry undisturbed for 3 minutes from the time the basket is put in the machine, just to warm up the meat.
2. Use kitchen tongs to transfer the corned beef to a cutting board. Spread 1 teaspoon mayonnaise on one side of each slice of rye bread, rubbing the mayonnaise into the bread with a small flatware knife.
3. Place the bread slices mayonnaise side down on a cutting board. Spread the Russian dressing over the "dry" side of each slice. For one sandwich, top one slice of bread with the corned beef, sauerkraut, and cheese (if using). For two sandwiches, top two slices of bread each with half of the corned beef, sauerkraut, and cheese (if using). Close the sandwiches with the remaining bread, setting it mayonnaise side up on top.
4. Set the sandwich(es) in the basket and air-fry undisturbed for 8 minutes, or until browned and crunchy.
5. Use a nonstick-safe spatula, and perhaps a flatware fork for balance, to transfer the sandwich(es) to a cutting board. Cool for 2 or 3 minutes before slicing in half and serving.

## Chili Cheese Dogs

Servings: 3
Cooking Time: 12 Minutes
**Ingredients:**
- ¾ pound Lean ground beef
- 1½ tablespoons Chile powder
- 1 cup plus 2 tablespoons Jarred sofrito
- 3 Hot dogs (gluten-free, if a concern)
- 3 Hot dog buns (gluten-free, if a concern), split open lengthwise
- 3 tablespoons Finely chopped scallion
- 9 tablespoons (a little more than 2 ounces) Shredded Cheddar cheese

**Directions:**
1. Crumble the ground beef into a medium or large saucepan set over medium heat. Brown well, stirring often to break up the clumps. Add the chile powder and cook for 30 seconds, stirring the whole time. Stir in the sofrito and bring to a simmer. Reduce the heat to low and simmer, stirring occasionally, for 5 minutes. Keep warm.
2. Preheat the air fryer to 400°F (205°C).
3. When the machine is at temperature, put the hot dogs in the basket and air-fry undisturbed for 10 minutes, or until the hot dogs are bubbling and blistered, even a little crisp.
4. Use kitchen tongs to put the hot dogs in the buns. Top each with a ½ cup of the ground beef mixture, 1 tablespoon of the minced scallion, and 3 tablespoons of the cheese. (The scallion should go under the cheese so it superheats and wilts a bit.) Set the filled hot dog buns in the basket and air-fry undisturbed for 2 minutes, or until the cheese has melted.
5. Remove the basket from the machine. Cool the chili cheese dogs in the basket for 5 minutes before serving.

## Chicken Club Sandwiches

Servings: 3
Cooking Time: 15 Minutes
**Ingredients:**
- 3 5- to 6-ounce boneless skinless chicken breasts
- 6 Thick-cut bacon strips (gluten-free, if a concern)
- 3 Long soft rolls, such as hero, hoagie, or Italian sub rolls (gluten-free, if a concern)
- 3 tablespoons Regular, low-fat, or fat-free mayonnaise (gluten-free, if a concern)
- 3 Lettuce leaves, preferably romaine or iceberg
- 6 ¼-inch-thick tomato slices

**Directions:**
1. Preheat the air fryer to 375°F (190°C).
2. Wrap each chicken breast with 2 strips of bacon, spiraling the bacon around the meat, slightly overlapping the

strips on each revolution. Start the second strip of bacon farther down the breast but on a line with the start of the first strip so they both end at a lined-up point on the chicken breast.

3. When the machine is at temperature, set the wrapped breasts bacon-seam side down in the basket with space between them. Air-fry undisturbed for 12 minutes, until the bacon is browned, crisp, and cooked through and an instant-read meat thermometer inserted into the center of a breast registers 165°F (75°C). You may need to add 2 minutes in the air fryer if the temperature is at 360°F (1805°C).

4. Use kitchen tongs to transfer the breasts to a wire rack. Split the rolls open lengthwise and set them cut side down in the basket. Air-fry for 1 minute, or until warmed through.

5. Use kitchen tongs to transfer the rolls to a cutting board. Spread 1 tablespoon mayonnaise on the cut side of one half of each roll. Top with a chicken breast, lettuce leaf, and tomato slice. Serve warm.

## Eggplant Parmesan Subs

Servings: 2
Cooking Time: 13 Minutes
**Ingredients:**
- 4 Peeled eggplant slices (about ½ inch thick and 3 inches in diameter)
- Olive oil spray
- 2 tablespoons plus 2 teaspoons Jarred pizza sauce, any variety except creamy
- ¼ cup (about ⅔ ounce) Finely grated Parmesan cheese
- 2 Small, long soft rolls, such as hero, hoagie, or Italian sub rolls (gluten-free, if a concern), split open lengthwise

**Directions:**
1. Preheat the air fryer to 350°F (175°C) .
2. When the machine is at temperature, coat both sides of the eggplant slices with olive oil spray. Set them in the basket in one layer and air-fry undisturbed for 10 minutes, until lightly browned and softened.
3. Increase the machine's temperature to 375°F (190°C) (or 370°F (1805°C), if that's the closest setting—unless the machine is already at 360°F (180°C), in which case leave it alone). Top each eggplant slice with 2 teaspoons pizza sauce, then 1 tablespoon cheese. Air-fry undisturbed for 2 minutes, or until the cheese has melted.
4. Use a nonstick-safe spatula, and perhaps a flatware fork for balance, to transfer the eggplant slices cheese side up to a cutting board. Set the roll(s) cut side down in the basket in one layer (working in batches as necessary) and air-fry undisturbed for 1 minute, to toast the rolls a bit and warm them up. Set 2 eggplant slices in each warm roll.

## Asian Glazed Meatballs

Servings: 4
Cooking Time: 10 Minutes
**Ingredients:**
- 1 large shallot, finely chopped
- 2 cloves garlic, minced
- 1 tablespoon grated fresh ginger
- 2 teaspoons fresh thyme, finely chopped
- 1½ cups brown mushrooms, very finely chopped (a food processor works well here)
- 2 tablespoons soy sauce
- freshly ground black pepper
- 1 pound ground beef
- ½ pound ground pork
- 3 egg yolks
- 1 cup Thai sweet chili sauce (spring roll sauce)
- ¼ cup toasted sesame seeds
- 2 scallions, sliced

**Directions:**
1. Combine the shallot, garlic, ginger, thyme, mushrooms, soy sauce, freshly ground black pepper, ground beef and pork, and egg yolks in a bowl and mix the ingredients together. Gently shape the mixture into 24 balls, about the size of a golf ball.
2. Preheat the air fryer to 380°F (195°C).
3. Working in batches, air-fry the meatballs for 8 minutes, turning the meatballs over halfway through the cooking time. Drizzle some of the Thai sweet chili sauce on top of each meatball and return the basket to the air fryer, air-frying for another 2 minutes. Reserve the remaining Thai sweet chili sauce for serving.
4. As soon as the meatballs are done, sprinkle with toasted sesame seeds and transfer them to a serving platter. Scatter the scallions around and serve warm.

## Best-ever Roast Beef Sandwiches

Servings: 6
Cooking Time: 30-50 Minutes
**Ingredients:**
- 2½ teaspoons Olive oil
- 1½ teaspoons Dried oregano
- 1½ teaspoons Dried thyme
- 1½ teaspoons Onion powder
- 1½ teaspoons Table salt
- 1½ teaspoons Ground black pepper
- 3 pounds Beef eye of round
- 6 Round soft rolls, such as Kaiser rolls or hamburger buns (gluten-free, if a concern), split open lengthwise
- ¾ cup Regular, low-fat, or fat-free mayonnaise (gluten-free, if a concern)
- 6 Romaine lettuce leaves, rinsed
- 6 Round tomato slices (¼ inch thick)

**Directions:**
1. Preheat the air fryer to 350°F (175°C).
2. Mix the oil, oregano, thyme, onion powder, salt, and pepper in a small bowl. Spread this mixture all over the eye of round.
3. When the machine is at temperature, set the beef in the basket and air-fry for 30 to 50 minutes (the range depends on the size of the cut), turning the meat twice, until an instant-read meat thermometer inserted into the thickest piece of the meat registers 130°F (55°C) for rare, 140°F (60°C) for medium, or 150°F (65°C) for well-done.
4. Use kitchen tongs to transfer the beef to a cutting board. Cool for 10 minutes. If serving now, carve into ⅛-inch-thick slices. Spread each roll with 2 tablespoons mayonnaise and divide the beef slices between the rolls. Top with a lettuce leaf and a tomato slice and serve. Or set the beef in a container, cover, and refrigerate for up to 3 days to make cold roast beef sandwiches anytime.

## Crunchy Falafel Balls

Servings: 8
Cooking Time: 16 Minutes
**Ingredients:**
- 2½ cups Drained and rinsed canned chickpeas
- ¼ cup Olive oil
- 3 tablespoons All-purpose flour
- 1½ teaspoons Dried oregano
- 1½ teaspoons Dried sage leaves
- 1½ teaspoons Dried thyme
- ¾ teaspoon Table salt
- Olive oil spray

**Directions:**
1. Preheat the air fryer to 400°F (205°C).
2. Place the chickpeas, olive oil, flour, oregano, sage, thyme, and salt in a food processor. Cover and process into a paste, stopping the machine at least once to scrape down the inside of the canister.
3. Scrape down and remove the blade. Using clean, wet hands, form 2 tablespoons of the paste into a ball, then continue making 9 more balls for a small batch, 15 more for a medium one, and 19 more for a large batch. Generously coat the balls in olive oil spray.
4. Set the balls in the basket in one layer with a little space between them and air-fry undisturbed for 16 minutes, or until well browned and crisp.
5. Dump the contents of the basket onto a wire rack. Cool for 5 minutes before serving.

# Appetizers And Snacks

## Cheesy Green Pitas

Servings: 4
Cooking Time: 15 Minutes
**Ingredients:**
- ½ cup canned artichoke hearts, sliced
- 2 whole-wheat pitas
- 2 tbsp olive oil, divided
- 2 garlic cloves, minced
- ¼ tsp salt
- ¼ cup green olives
- ¼ cup grated Pecorino
- ¼ cup crumbled feta
- 2 tbsp chopped chervil

**Directions:**
1. Preheat air fryer to 380°F (195°C). Lightly brush each pita with some olive oil, then top with garlic and salt. Divide the artichoke hearts, green olives, and cheeses evenly between the two pitas, and put both into the air fryer. Bake for 10 minutes. Remove the pitas and cut them into 4 pieces each before serving. Top with chervil. Enjoy!
2. Roast the shrimp for 4 minutes, then open the air fryer and place the ramekin with oil and garlic in the basket beside the shrimp packet. Cook for 2 more minutes. Place the shrimp on a serving plate or platter with the ramekin of garlic olive oil on the side for dipping.

## Pork Pot Stickers With Yum Yum Sauce

Servings: 48
Cooking Time: 8 Minutes
**Ingredients:**
- 1 pound ground pork
- 2 cups shredded green cabbage
- ¼ cup shredded carrot
- ½ cup finely chopped water chestnuts
- 2 teaspoons minced fresh ginger
- ¼ cup hoisin sauce
- 2 tablespoons soy sauce
- 1 tablespoon sesame oil
- freshly ground black pepper
- 3 scallions, minced
- 48 round dumpling wrappers (or wonton wrappers with the corners cut off to make them round)
- 1 tablespoon vegetable oil
- soy sauce, for serving
- Yum Yum Sauce:
- 1½ cups mayonnaise
- 2 tablespoons sugar
- 3 tablespoons rice vinegar
- 1 teaspoon soy sauce
- 2 tablespoons ketchup
- 1½ teaspoons paprika
- ¼ teaspoon ground cayenne pepper
- ¼ teaspoon garlic powder

**Directions:**
1. Preheat a large sauté pan over medium-high heat. Add the ground pork and brown for a few minutes. Remove the cooked pork to a bowl using a slotted spoon and discard the fat from the pan. Return the cooked pork to the sauté pan and add the cabbage, carrots and water chestnuts. Sauté for a minute and then add the fresh ginger, hoisin sauce, soy sauce, sesame oil, and freshly ground black pepper. Sauté for a few more minutes, just until cabbage and carrots are soft. Then stir in the scallions and transfer the pork filling to a bowl to cool.
2. Make the pot stickers in batches of 1 Place 12 dumpling wrappers on a flat surface. Brush a little water around the perimeter of the wrappers. Place a rounded teaspoon of the filling into the center of each wrapper. Fold the wrapper over the filling, bringing the edges together to form a half moon, sealing the edges shut. Brush a little more water on the top surface of the sealed edge of the pot sticker. Make pleats in the dough around the sealed edge by pinching the dough and folding the edge over on itself. You should have about 5 to 6 pleats in the dough. Repeat this three times until you have 48 pot stickers. Freeze the pot stickers for 2 hours (or as long as 3 weeks in an airtight container).
3. Preheat the air fryer to 400°F (205°C).
4. Air-fry the pot stickers in batches of 16. Brush or spray the pot stickers with vegetable oil just before putting them in the air fryer basket. Air-fry for 8 minutes, turning the pot stickers once or twice during the cooking process.
5. While the pot stickers are cooking, combine all the ingredients for the Yum Yum sauce in a bowl. Serve the pot stickers warm with the Yum Yum sauce and soy sauce for dipping.

## Beet Chips With Guacamole

Servings: 4
Cooking Time: 40 Minutes
**Ingredients:**
- 2 avocados, cubed
- 2 tbsp lime juice
- Celery salt to taste
- 2 beets, peeled
- 2 eggs, beaten
- 1 cup panko bread crumbs
- ½ tsp paprika

**Directions:**
1. Preheat the air fryer to 375°F (175°C). Mash the avocados, lime juice, and celery salt in a bowl, then pour the guacamole into a serving bowl, cover, and refrigerate. Slice the beets into 3-inch long sticks that are ½ inch thick. Beat the eggs in a shallow bowl and combine the panko and paprika on a plate. Dip the fries in the egg, then the panko mixture, coating well. Put the beets in the frying basket and spray with cooking oil, then Air Fry for 18-22 minutes or until crispy and golden. Serve with guacamole.

## Kale Chips

Servings: 2
Cooking Time: 5 Minutes
**Ingredients:**
- 4 Medium kale leaves, about 1 ounce each
- 2 teaspoons Olive oil
- 2 teaspoons Regular or low-sodium soy sauce or gluten-free tamari sauce

**Directions:**
1. Preheat the air fryer to 400°F (205°C).
2. Cut the stems from the leaves (all the stems, all the way up the leaf). Tear each leaf into three pieces. Put them in a large bowl.
3. Add the olive oil and soy or tamari sauce. Toss well to coat. You can even gently rub the leaves along the side of the bowl to get the liquids to stick to them.
4. When the machine is at temperature, put the leaf pieces in the basket in one layer. Air-fry for 5 minutes, turning and rearranging with kitchen tongs once halfway through, until the chips are dried out and crunchy. Watch carefully so they don't turn dark brown at the edges.
5. Gently pour the contents of the basket onto a wire rack. Cool for at least 5 minutes before serving. The chips can keep for up to 8 hours uncovered on the rack (provided it's not a humid day).

## Country Wings

Servings: 4
Cooking Time: 19 Minutes
**Ingredients:**
- 2 pounds chicken wings
- Marinade
- 1 cup buttermilk
- ½ teaspoon black pepper
- ½ teaspoon salt
- Coating
- 1 cup flour
- 1 cup panko breadcrumbs
- 2 teaspoons salt
- 2 tablespoons poultry seasoning
- oil for misting or cooking spray

**Directions:**
1. Cut the tips off the wings. Discard or freeze for stock. Cut remaining wing sections apart at the joint to make 2 pieces per wing. Place wings in a large bowl or plastic bag.
2. Mix together all marinade ingredients and pour over wings. Refrigerate for at least 1 hour but for no more than 8 hours.
3. Preheat air fryer to 360°F (180°C).
4. Mix all coating ingredients together in a shallow dish or on wax paper.
5. Remove wings from marinade, shaking off excess, and roll in coating mixture.
6. Spray both sides of each wing with oil or cooking spray.
7. Place wings in air fryer basket in single layer, close but not too crowded. Cook for 19 minutes or until chicken is done and juices run clear.
8. Repeat step 7 to cook remaining wings.

## Crunchy Parmesan Edamame

Servings: 4
Cooking Time: 25 Minutes + Cooling Time
**Ingredients:**
- 1 cup edamame, shelled
- 1 tbsp sesame oil
- 1 tsp five-spice powder
- ½ tsp salt
- ½ tsp garlic powder
- ¼ cup grated Parmesan

**Directions:**
1. Cook the edamame in boiling salted water until crisp-tender, about 10 minutes. Drain and leave to cool. Preheat air fryer to 350°F. Combine edamame, garlic, and sesame oil in a bowl. Place them in the frying basket and Air Fry for 16 minutes, shaking twice. Transfer to a small bowl and toss with five-spice powder and salt. Serve chilled topped with Parmesan cheese. Enjoy!

## Curly Kale Chips With Greek Sauce

Servings: 4
Cooking Time: 15 Minutes
**Ingredients:**
- 1 cup Greek yogurt
- 3 tbsp lemon juice
- ½ tsp mustard powder
- ½ tsp dried dill
- 1 tbsp ground walnuts
- 1 bunch curly kale
- 2 tbsp olive oil
- Salt and pepper to taste

**Directions:**
1. Preheat air fryer to 390°F (200°C). Mix together yogurt, lemon juice, mustard powder, ground walnuts, and dill until well blended. Set aside. Cut off the stems and ribs from the kale, then cut the leaves into 3-inch pieces.
2. In a bowl, toss the kale with olive oil, salt and pepper. Arrange the kale in the fryer and Air Fry for 2-3 minutes. Shake the basket, then cook for another 2-3 minutes or until the kale is crisp. Serve the chips with Greek sauce.

## Hot Nachos With Chile Salsa

Servings: 4
Cooking Time: 20 Minutes
**Ingredients:**
- ½ chile de árbol pepper, seeds removed
- 1 tbsp olive oil
- Salt to taste
- 1 shallot, chopped
- 2 garlic cloves
- 1 can diced tomatoes
- 2 tbsp fresh cilantro
- Juice of 1 lime
- ¼ tsp chili-lime seasoning
- 6 corn tortillas

**Directions:**
1. Add the shallot, garlic, chile de árbol, tomatoes, cilantro, lime juice and salt in a food processor. Pulse until combined and chunky. Pour the salsa into a serving bowl and set aside. Drizzle olive oil on both sides of the tortillas. Stack the tortilla and cut them in half with a sharp knife. Continue to cut into quarters, then cut again so that each tortilla is cut into 8 equal wedges. Season both sides of each wedge with chile-lime seasoning.
2. Preheat air fryer to 400°F (205°C). Place the tortilla wedges in the greased frying basket and Air Fry for 4-7 minutes, shaking once until the chips are golden and crisp.

Allow to cool slightly and serve with previously prepared salsa.

## Mozzarella En Carrozza With Puttanesca Sauce

Servings: 6
Cooking Time: 8 Minutes
**Ingredients:**
- Puttanesca Sauce
- 2 teaspoons olive oil
- 1 anchovy, chopped (optional)
- 2 cloves garlic, minced
- 1 (14-ounce) can petite diced tomatoes
- ½ cup chicken stock or water
- ⅓ cup Kalamata olives, chopped
- 2 tablespoons capers
- ½ teaspoon dried oregano
- ¼ teaspoon crushed red pepper flakes
- salt and freshly ground black pepper
- 1 tablespoon fresh parsley, chopped
- 8 slices of thinly sliced white bread (Pepperidge Farm®)
- 8 ounces mozzarella cheese, cut into ¼-inch slices
- ½ cup all-purpose flour
- 3 eggs, beaten
- 1½ cups seasoned panko breadcrumbs
- ½ teaspoon garlic powder
- ½ teaspoon salt
- freshly ground black pepper
- olive oil, in a spray bottle

**Directions:**
1. Start by making the puttanesca sauce. Heat the olive oil in a medium saucepan on the stovetop. Add the anchovies (if using, and I really think you should!) and garlic and sauté for 3 minutes, or until the anchovies have "melted" into the oil. Add the tomatoes, chicken stock, olives, capers, oregano and crushed red pepper flakes and simmer the sauce for 20 minutes. Season with salt and freshly ground black pepper and stir in the fresh parsley.
2. Cut the crusts off the slices of bread. Place four slices of the bread on a cutting board. Divide the cheese between the four slices of bread. Top the cheese with the remaining four slices of bread to make little sandwiches and cut each sandwich into 4 triangles.
3. Set up a dredging station using three shallow dishes. Place the flour in the first shallow dish, the eggs in the second dish and in the third dish, combine the panko breadcrumbs, garlic powder, salt and black pepper. Dredge each little triangle in the flour first (you might think this is

redundant, but it helps to get the coating to adhere to the edges of the sandwiches) and then dip them into the egg, making sure both the sides and the edges are coated. Let the excess egg drip off and then press the triangles into the breadcrumb mixture, pressing the crumbs on with your hands so they adhere. Place the coated triangles in the freezer for 2 hours, until the cheese is frozen.

4. Preheat the air fryer to 390°F (200°C). Spray all sides of the mozzarella triangles with oil and transfer a single layer of triangles to the air fryer basket. Air-fry in batches at 390°F (200°C) for 5 minutes. Turn the triangles over and air-fry for an additional 3 minutes.

5. Serve mozzarella triangles immediately with the warm puttanesca sauce.

## Eggs In Avocado Halves

Servings: 3
Cooking Time: 23 Minutes
**Ingredients:**
- 3 Hass avocados, halved and pitted but not peeled
- 6 Medium eggs
- Vegetable oil spray
- 3 tablespoons Heavy or light cream (not fat-free cream)
- To taste Table salt
- To taste Ground black pepper

**Directions:**
1. Preheat the air fryer to 350°F (175°C).
2. Slice a small amount off the (skin) side of each avocado half so it can sit stable, without rocking. Lightly coat the skin of the avocado half (the side that will now sit stable) with vegetable oil spray.
3. Arrange the avocado halves open side up on a cutting board, then crack an egg into the indentation in each where the pit had been. If any white overflows the avocado half, wipe that bit of white off the cut edge of the avocado before proceeding.
4. Remove the basket (or its attachment) from the machine and set the filled avocado halves in it in one layer. Return it to the machine without pushing it in. Drizzle each avocado half with about 1½ teaspoons cream, a little salt, and a little ground black pepper.
5. Air-fry undisturbed for 10 minutes for a soft-set yolk, or air-fry for 13 minutes for more-set eggs.
6. Use a nonstick-safe spatula and a flatware fork for balance to transfer the avocado halves to serving plates. Cool a minute or two before serving.

## Curried Pickle Chips

Servings: 4
Cooking Time: 25 Minutes
**Ingredients:**
- 2 dill pickles, sliced
- 1 cup breadcrumbs
- 2 eggs, beaten
- A pinch of white pepper
- 1 tsp curry powder
- ½ tsp mustard powder

**Directions:**
1. Preheat air fryer to 350°F (175°C). Combine the breadcrumbs, curry, mustard powder, and white pepper in a mixing bowl. Coat the pickle slices with the crumb mixture; then dip into the eggs, then dip again into the dry ingredients. Arrange the coated pickle pieces on the greased frying basket in an even layer. Air Fry for 15 minutes, shaking the basket several times during cooking until crispy, golden brown and perfect. Serve warm.

## Russian Pierogi With Cheese Dip

Servings: 6
Cooking Time: 20 Minutes
**Ingredients:**
- 1 package frozen pierogi
- 1 cup sour cream
- 1 tbsp fresh lemon juice
- ½ chopped red bell pepper
- 3 spring onions, chopped
- ½ cup shredded carrot
- 1 tsp dried rosemary

**Directions:**
1. Preheat the air fryer to 400°F (205°C). Mix the sour cream and lemon juice in a bowl, then add the bell pepper, spring onions, carrot, and rosemary and mix well. Set the dip aside. Put as many frozen pierogi as will fit in the frying basket in a single layer and spray with cooking oil. Air Fry for 11-14 minutes, rotating pierogis once until golden. Repeat with the remaining pierogi. Serve with the dip.

## Onion Puffs

Servings: 14
Cooking Time: 8 Minutes
**Ingredients:**
- Vegetable oil spray
- ¾ cup Chopped yellow or white onion
- ½ cup Seasoned Italian-style panko bread crumbs
- 4½ tablespoons All-purpose flour
- 4½ tablespoons Whole, low-fat, or fat-free milk
- 1½ tablespoons Yellow cornmeal
- 1¼ teaspoons Granulated white sugar
- ½ teaspoon Baking powder

- ¼ teaspoon Table salt

**Directions:**
1. Cut or tear a piece of aluminum foil so that it lines the air fryer's basket with a ½-inch space on each of its four sides. Lightly coat the foil with vegetable oil spray, then set the foil sprayed side up inside the basket.
2. Preheat the air fryer to 400°F (205°C).
3. Stir the onion, bread crumbs, flour, milk, cornmeal, sugar, baking powder, and salt in a bowl to form a thick batter.
4. Remove the basket from the machine. Drop the onion batter by 2-tablespoon measures onto the foil, spacing the mounds evenly across its surface. Return the basket to the machine and air-fry undisturbed for 4 minutes.
5. Remove the basket from the machine. Lightly coat the puffs with vegetable oil spray. Use kitchen tongs to pick up a corner of the foil, then gently pull it out of the basket, letting the puffs slip onto the basket directly. Return the basket to the machine and continue air-frying undisturbed for 8 minutes, or until brown and crunchy.
6. Use kitchen tongs to transfer the puffs to a wire rack or a serving platter. Cool for 5 minutes before serving.

## Fried Green Tomatoes

Servings: 4
Cooking Time: 15 Minutes
**Ingredients:**
- 2 eggs
- ¼ cup buttermilk
- ½ cup cornmeal
- ½ cup breadcrumbs
- ¼ teaspoon salt
- 1½ pounds firm green tomatoes, cut in ¼-inch slices
- oil for misting or cooking spray
- Horseradish Drizzle
- ¼ cup mayonnaise
- ¼ cup sour cream
- 2 teaspoons prepared horseradish
- ½ teaspoon Worcestershire sauce
- ½ teaspoon lemon juice
- ⅛ teaspoon black pepper

**Directions:**
1. Mix all ingredients for Horseradish Drizzle together and chill while you prepare the green tomatoes.
2. Preheat air fryer to 390°F (200°C).
3. Beat the eggs and buttermilk together in a shallow bowl.
4. Mix cornmeal, breadcrumbs, and salt together in a plate or shallow dish.
5. Dip 4 tomato slices in the egg mixture, then roll in the breadcrumb mixture.
6. Mist one side with oil and place in air fryer basket, oil-side down, in a single layer.
7. Mist the top with oil.
8. Cook for 15minutes, turning once, until brown and crispy.
9. Repeat steps 5 through 8 to cook remaining tomatoes.
10. Drizzle horseradish sauce over tomatoes just before serving.

## Cauliflower "tater" Tots

Servings: 6
Cooking Time: 10 Minutes
**Ingredients:**
- 1 head of cauliflower
- 2 eggs
- ¼ cup all-purpose flour*
- ½ cup grated Parmesan cheese
- 1 teaspoon salt
- freshly ground black pepper
- vegetable or olive oil, in a spray bottle

**Directions:**
1. Grate the head of cauliflower with a box grater or finely chop it in a food processor. You should have about 3½ cups. Place the chopped cauliflower in the center of a clean kitchen towel and twist the towel tightly to squeeze all the water out of the cauliflower. (This can be done in two batches to make it easier to drain all the water from the cauliflower.)
2. Place the squeezed cauliflower in a large bowl. Add the eggs, flour, Parmesan cheese, salt and freshly ground black pepper. Shape the cauliflower into small cylinders or "tater tot" shapes, rolling roughly one tablespoon of the mixture at a time. Place the tots on a cookie sheet lined with paper towel to absorb any residual moisture. Spray the cauliflower tots all over with oil.
3. Preheat the air fryer to 400°F (205°C).
4. Air-fry the tots at 400°F (205°C), one layer at a time for 10 minutes, turning them over for the last few minutes of the cooking process for even browning. Season with salt and black pepper. Serve hot with your favorite dipping sauce.

## Enchilada Chicken Dip

Servings: 6
Cooking Time: 20 Minutes
**Ingredients:**
- 1 cup chopped cooked chicken breasts
- 1 can diced green chiles, including juice
- 8 oz cream cheese, softened
- ¼ cup mayonnaise
- ¼ cup sour cream
- 2 tbsp chopped onion
- 1 jalapeño pepper, minced
- 1 cup shredded mozzarella
- ¼ cup diced tomatoes
- 1 tsp chili powder

**Directions:**
1. Preheat air fryer to 400°F. Beat the cream cheese, mayonnaise, and sour cream in a bowl until smooth. Stir in the cooked chicken, onion, green chiles, jalapeño, and ½ cup of mozzarella cheese. Spoon the mixture into a baking dish. Sprinkle the remaining cheese on top, and place the dish in the fryer. Bake for 10 minutes. Garnish the dip with diced tomatoes and chili powder. Serve.

## Chili Corn On The Cob

Servings: 4
Cooking Time: 30 Minutes
**Ingredients:**
- Salt and pepper to taste
- ½ tsp smoked paprika
- ¼ tsp chili powder
- 4 ears corn, halved
- 1 tbsp butter, melted
- ¼ cup lime juice
- 1 tsp lime zest
- 1 lime, quartered

**Directions:**
1. Preheat air fryer to 400°F (205°C). Combine salt, pepper, lime juice, lime zest, paprika, and chili powder in a small bowl. Toss corn and butter in a large bowl, then add the seasonings from the small bowl. Toss until coated. Arrange the corn in a single layer in the frying basket. Air Fry for 10 minutes, then turn the corn. Air Fry for another 8 minutes. Squeeze lime over the corn and serve.

## Buffalo Wings

Servings: 2
Cooking Time: 12 Minutes Per Batch
**Ingredients:**
- 2 pounds chicken wings
- 3 tablespoons butter, melted
- ¼ cup hot sauce (like Crystal® or Frank's®)
- Finishing Sauce:
- 3 tablespoons butter, melted
- ¼ cup hot sauce (like Crystal® or Frank's®)
- 1 teaspoon Worcestershire sauce

**Directions:**
1. Prepare the chicken wings by cutting off the wing tips and discarding (or freezing for chicken stock). Divide the drumettes from the wingettes by cutting through the joint. Place the chicken wing pieces in a large bowl.
2. Combine the melted butter and the hot sauce and stir to blend well. Pour the marinade over the chicken wings, cover and let the wings marinate for 2 hours or up to overnight in the refrigerator.
3. Preheat the air fryer to 400°F (205°C).
4. Air-fry the wings in two batches for 10 minutes per batch, shaking the basket halfway through the cooking process. When both batches are done, toss all the wings back into the basket for another 2 minutes to heat through and finish cooking.
5. While the wings are air-frying, combine the remaining 3 tablespoons of butter, ¼ cup of hot sauce and the Worcestershire sauce. Remove the wings from the air fryer, toss them in the finishing sauce and serve with some cooling blue cheese dip and celery sticks.

## No-guilty Spring Rolls

Servings: 6
Cooking Time: 20 Minutes
**Ingredients:**
- 2 cups shiitake mushrooms, thinly sliced
- 4 cups green cabbage, shredded
- 4 tsp sesame oil
- 6 garlic cloves, minced
- 1 tbsp grated ginger
- 1 cup grated carrots
- Salt to taste
- 16 rice paper wraps
- ½ tsp ground cumin
- ½ tsp ground coriander

**Directions:**
1. Warm the sesame oil in a pan over medium heat. Add garlic, ginger, mushrooms, cabbage, carrots, cumin, coriander, and salt and stir-fry for 3-4 minutes or until the cabbage is wilted. Remove from heat. Get a piece of rice paper, wet with water, and lay it on a flat, non-absorbent surface. Place ¼ cup of the filling in the middle, then fold the bottom over the filling and fold the sides in. Roll up to make a mini burrito. Repeat until you have the number of spring rolls you want.
2. Preheat air fryer to 390°F (200°C). Place the spring rolls in the greased frying basket. Spray the tops with cooking oil and Air Fry for 8-10 minutes until golden. Serve immediately.

# Corn Tortilla Chips

Servings: 4
Cooking Time: 12 Minutes
**Ingredients:**
- Eight 6-inch corn tortillas
- ½ teaspoon sea salt
- ¼ teaspoon ground cumin
- ¼ teaspoon chili powder
- ¼ teaspoon garlic powder
- ⅛ teaspoon onion powder
- 1 tablespoon avocado oil

**Directions:**
1. Cut each corn tortilla into quarters, creating 32 chips in total.
2. Preheat the air fryer to 350°F (175°C).
3. In a small bowl, mix together the sea salt, cumin, chili powder, garlic powder, and onion powder.
4. Spray or brush one side of the tortillas with avocado oil. Sprinkle the seasoning mixture evenly over the oiled side of the chips.
5. Working in batches, place half the chips in the air fryer basket. Cook for 8 minutes, shake the basket, and cook another 2 to 4 minutes, checking for crispness. When the chips are golden brown, spread them out onto paper towels and allow them to cool for 3 minutes before serving. Repeat with the remaining chips.

# Crunchy Lobster Bites

Servings: 3
Cooking Time: 6 Minutes
**Ingredients:**
- 1 Large egg white(s)
- 2 tablespoons Water
- ½ cup All-purpose flour or gluten-free all-purpose flour
- ½ cup Yellow cornmeal
- 1 teaspoon Mild paprika
- 1 teaspoon Garlic powder
- 1 teaspoon Onion powder
- 1 teaspoon Table salt
- 4 Small (3- to 4-ounce) lobster tails
- Vegetable oil spray

**Directions:**
1. Preheat the air fryer to 400°F (205°C).
2. Whisk the egg white(s) and water in a shallow soup plate or small pie plate until foamy.
3. Stir the flour, cornmeal, paprika, garlic powder, onion powder, and salt in a large bowl until uniform.
4. Slice each lobster tail (shell and all) in half lengthwise, then pull the meat out of each half of the tail shell. Cut each strip of meat into 1-inch segments (2 or 3 segments per strip).
5. Dip a piece of lobster meat in the egg white mixture to coat it on all sides, letting any excess egg white slip back into the rest. Drop the piece of lobster meat into the bowl with the flour mixture. Continue on with the remaining pieces of lobster meat, getting them all in that bowl. Gently toss them all in the flour mixture until well coated.
6. Use two flatware forks to transfer the lobster pieces to a cutting board with the coating intact. Coat them on all sides with vegetable oil spray.
7. Set the lobster pieces in the basket in one layer. Air-fry undisturbed for 6 minutes, or until golden brown and crunchy. Gently dump the contents of the basket onto a wire rack and cool for 2 or 3 minutes before serving.

# Buffalo Cauliflower

Servings: 6
Cooking Time: 12 Minutes
**Ingredients:**
- 1 large head of cauliflower, washed and cut into medium-size florets
- ½ cup all-purpose flour
- ¼ cup melted butter
- 3 tablespoons hot sauce
- ½ teaspoon garlic powder
- ½ cup blue cheese dip or ranch dressing (optional)

**Directions:**
1. Preheat the air fryer to 350°F (175°C).
2. Make sure the cauliflower florets are dry, and then coat them in flour.
3. Liberally spray the air fryer basket with an olive oil mist. Place the cauliflower into the basket, making sure not to stack them on top of each other. Depending on the size of your air fryer, you may need to do this in two batches.
4. Cook for 6 minutes, then shake the basket, and cook another 6 minutes.
5. While cooking, mix the melted butter, hot sauce, and garlic powder in a large bowl.
6. Carefully remove the cauliflower from the air fryer. Toss the cauliflower into the butter mixture to coat. Repeat Steps 2–4 for any leftover cauliflower. Serve warm with the dip of your choice.

# Baba Ghanouj

Servings: 2
Cooking Time: 40 Minutes
**Ingredients:**
- 2 Small (12-ounce) purple Italian eggplant(s)
- ¼ cup Olive oil
- ¼ cup Tahini
- ½ teaspoon Ground black pepper
- ¼ teaspoon Onion powder
- ¼ teaspoon Mild smoked paprika (optional)
- Up to 1 teaspoon Table salt

**Directions:**
1. Preheat the air fryer to 400°F (205°C).
2. Prick the eggplant(s) on all sides with a fork. When the machine is at temperature, set the eggplant(s) in the basket in one layer. Air-fry undisturbed for 40 minutes, or until blackened and soft.
3. Remove the basket from the machine. Cool the eggplant(s) in the basket for 20 minutes.
4. Use a nonstick-safe spatula, and perhaps a flatware tablespoon for balance, to gently transfer the eggplant(s) to a bowl. The juices will run out. Make sure the bowl is close to the basket. Split the eggplant(s) open.
5. Scrape the soft insides of half an eggplant into a food processor. Repeat with the remaining piece(s). Add any juices from the bowl to the eggplant in the food processor, but discard the skins and stems.
6. Add the olive oil, tahini, pepper, onion powder, and smoked paprika (if using). Add about half the salt, then cover and process until smooth, stopping the machine at least once to scrape down the inside of the canister. Check the spread for salt and add more as needed. Scrape the baba ghanouj into a bowl and serve warm, or set aside at room temperature for up to 2 hours, or cover and store in the refrigerator for up to 4 days.

# Skinny Fries

Servings: 2
Cooking Time: 15 Minutes
**Ingredients:**
- 2 to 3 russet potatoes, peeled and cut into ¼-inch sticks
- 2 to 3 teaspoons olive or vegetable oil
- salt

**Directions:**
1. Cut the potatoes into ¼-inch strips. (A mandolin with a julienne blade is really helpful here.) Rinse the potatoes with cold water several times and let them soak in cold water for at least 10 minutes or as long as overnight.
2. Preheat the air fryer to 380°F (195°C).
3. Drain and dry the potato sticks really well, using a clean kitchen towel. Toss the fries with the oil in a bowl and then air-fry the fries in two batches at 380°F (195°C) for 15 minutes, shaking the basket a couple of times while they cook.
4. Add the first batch of French fries back into the air fryer basket with the finishing batch and let everything warm through for a few minutes. As soon as the fries are done, season them with salt and transfer to a plate or basket. Serve them warm with ketchup or your favorite dip.

# Roasted Red Pepper Dip

Servings: 2
Cooking Time: 15 Minutes
**Ingredients:**
- 2 Medium-size red bell pepper(s)
- 1¾ cups (one 15-ounce can) Canned white beans, drained and rinsed
- 1 tablespoon Fresh oregano leaves, packed
- 3 tablespoons Olive oil
- 1 tablespoon Lemon juice
- ½ teaspoon Table salt
- ½ teaspoon Ground black pepper

**Directions:**
1. Preheat the air fryer to 400°F (205°C).
2. Set the pepper(s) in the basket and air-fry undisturbed for 15 minutes, until blistered and even blackened.
3. Use kitchen tongs to transfer the pepper(s) to a zip-closed plastic bag or small bowl. Seal the bag or cover the bowl with plastic wrap. Set aside for 20 minutes.
4. Peel each pepper, then stem it, cut it in half, and remove all its seeds and their white membranes.
5. Set the pieces of the pepper in a food processor. Add the beans, oregano, olive oil, lemon juice, salt, and pepper. Cover and process until smooth, stopping the machine at least once to scrape down the inside of the canister. Scrape the dip into a bowl and serve warm, or cover and refrigerate for up to 3 days (although the dip tastes best if it's allowed to come back to room temperature).

# Canadian-inspired Waffle Poutine

Servings: 4
Cooking Time: 30 Minutes
**Ingredients:**
- 1 cup frozen waffle cut fries
- 2 tsp olive oil
- 1 red bell pepper, chopped
- 2 green onions, sliced
- 1 cup grated mozzarella
- ½ cup beef gravy

**Directions:**
1. Preheat air fryer to 380°F (195°C). Toss the waffle fries with olive oil, then place in the frying basket. Air Fry for

about 10-12 minutes, shake the basket once until crisp and lightly golden. Take the fries out of the basket and place in a baking pan. Top with peppers, green onions, and mozzarella cheese. Cook until the vegetables are tender, about 3 minutes. Remove the pan from the fryer and drizzle beef gravy over all of the fries and vegetables. Heat the gravy through for about 2 minutes, then serve.

## Cheeseburger Slider Pockets

Servings: 4
Cooking Time: 13 Minutes
**Ingredients:**
- 1 pound extra lean ground beef
- 2 teaspoons steak seasoning
- 2 tablespoons Worcestershire sauce
- 8 ounces Cheddar cheese
- ⅓ cup ketchup
- ¼ cup light mayonnaise
- 1 tablespoon pickle relish
- 1 pound frozen bread dough, defrosted
- 1 egg, beaten
- sesame seeds
- vegetable or olive oil, in a spray bottle

**Directions:**
1. Combine the ground beef, steak seasoning and Worcestershire sauce in a large bowl. Divide the meat mixture into 12 equal portions. Cut the Cheddar cheese into twelve 2-inch squares, about ¼-inch thick. Stuff a square of cheese into the center of each portion of meat and shape into a 3-inch patty.
2. Make the slider sauce by combining the ketchup, mayonnaise, and relish in a small bowl. Set aside.
3. Cut the bread dough into twelve pieces. Shape each piece of dough into a ball and use a rolling pin to roll them out into 4-inch circles. Dollop ½ teaspoon of the slider sauce into the center of each dough circle. Place a beef patty on top of the sauce and wrap the dough around the patty, pinching the dough together to seal the pocket shut. Try not to stretch the dough too much when bringing the edges together. Brush both sides of the slider pocket with the beaten egg. Sprinkle sesame seeds on top of each pocket.
4. Preheat the air fryer to 350°F (175°C).
5. Spray or brush the bottom of the air fryer basket with oil. Air-fry the slider pockets four at a time. Transfer the slider pockets to the air fryer basket, seam side down and air-fry at 350°F (175°C) for 10 minutes, until the dough is golden brown. Flip the slider pockets over and air-fry for another 3 minutes. When all the batches are done, pop all the sliders into the air fryer for a few minutes to re-heat and serve them hot out of the fryer.

## Charred Shishito Peppers

Servings: 4
Cooking Time: 5 Minutes
**Ingredients:**
- 20 shishito peppers (about 6 ounces)
- 1 teaspoon vegetable oil
- coarse sea salt
- 1 lemon

**Directions:**
1. Preheat the air fryer to 390°F (200°C).
2. Toss the shishito peppers with the oil and salt. You can do this in a bowl or directly in the air fryer basket.
3. Air-fry at 390°F (200°C) for 5 minutes, shaking the basket once or twice while they cook.
4. Turn the charred peppers out into a bowl. Squeeze some lemon juice over the top and season with coarse sea salt. These should be served as finger foods – pick the pepper up by the stem and eat the whole pepper, seeds and all. Watch for that surprise spicy one!

## Sausage And Cheese Rolls

Servings: 3
Cooking Time: 18 Minutes
**Ingredients:**
- 3 3- to 3½-ounce sweet or hot Italian sausage links
- 2 1-ounce string cheese stick(s), unwrapped and cut in half lengthwise
- Three quarters from one thawed sheet (cut the sheet into four quarters; wrap and refreeze one of them) A 17.25-ounce box frozen puff pastry

**Directions:**
1. Preheat the air fryer to 400°F (205°C).
2. When the machine is at temperature, set the sausage links in the basket and air-fry undisturbed for 12 minutes, or until cooked through.
3. Use kitchen tongs to transfer the links to a wire rack. Cool for 15 minutes. (If necessary, pour out any rendered fat that has collected below the basket in the machine.)
4. Cut the sausage links in half lengthwise. Sandwich half a string cheese stick between two sausage halves, trimming the ends so the cheese doesn't stick out beyond the meat.
5. Roll each piece of puff pastry into a 6 x 6-inch square on a clean, dry work surface. Set the sausage-cheese sandwich at one edge and roll it up in the dough. The ends will be open like a pig-in-a-blanket. Repeat with the remaining puff pastry, sausage, and cheese.
6. Set the rolls seam side down in the basket. Air-fry undisturbed for 6 minutes, or until puffed and golden brown.
7. Use a nonstick-safe spatula, and perhaps a flatware fork for balance, to transfer the rolls to a wire rack. Cool for at least 5 minutes before serving.

# Mustard Greens Chips With Curried Sauce

Servings: 4
Cooking Time: 20 Minutes
**Ingredients:**
- 1 cup plain yogurt
- 1 tbsp lemon juice
- 1 tbsp curry powder
- 1 bunch of mustard greens
- 2 tsp olive oil
- Sea salt to taste

**Directions:**
1. Preheat air fryer to 390°F (200°C). Using a sharp knife, remove and discard the ribs from the mustard greens. Slice the leaves into 2-3-inch pieces. Transfer them to a large bowl, then pour in olive oil and toss to coat. Air Fry for 5-6 minutes. Shake at least once. The chips should be crispy when finished. Sprinkle with a little bit of sea salt. Mix the yogurt, lemon juice, salt, and curry in a small bowl. Serve the greens with the sauce.

# Piri Piri Chicken Wings

Servings: 4
Cooking Time: 45 Minutes
**Ingredients:**
- 1 cup crushed cracker crumbs
- 1 tbsp sweet paprika
- 1 tbsp smoked paprika
- 1 tbsp Piri Piri seasoning
- 1 tsp sea salt
- 2 tsp onion powder
- 1 tsp garlic powder
- 2 lb chicken drumettes
- 2 tbsp olive oil

**Directions:**
1. Preheat the air fryer to 380°F (195°C). Combine the cracker crumbs, paprikas, Piri Piri seasoning, sea salt, onion and garlic powders in a bowl and mix well. Pour into a screw-top glass jar and set aside. Put the drumettes in a large bowl, drizzle with the olive oil, and toss to coat. Sprinkle 1/3 cup of the breading mix over the meat and press the mix into the drumettes. Put half the drumettes in the frying basket and Air Fry for 20-25 minutes, shaking the basket once until golden and crisp. Serve hot.

# Cherry Chipotle Bbq Chicken Wings

Servings: 2
Cooking Time: 12 Minutes
**Ingredients:**
- 1 teaspoon smoked paprika
- ½ teaspoon dry mustard powder
- 1 teaspoon dried oregano
- 1 teaspoon dried thyme
- ½ teaspoon chili powder
- 1 teaspoon salt
- 2 pounds chicken wings
- vegetable oil or spray
- salt and freshly ground black pepper
- 1 to 2 tablespoons chopped chipotle peppers in adobo sauce
- ⅓ cup cherry preserves ¼ cup tomato ketchup

**Directions:**
1. Combine the first six ingredients in a large bowl. Prepare the chicken wings by cutting off the wing tips and discarding (or freezing for chicken stock). Divide the drumettes from the win-gettes by cutting through the joint. Place the chicken wing pieces in the bowl with the spice mix. Toss or shake well to coat.
2. Preheat the air fryer to 400°F (205°C).
3. Spray the wings lightly with the vegetable oil and air-fry the wings in two batches for 10 minutes per batch, shaking the basket halfway through the cooking process. When both batches are done, toss all the wings back into the basket for another 2 minutes to heat through and finish cooking.
4. While the wings are air-frying, combine the chopped chipotle peppers, cherry preserves and ketchup in a bowl.
5. Remove the wings from the air fryer, toss them in the cherry chipotle BBQ sauce and serve with napkins!

# Sweet And Salty Snack Mix

Servings: 10
Cooking Time: 12 Minutes
**Ingredients:**
- ½ cup honey
- 3 tablespoons butter, melted
- 1 teaspoon salt
- 2 cups sesame sticks
- 1 cup pepitas (pumpkin seeds)
- 2 cups granola
- 1 cup cashews
- 2 cups crispy corn puff cereal (Kix® or Corn Pops®)
- 2 cups mini pretzel crisps
- 1 cup dried cherries

**Directions:**
1. Combine the honey, butter and salt in a small bowl or measuring cup and stir until combined.
2. Combine the sesame sticks, pepitas, granola, cashews, corn puff cereal and pretzel crisps in a large bowl. Pour the honey mixture over the top and toss to combine.
3. Preheat air fryer to 370°F (185°C).

4. Air-fry the snack mix in two batches. Place half the mixture in the air fryer basket and air-fry for 12 minutes, or until the snack mix is lightly toasted. Toss the basket several times throughout the process so that the mix cooks evenly and doesn't get too dark on top.
5. Transfer the snack mix to a cookie sheet and let it cool completely. Mix in the dried cherries and store the mix in an airtight container for up to a week or two.

## Homemade Pretzel Bites

Servings: 8
Cooking Time: 6 Minutes
**Ingredients:**
- 4¾ cups filtered water, divided
- 1 tablespoon butter
- 1 package fast-rising yeast
- ½ teaspoon salt
- 2⅓ cups bread flour
- 2 tablespoons baking soda
- 2 egg whites
- 1 teaspoon kosher salt

**Directions:**
1. Preheat the air fryer to 370°F (185°C).
2. In a large microwave-safe bowl, add ¾ cup of the water. Heat for 40 seconds in the microwave. Remove and whisk in the butter; then mix in the yeast and salt. Let sit 5 minutes.
3. Using a stand mixer with a dough hook attachment, add the yeast liquid and mix in the bread flour ⅓ cup at a time until all the flour is added and a dough is formed.
4. Remove the bowl from the stand; then let the dough rise 1 hour in a warm space, covered with a kitchen towel.
5. After the dough has doubled in size, remove from the bowl and punch down a few times on a lightly floured flat surface.
6. Divide the dough into 4 balls; then roll each ball out into a long, skinny, sticklike shape. Using a sharp knife, cut each dough stick into 6 pieces.
7. Repeat Step 6 for the remaining dough balls until you have about 24 bites formed.
8. Heat the remaining 4 cups of water over the stovetop in a medium pot with the baking soda stirred in.
9. Drop the pretzel bite dough into the hot water and let boil for 60 seconds, remove, and let slightly cool.
10. Lightly brush the top of each bite with the egg whites, and then cover with a pinch of kosher salt.
11. Spray the air fryer basket with olive oil spray and place the pretzel bites on top. Cook for 6 to 8 minutes, or until lightly browned. Remove and keep warm.
12. Repeat until all pretzel bites are cooked.
13. Serve warm.

## Crispy Wontons

Servings: 8
Cooking Time: 10 Minutes
**Ingredients:**
- ½ cup refried beans
- 3 tablespoons salsa
- ¼ cup canned artichoke hearts, drained and patted dry
- ¼ cup frozen spinach, defrosted and squeezed dry
- 2 ounces cream cheese
- 1½ teaspoons dried oregano, divided
- ¼ teaspoon garlic powder
- ¼ teaspoon onion powder
- ½ teaspoon salt
- ¼ cup chopped pepperoni
- ¼ cup grated mozzarella cheese
- 1 tablespoon grated Parmesan
- 2 ounces cream cheese
- ½ teaspoon dried oregano
- 32 wontons
- 1 cup water

**Directions:**
1. Preheat the air fryer to 370°F (185°C).
2. In a medium bowl, mix together the refried beans and salsa.
3. In a second medium bowl, mix together the artichoke hearts, spinach, cream cheese, oregano, garlic powder, onion powder, and salt.
4. In a third medium bowl, mix together the pepperoni, mozzarella cheese, Parmesan cheese, cream cheese, and the remaining ½ teaspoon of oregano.
5. Get a towel lightly damp with water and ring it out. While working with the wontons, leave the unfilled wontons under the damp towel so they don't dry out.
6. Working with 8 wontons at a time, place 2 teaspoons of one of the fillings into the center of the wonton, rotating among the different fillings (one filling per wonton). Working one at a time, use a pastry brush, dip the pastry brush into the water, and brush the edges of the dough with the water. Fold the dough in half to form a triangle and set aside. Continue until 8 wontons are formed. Spray the wontons with cooking spray and cover with a dry towel. Repeat until all 32 wontons have been filled.
7. Place the wontons into the air fryer basket, leaving space between the wontons, and cook for 5 minutes. Turn over and check for brownness, and then cook for another 5 minutes.

# Bread And Breakfast

## Cheesy Egg Bites

Servings: 6
Cooking Time: 35 Minutes
**Ingredients:**
- ½ cup shredded Muenster cheese
- 5 eggs, beaten
- 3 tbsp sour cream
- ½ tsp dried oregano
- Salt and pepper to taste
- 1/3 cup minced bell pepper
- 3 tbsp minced scallions

**Directions:**
1. Preheat the air fryer to 325°F (160°C). Make a foil sling: Fold an 18-inch-long piece of heavy-duty aluminum foil lengthwise into thirds. Combine the eggs, sour cream, oregano, salt, and pepper in a bowl. Add the bell peppers, scallions, and cheese and stir. Add the mixture to 6 egg bite cups, making sure to get some of the solids in each cup.
2. Put the egg bite pan on the sling you made and lower it into the fryer. Leave the foil in but bend down the edges so they fit. Bake the bites for 10-15 minutes or until a toothpick inserted into the center comes out clean. Remove the egg bite pan using the foil sling. Cool for 5 minutes, then turn the pan upside down over a plate to remove the egg bites. Serve warm.

## Carrot Muffins

Servings: 4
Cooking Time: 35 Minutes + Cooling Time
**Ingredients:**
- 1 ½ cups flour
- ½ tsp baking soda
- ½ tsp baking powder
- 1/3 cup brown sugar
- ½ tsp ground cinnamon
- 2 eggs
- 2/3 cup almond milk
- 3 tbsp sunflower oil
- ½ cup shredded carrots
- 1/3 cup golden raisins

**Directions:**
1. Preheat air fryer to 320°F (160°C). Mix the flour, baking powder, baking soda, brown sugar, and cinnamon in a bowl. In a smaller bowl, whisk the eggs, almond milk, and oil. Combine the mixtures, stir, but leave some lumps in the batter. Add the carrots and raisins and stir. Make 8 foil muffin cups by doubling 16 cups. Set 4 cups in the air fryer and put the batter in the cups until they're ¾ full. Bake in the fryer for 13-17 minutes; the muffin tops should bounce when touched. Repeat until all muffins are done. Let the muffins cool on a rack, then serve.

## Pumpkin Loaf

Servings: 6
Cooking Time: 22 Minutes
**Ingredients:**
- cooking spray
- 1 large egg
- ½ cup granulated sugar
- 1/3 cup oil
- ½ cup canned pumpkin (not pie filling)
- ½ teaspoon vanilla
- ⅔ cup flour plus 1 tablespoon
- ½ teaspoon baking powder
- ½ teaspoon baking soda
- ½ teaspoon salt
- 1 teaspoon pumpkin pie spice
- ¼ teaspoon cinnamon

**Directions:**
1. Spray 6 x 6-inch baking dish lightly with cooking spray.
2. Place baking dish in air fryer basket and preheat air fryer to 330°F (165°C).
3. In a large bowl, beat eggs and sugar together with a hand mixer.
4. Add oil, pumpkin, and vanilla and mix well.
5. Sift together all dry ingredients. Add to pumpkin mixture and beat well, about 1 minute.
6. Pour batter in baking dish and cook at 330°F (165°C) for 22 minutes or until toothpick inserted in center of loaf comes out clean.

## Smoked Salmon Croissant Sandwich

Servings: 1
Cooking Time: 30 Minutes
**Ingredients:**
- 1 croissant, halved
- 2 eggs
- 1 tbsp guacamole
- 1 smoked salmon slice
- Salt and pepper to taste

**Directions:**

1. Preheat air fryer to 360°F (180°C). Place the croissant, crusty side up, in the frying basket side by side. Whisk the eggs in a small ceramic dish until fluffy. Place in the air fryer. Bake for 10 minutes. Gently scramble the half-cooked egg in the baking dish with a fork. Flip the croissant and cook for another 10 minutes until the scrambled eggs are cooked, but still fluffy, and the croissant is toasted.

2. Place one croissant on a serving plate, then spread the guacamole on top. Scoop the scrambled eggs onto guacamole, then top with smoked salmon. Sprinkle with salt and pepper. Top with the second slice of toasted croissant, close sandwich, and serve hot.

## Walnut Pancake

Servings: 4
Cooking Time: 20 Minutes
**Ingredients:**
- 3 tablespoons butter, divided into thirds
- 1 cup flour
- 1½ teaspoons baking powder
- ¼ teaspoon salt
- 2 tablespoons sugar
- ¾ cup milk
- 1 egg, beaten
- 1 teaspoon pure vanilla extract
- ½ cup walnuts, roughly chopped
- maple syrup or fresh sliced fruit, for serving

**Directions:**
1. Place 1 tablespoon of the butter in air fryer baking pan. Cook at 330°F (165°C) for 3minutes to melt.
2. In a small dish or pan, melt the remaining 2 tablespoons of butter either in the microwave or on the stove.
3. In a medium bowl, stir together the flour, baking powder, salt, and sugar. Add milk, beaten egg, the 2 tablespoons of melted butter, and vanilla. Stir until combined but do not beat. Batter may be slightly lumpy.
4. Pour batter over the melted butter in air fryer baking pan. Sprinkle nuts evenly over top.
5. Cook for 20minutes or until toothpick inserted in center comes out clean. Turn air fryer off, close the machine, and let pancake rest for 2minutes.
6. Remove pancake from pan, slice, and serve with syrup or fresh fruit.

## Parsley Egg Scramble With Cottage Cheese

Servings:2
Cooking Time: 15 Minutes
**Ingredients:**
- 1 tbsp cottage cheese, crumbled
- 4 eggs
- Salt and pepper to taste
- 2 tsp heavy cream
- 1 tbsp chopped parsley

**Directions:**
1. Preheat air fryer to 400°F. Grease a baking pan with olive oil. Beat the eggs, salt, and pepper in a bowl. Pour it into the pan, place the pan in the frying basket, and Air Fry for 5 minutes. Using a silicone spatula, stir in heavy cream, cottage cheese, and half of parsley and Air Fry for another 2 minutes. Scatter with parsley to serve.

## Green Strata

Servings: 4
Cooking Time: 35 Minutes
**Ingredients:**
- 5 asparagus, chopped
- 4 eggs
- 3 tbsp milk
- 1 cup baby spinach, torn
- 2 bread slices, cubed
- ½ cup grated Gruyere cheese
- 2 tbsp chopped parsley
- Salt and pepper to taste

**Directions:**
1. Preheat air fryer to 340°F (170°C). Add asparagus spears and 1 tbsp water in a baking pan. Place the pan into the air fryer. Bake until crisp and tender, 3-5 minutes. Remove. Wipe to basket clean and spray with cooking spray. Return asparagus to the pan and arrange the bread cubes.
2. Beat the eggs and milk in a bowl. Then mix in baby spinach and Gruyere cheese, parsley, salt, and pepper. Pour over the asparagus and bread. Return to the fryer and Bake until eggs are set, and the tops browned, 12-14 minutes. Serve warm.

## Apple-cinnamon-walnut Muffins

Servings: 8
Cooking Time: 11 Minutes
**Ingredients:**
- 1 cup flour
- ⅓ cup sugar
- 1 teaspoon baking powder
- ¼ teaspoon baking soda
- ¼ teaspoon salt
- 1 teaspoon cinnamon
- ¼ teaspoon ginger
- ¼ teaspoon nutmeg

- 1 egg
- 2 tablespoons pancake syrup, plus 2 teaspoons
- 2 tablespoons melted butter, plus 2 teaspoons
- ¾ cup unsweetened applesauce
- ½ teaspoon vanilla extract
- ¼ cup chopped walnuts
- ¼ cup diced apple
- 8 foil muffin cups, liners removed and sprayed with cooking spray

**Directions:**
1. Preheat air fryer to 330°F (165°C).
2. In a large bowl, stir together flour, sugar, baking powder, baking soda, salt, cinnamon, ginger, and nutmeg.
3. In a small bowl, beat egg until frothy. Add syrup, butter, applesauce, and vanilla and mix well.
4. Pour egg mixture into dry ingredients and stir just until moistened.
5. Gently stir in nuts and diced apple.
6. Divide batter among the 8 muffin cups.
7. Place 4 muffin cups in air fryer basket and cook at 330°F (165°C) for 11 minutes.
8. Repeat with remaining 4 muffins or until toothpick inserted in center comes out clean.

## Spiced Apple Roll-ups

Servings: 8
Cooking Time: 40 Minutes
**Ingredients:**
- 2 Granny Smith apples, peeled and cored
- 3 tbsp ground cinnamon
- 3 tbsp granulated sugar
- 2 tsp ground nutmeg
- 1 tsp ground cardamom
- ½ tsp ground allspice
- ½ lemon, juiced and zested
- 10 tbsp butter, melted
- 2 tbsp brown sugar
- 8 thin slices white sandwich bread, crusts cut off

**Directions:**
1. Preheat the air fryer to 350°F (175°C). Combine the cinnamon, granulated sugar, nutmeg, lemon juice and zest, cardamom, and allspice in a bowl and mix well. Pour the spice mix into a small glass jar and set aside. Cut the apples into ½-inch pieces and put the pieces in a cake pan. Drizzle 2 tbsp of melted butter on top, then sprinkle brown sugar and a tsp of the spice mix; toss.
2. Put the pan in the frying basket and Bake the apples for 8-12 minutes or until tender without losing their shape. Remove from the air fryer and put them into a bowl to cool. Lay the sandwich bread slices on a clean workspace and roll with a rolling pin to about ¼ inch thickness.
3. Top the rolled bread with 2 tbsp of the apple mixture, then roll it up. Dip the roll-ups in the melted butter and sprinkle with ½ tsp of spice mix. Line a pan with round parchment paper, Put the rolls in a parchment-lined baking pan, seam side down, and Air Fry for 6-9 minutes or until brown and crisp. Serve warm.

## Lemon-blueberry Morning Bread

Servings: 2
Cooking Time: 15 Minutes
**Ingredients:**
- ½ cup flour
- ¼ cup powdered sugar
- ½ tsp baking powder
- ⅛ tsp salt
- 2 tbsp butter, melted
- 1 egg
- ½ tsp gelatin
- ½ tsp vanilla extract
- 1 tsp lemon zest
- ½ cup blueberries

**Directions:**
1. Preheat air fryer to 300°F. Mix the flour, sugar, baking powder, and salt in a bowl. In another bowl, whisk the butter, egg, gelatin, lemon zest, vanilla extract, and blueberries. Add egg mixture to flour mixture and stir until smooth. Spoon mixture into a pizza pan. Place pan in the frying basket and Bake for 10 minutes. Let sit for 5 minutes before slicing. Serve immediately.

## Spring Vegetable Omelet

Servings: 4
Cooking Time: 20 Minutes
**Ingredients:**
- ¼ cup chopped broccoli, lightly steamed
- ½ cup grated cheddar cheese
- 6 eggs
- ¼ cup steamed kale
- 1 green onion, chopped
- Salt and pepper to taste

**Directions:**
1. Preheat air fryer to 360°F (180°C). In a bowl, beat the eggs. Stir in kale, broccoli, green onion, and cheddar cheese. Transfer the mixture to a greased baking dish and Bake in the fryer for 15 minutes until golden and crisp. Season to taste and serve immediately.

# Peppered Maple Bacon Knots

Servings: 6
Cooking Time: 8 Minutes
**Ingredients:**
- 1 pound maple smoked center-cut bacon
- ¼ cup maple syrup
- ¼ cup brown sugar
- coarsely cracked black peppercorns

**Directions:**
1. Tie each bacon strip in a loose knot and place them on a baking sheet.
2. Combine the maple syrup and brown sugar in a bowl. Brush each knot generously with this mixture and sprinkle with coarsely cracked black pepper.
3. Preheat the air fryer to 390°F (200°C).
4. Air-fry the bacon knots in batches. Place one layer of knots in the air fryer basket and air-fry for 5 minutes. Turn the bacon knots over and air-fry for an additional 3 minutes.
5. Serve warm.

# White Wheat Walnut Bread

Servings: 8
Cooking Time: 25 Minutes
**Ingredients:**
- 1 cup lukewarm water (105–115°F) (40 - 45°C)
- 1 packet RapidRise yeast
- 1 tablespoon light brown sugar
- 2 cups whole-grain white wheat flour
- 1 egg, room temperature, beaten with a fork
- 2 teaspoons olive oil
- ½ teaspoon salt
- ½ cup chopped walnuts
- cooking spray

**Directions:**
1. In a small bowl, mix the water, yeast, and brown sugar.
2. Pour yeast mixture over flour and mix until smooth.
3. Add the egg, olive oil, and salt and beat with a wooden spoon for 2minutes.
4. Stir in chopped walnuts. You will have very thick batter rather than stiff bread dough.
5. Spray air fryer baking pan with cooking spray and pour in batter, smoothing the top.
6. Let batter rise for 15minutes.
7. Preheat air fryer to 360°F (180°C).
8. Cook bread for 25 minutes, until toothpick pushed into center comes out with crumbs clinging. Let bread rest for 10minutes before removing from pan.

# Hashbrown Potatoes Lyonnaise

Servings: 4
Cooking Time: 33 Minutes
**Ingredients:**
- 1 Vidalia (or other sweet) onion, sliced
- 1 teaspoon butter, melted
- 1 teaspoon brown sugar
- 2 large russet potatoes (about 1 pound), sliced ½-inch thick
- 1 tablespoon vegetable oil
- salt and freshly ground black pepper

**Directions:**
1. Preheat the air fryer to 370°F (185°C).
2. Toss the sliced onions, melted butter and brown sugar together in the air fryer basket. Air-fry for 8 minutes, shaking the basket occasionally to help the onions cook evenly.
3. While the onions are cooking, bring a 3-quart saucepan of salted water to a boil on the stovetop. Par-cook the potatoes in boiling water for 3 minutes. Drain the potatoes and pat them dry with a clean kitchen towel.
4. Add the potatoes to the onions in the air fryer basket and drizzle with vegetable oil. Toss to coat the potatoes with the oil and season with salt and freshly ground black pepper.
5. Increase the air fryer temperature to 400°F (205°C) and air-fry for 22 minutes tossing the vegetables a few times during the cooking time to help the potatoes brown evenly. Season to taste again with salt and freshly ground black pepper and serve warm.

# Egg & Bacon Toasts

Servings: 4
Cooking Time: 25 Minutes
**Ingredients:**
- 4 French bread slices, cut diagonally
- 1 + tsp butter
- 4 eggs
- 2 tbsp milk
- ½ tsp dried thyme
- Salt and pepper to taste
- 4 oz cooked bacon, crumbled
- 2/3 cup grated Colby cheese

**Directions:**
1. Preheat the air fryer to 350°F (175°C). Spray each slice of bread with oil and Bake in the frying basket for 2-3 minutes until light brown; set aside. Beat together the eggs, milk, thyme, salt, and pepper in a bowl and add the melted butter. Transfer to a 6-inch cake pan and place the pan into the fryer. Bake for 7-8 minutes, stirring once or until the eggs are set. Transfer the egg mixture into a bowl.
2. Top the bread slices with egg mixture, bacon, and cheese. Return to the fryer and Bake for 4-8 minutes or until the cheese melts and browns in spots. Serve.

# Almond Cranberry Granola

Servings: 12
Cooking Time: 9 Minutes
**Ingredients:**
- 2 tablespoons sesame seeds
- ¼ cup chopped almonds
- ¼ cup sunflower seeds
- ½ cup unsweetened shredded coconut
- 2 tablespoons unsalted butter, melted or at least softened
- 2 tablespoons coconut oil
- ⅓ cup honey
- 2½ cups oats
- ¼ teaspoon sea salt
- ½ cup dried cranberries

**Directions:**
1. In a large mixing bowl, stir together the sesame seeds, almonds, sunflower seeds, coconut, butter, coconut oil, honey, oats, and salt.
2. Line the air fryer basket with parchment paper. Punch 8 to 10 holes into the parchment paper with a fork so air can circulate. Pour the granola mixture onto the parchment paper.
3. Air fry the granola at 350°F (175°C) for 9 minutes, stirring every 3 minutes.
4. When cooking is complete, stir in the dried cranberries and allow the mixture to cool. Store in an airtight container up to 2 weeks or freeze for 6 months.

# Chorizo Sausage & Cheese Balls

Servings: 4
Cooking Time: 25 Minutes
**Ingredients:**
- 1 egg white
- 1 lb chorizo ground sausage
- ¼ tsp smoked paprika
- 2 tbsp canned green chiles
- ¼ cup bread crumbs
- ¼ cup grated cheddar

**Directions:**
1. Preheat air fryer to 400°F (205°C). Mix all ingredients in a large bowl. Form into 16 balls. Put the sausage balls in the frying basket and Air Fry for 6 minutes. When done, shake the basket and cook for an additional 6 minutes. Transfer to a serving plate and serve.

# Chocolate Chip Banana Muffins

Servings: 12
Cooking Time: 14 Minutes
**Ingredients:**
- 2 medium bananas, mashed
- ¼ cup brown sugar
- 1½ teaspoons vanilla extract
- ⅔ cup milk
- 2 tablespoons butter
- 1 large egg
- 1 cup white whole-wheat flour
- ½ cup old-fashioned oats
- 1 teaspoon baking soda
- ½ teaspoon baking powder
- ⅛ teaspoon sea salt
- ¼ cup mini chocolate chips

**Directions:**
1. Preheat the air fryer to 330°F (165°C).
2. In a large bowl, combine the bananas, brown sugar, vanilla extract, milk, butter, and egg; set aside.
3. In a separate bowl, combine the flour, oats, baking soda, baking powder, and salt.
4. Slowly add the dry ingredients into the wet ingredients, folding in the flour mixture ⅓ cup at a time.
5. Mix in the chocolate chips and set aside.
6. Using silicone muffin liners, fill 6 muffin liners two-thirds full. Carefully place the muffin liners in the air fryer basket and bake for 20 minutes (or until the tops are browned and a toothpick inserted in the center comes out clean). Carefully remove the muffins from the basket and repeat with the remaining batter.
7. Serve warm.

# Maple-peach And Apple Oatmeal

Servings: 4
Cooking Time: 15 Minutes
**Ingredients:**
- 2 cups old-fashioned rolled oats
- ½ tsp baking powder
- 1 ½ tsp ground cinnamon
- ¼ tsp ground flaxseeds
- ⅛ tsp salt
- 1 ¼ cups vanilla almond milk
- ¼ cup maple syrup
- 1 tsp vanilla extract
- 1 peeled peach, diced
- 1 peeled apple, diced

**Directions:**
1. Preheat air fryer to 350°F (175°C). Mix oats, baking powder, cinnamon, flaxseed, and salt in a large bowl. Next, stir in almond milk, maple syrup, vanilla, and ¾ of the diced peaches, and ¾ of the diced apple. Grease 6 ramekins. Divide the batter evenly between the ramekins and transfer the ramekins to the frying basket. Bake in the air fryer for 8-10 minutes until the top is golden and set. Garnish with the rest of the peaches and apples. Serve.

# Viking Toast

Servings: 2
Cooking Time: 20 Minutes
**Ingredients:**
- 2 tbsp minced green chili pepper
- 1 avocado, pressed
- 1 clove garlic, minced
- ¼ tsp lemon juice
- Salt and pepper to taste
- 2 bread slices
- 2 plum tomatoes, sliced
- 4 oz smoked salmon
- ¼ diced peeled red onion

**Directions:**
1. Preheat air fryer at 350°F. Combine the avocado, garlic, lemon juice, and salt in a bowl until you reach your desired consistency. Spread avocado mixture on the bread slices.
2. Top with tomato slices and sprinkle with black pepper. Place bread slices in the frying basket and Bake for 5 minutes. Transfer to a plate. Top each bread slice with salmon, green chili pepper, and red onion. Serve.

# Morning Loaded Potato Skins

Servings: 4
Cooking Time: 55 Minutes
**Ingredients:**
- 2 large potatoes
- 1 fried bacon slice, chopped
- Salt and pepper to taste
- 1 tbsp chopped dill
- 1 ½ tbsp butter
- 2 tbsp milk
- 4 eggs
- 1 scallion, sliced
- ¼ cup grated fontina cheese
- 2 tbsp chopped parsley

**Directions:**
1. Preheat air fryer to 400°F (205°C). Wash each potato and poke with fork 3 or 4 times. Place in the frying basket and bake for 40-45 minutes. Remove the potatoes and let cool until they can be handled. Cut each potato in half lengthwise. Scoop out potato flesh but leave enough to maintain the structure of the potato. Transfer the potato flesh to a medium bowl and stir in salt, pepper, dill, bacon, butter, and milk until mashed with some chunky pieces.
2. Fill the potato skin halves with the potato mixture and press the center of the filling with a spoon about ½-inch deep. Crack an egg in the center of each potato, then top with scallions and cheese. Return the potatoes to the air fryer and bake for 3 to 5 minutes until the egg is cooked to preferred doneness and cheese is melted. Serve immediately sprinkled with parsley.

# Vegetarian Quinoa Cups

Servings: 6
Cooking Time: 25 Minutes
**Ingredients:**
- 1 carrot, chopped
- 1 zucchini, chopped
- 4 asparagus, chopped
- ¾ cup quinoa flour
- 2 tbsp lemon juice
- ¼ cup nutritional yeast
- ¼ tsp garlic powder
- Salt and pepper to taste

**Directions:**
1. Preheat air fryer to 340°F (170°C). Combine the vegetables, quinoa flour, water, lemon juice, nutritional yeast, garlic powder, salt, and pepper in a medium bowl, and mix well. Divide the mixture between 6 cupcake molds. Place the filled molds into the air fryer and Bake for 20 minutes, or until the tops are lightly browned and a toothpick inserted into the center comes out clean. Serve cooled.

# Eggless Mung Bean Tart

Servings: 2
Cooking Time: 20 Minutes
**Ingredients:**
- 2 tsp soy sauce
- 1 tsp lime juice
- 1 large garlic clove, minced or pressed
- ½ tsp red chili flakes
- ½ cup mung beans, soaked
- Salt and pepper to taste
- ½ minced shallot
- 1 green onion, chopped

**Directions:**
1. Preheat the air fryer to 390°F (200°C). Add the soy sauce, lime juice, garlic, and chili flakes to a bowl and stir. Set aside. Place the drained beans in a blender along with ½ cup of water, salt, and pepper. Blend until smooth. Stir in shallot and green onion, but do not blend.
2. Pour the batter into a greased baking pan. Bake for 15 minutes in the air fryer until golden. A knife inserted in the center should come out clean. Once cooked, cut the "quiche" into quarters. Drizzle with sauce and serve.

# Coconut Mini Tarts

Servings: 2
Cooking Time: 25 Minutes
**Ingredients:**
- ¼ cup almond butter
- 1 tbsp coconut sugar
- 2 tbsp coconut yogurt
- ½ cup oat flour
- 2 tbsp strawberry jam

**Directions:**
1. Preheat air fryer to 350°F (175°C). Use 2 pieces of parchment paper, each 8-inches long. Draw a rectangle on one piece. Beat the almond butter, coconut sugar, and coconut yogurt in a shallow bowl until well combined. Mix in oat flour until you get a dough. Put the dough onto the undrawing paper and cover it with the other one, rectangle-side up. Using a rolling pin, roll out until you get a rectangle. Discard top paper.
2. Cut it into 4 equal rectangles. Spread on 2 rectangles, 1 tbsp of strawberry jam each, then top with the remaining rectangles. Using a fork, press all edges to seal them. Bake in the fryer for 8 minutes. Serve right away.

# Tri-color Frittata

Servings: 4
Cooking Time: 30 Minutes
**Ingredients:**
- 8 eggs, beaten
- 1 red bell pepper, diced
- Salt and pepper to taste
- 1 garlic clove, minced
- ½ tsp dried oregano
- ½ cup ricotta

**Directions:**
1. Preheat air fryer to 360°F (180°C). Place the beaten eggs, bell pepper, oregano, salt, black pepper, and garlic and mix well. Fold in ¼ cup half of ricotta cheese.
2. Pour the egg mixture into a greased cake pan and top with the remaining ricotta. Place into the air fryer and Bake for 18-20 minutes or until the eggs are set in the center. Let the frittata cool for 5 minutes. Serve sliced.

# Blueberry French Toast Sticks

Servings: 4
Cooking Time: 20 Minutes
**Ingredients:**
- 3 bread slices, cut into strips
- 1 tbsp butter, melted
- 2 eggs
- 1 tbsp milk
- 1 tbsp sugar
- ½ tsp vanilla extract
- 1 cup fresh blueberries
- 1 tbsp lemon juice

**Directions:**
1. Preheat air fryer to 380°F (195°C). After laying the bread strips on a plate, sprinkle some melted butter over each piece. Whisk the eggs, milk, vanilla, and sugar, then dip the bread in the mix. Place on a wire rack to let the batter drip. Put the bread strips in the air fryer and Air Fry for 5-7 minutes. Use tongs to flip them once and cook until golden. With a fork, smash the blueberries and lemon juice together. Spoon the blueberries sauce over the French sticks. Serve immediately.

# Egg & Bacon Pockets

Servings: 4
Cooking Time: 50 Minutes
**Ingredients:**
- 2 tbsp olive oil
- 4 bacon slices, chopped
- ¼ red bell pepper, diced
- 1/3 cup scallions, chopped
- 4 eggs, beaten
- 1/3 cup grated Swiss cheese
- 1 cup flour
- 1 ½ tsp baking powder
- ½ tsp salt
- 1 cup Greek yogurt
- 1 egg white, beaten
- 2 tsp Italian seasoning
- 1 tbsp Tabasco sauce

**Directions:**
1. Warm the olive oil in a skillet over medium heat and add the bacon. Stir-fry for 3-4 minutes or until crispy. Add the bell pepper and scallions and sauté for 3-4 minutes. Pour in the beaten eggs and stir-fry to scramble them, 3 minutes. Stir in the Swiss cheese and set aside to cool.
2. Sift the flour, baking powder, and salt in a bowl. Add yogurt and mix together until combined. Transfer the dough to a floured workspace. Knead it for 3 minutes or until smooth. Form the dough into 4 equal balls. Roll out the balls into round discs. Divide the bacon-egg mixture between the rounds. Fold the dough over the filling and seal the edges with a fork. Brush the pockets with egg white and sprinkle with Italian seasoning.
3. Preheat air fryer to 350°F (175°C). Arrange the pockets on the greased frying basket and Bake for 9-11 minutes, flipping once until golden. Serve with Tabasco sauce.

## Matcha Granola

Servings: 4
Cooking Time: 15 Minutes
**Ingredients:**
- 2 tsp matcha green tea
- ½ cup slivered almonds
- ½ cup pecan pieces
- ½ cup sunflower seeds
- ½ cup pumpkin seeds
- 1 cup coconut flakes
- ¼ cup coconut sugar
- ⅛ cup flour
- ⅛ cup almond flour
- 1 tsp vanilla extract
- 2 tbsp melted butter
- 2 tbsp almond butter
- ⅛ tsp salt

**Directions:**
1. Preheat air fryer to 300°F. Mix the green tea, almonds, pecan, sunflower seeds, pumpkin seeds, coconut flakes, sugar, and flour, almond flour, vanilla extract, butter, almond butter, and salt in a bowl. Spoon the mixture into an ungreased round 4-cup baking dish. Place it in the fryer and Bake for 6 minutes, stirring once. Transfer to an airtight container, let cool for 10 minutes, then cover and store at room temperature until ready to serve.

## Easy Caprese Flatbread

Servings: 2
Cooking Time: 15 Minutes
**Ingredients:**
- 1 fresh mozzarella ball, sliced
- 1 flatbread
- 2 tsp olive oil
- ¼ garlic clove, minced
- 1 egg
- ⅛ tsp salt
- ¼ cup diced tomato
- 6 basil leaves
- ½ tsp dried oregano
- ½ tsp balsamic vinegar

**Directions:**
1. Preheat air fryer to 380°F (195°C). Lightly brush the top of the bread with olive oil, then top with garlic. Crack the egg into a small bowl and sprinkle with salt. Place the bread into the frying basket and gently pour the egg onto the top of the pita. Top with tomato, mozzarella, oregano and basil. Bake for 6 minutes. When ready, remove the pita pizza and drizzle with balsamic vinegar. Let it cool for 5 minutes. Slice and serve.

## Farmers Market Quiche

Servings: 4
Cooking Time: 35 Minutes
**Ingredients:**
- 4 button mushrooms
- ¼ medium red bell pepper
- 1 teaspoon extra-virgin olive oil
- One 9-inch pie crust, at room temperature
- ¼ cup grated carrot
- ¼ cup chopped, fresh baby spinach leaves
- 3 eggs, whisked
- ¼ cup half-and-half
- ½ teaspoon thyme
- ½ teaspoon sea salt
- 2 ounces crumbled goat cheese or feta

**Directions:**
1. In a medium bowl, toss the mushrooms and bell pepper with extra-virgin olive oil; place into the air fryer basket. Set the temperature to 400°F (205°C) for 8 minutes, stirring after 4 minutes. Remove from the air fryer, and roughly chop the mushrooms and bell peppers. Wipe the air fryer clean.
2. Prep a 7-inch oven-safe baking dish by spraying the bottom of the pan with cooking spray.
3. Place the pie crust into the baking dish; fold over and crimp the edges or use a fork to press to give the edges some shape.
4. In a medium bowl, mix together the mushrooms, bell peppers, carrots, spinach, and eggs. Stir in the half-and-half, thyme, and salt.
5. Pour the quiche mixture into the base of the pie shell. Top with crumbled cheese.
6. Place the quiche into the air fryer basket. Set the temperature to 325°F (160°C) for 30 minutes.
7. When complete, turn the quiche halfway and cook an additional 5 minutes. Allow the quiche to rest 20 minutes prior to slicing and serving.

# Poultry Recipes

## Spicy Black Bean Turkey Burgers With Cumin-avocado Spread

Servings: 2
Cooking Time: 20 Minutes
**Ingredients:**
- 1 cup canned black beans, drained and rinsed
- ¾ pound lean ground turkey
- 2 tablespoons minced red onion
- 1 Jalapeño pepper, seeded and minced
- 2 tablespoons plain breadcrumbs
- ½ teaspoon chili powder
- ¼ teaspoon cayenne pepper
- salt, to taste
- olive or vegetable oil
- 2 slices pepper jack cheese
- toasted burger rolls, sliced tomatoes, lettuce leaves
- Cumin-Avocado Spread:
- 1 ripe avocado
- juice of 1 lime
- 1 teaspoon ground cumin
- ½ teaspoon salt
- 1 tablespoon chopped fresh cilantro
- freshly ground black pepper

**Directions:**
1. Place the black beans in a large bowl and smash them slightly with the back of a fork. Add the ground turkey, red onion, Jalapeño pepper, breadcrumbs, chili powder and cayenne pepper. Season with salt. Mix with your hands to combine all the ingredients and then shape them into 2 patties. Brush both sides of the burger patties with a little olive or vegetable oil.
2. Preheat the air fryer to 380°F (195°C).
3. Transfer the burgers to the air fryer basket and air-fry for 20 minutes, flipping them over halfway through the cooking process. Top the burgers with the pepper jack cheese (securing the slices to the burgers with a toothpick) for the last 2 minutes of the cooking process.
4. While the burgers are cooking, make the cumin avocado spread. Place the avocado, lime juice, cumin and salt in food processor and process until smooth. (For a chunkier spread, you can mash this by hand in a bowl.) Stir in the cilantro and season with freshly ground black pepper. Chill the spread until you are ready to serve.
5. When the burgers have finished cooking, remove them from the air fryer and let them rest on a plate, covered gently with aluminum foil. Brush a little olive oil on the insides of the burger rolls. Place the rolls, cut side up, into the air fryer basket and air-fry at 400°F (205°C) for 1 minute to toast and warm them.
6. Spread the cumin-avocado spread on the rolls and build your burgers with lettuce and sliced tomatoes and any other ingredient you like. Serve warm with a side of sweet potato fries.

## Chicken & Fruit Biryani

Servings: 4
Cooking Time: 30 Minutes
**Ingredients:**
- 3 chicken breasts, cubed
- 2 tsp olive oil
- 2 tbsp cornstarch
- 1 tbsp curry powder
- 1 apple, chopped
- ½ cup chicken broth
- 1/3 cup dried cranberries
- 1 cooked basmati rice

**Directions:**
1. Preheat air fryer to 380°F (195°C). Combine the chicken and olive oil, then add some corn starch and curry powder. Mix to coat, then add the apple and pour the mix in a baking pan. Put the pan in the air fryer and Bake for 8 minutes, stirring once. Add the chicken broth, cranberries, and 2 tbsp of water and continue baking for 10 minutes, letting the sauce thicken. The chicken should be lightly charred and cooked through. Serve warm with basmati rice.

## Chicken Fried Steak With Gravy

Servings: 4
Cooking Time: 10 Minutes Per Batch
**Ingredients:**
- ½ cup flour
- 2 teaspoons salt, divided
- freshly ground black pepper
- ¼ teaspoon garlic powder
- 1 cup buttermilk
- 1 cup fine breadcrumbs
- 4 tenderized top round steaks (about 6 to 8 ounces each; ½-inch thick)
- vegetable or canola oil
- For the Gravy:
- 2 tablespoons butter or bacon drippings

- ¼ onion, minced (about ¼ cup)
- 1 clove garlic, smashed
- ¼ teaspoon dried thyme
- 3 tablespoons flour
- 1 cup milk
- salt and lots of freshly ground black pepper
- a few dashes of Worcestershire sauce

**Directions:**
1. Set up a dredging station. Combine the flour, 1 teaspoon of salt, black pepper and garlic powder in a shallow bowl. Pour the buttermilk into a second shallow bowl. Finally, put the breadcrumbs and 1 teaspoon of salt in a third shallow bowl.
2. Dip the tenderized steaks into the flour, then the buttermilk, and then the breadcrumb mixture, pressing the crumbs onto the steak. Place them on a baking sheet and spray both sides generously with vegetable or canola oil.
3. Preheat the air fryer to 400°F (205°C).
4. Transfer the steaks to the air fryer basket, two at a time, and air-fry for 10 minutes, flipping the steaks over halfway through the cooking time. This will cook your steaks to medium. If you want the steaks cooked a little more or less, add or subtract a minute or two. Hold the first batch of steaks warm in a 170°F (75°C) oven while you cook the second batch.
5. While the steaks are cooking, make the gravy. Melt the butter in a small saucepan over medium heat on the stovetop. Add the onion, garlic and thyme and cook for five minutes, until the onion is soft and just starting to brown. Stir in the flour and cook for another five minutes, stirring regularly, until the mixture starts to brown. Whisk in the milk and bring the mixture to a boil to thicken. Season to taste with salt, lots of freshly ground black pepper and a few dashes of Worcestershire sauce.
6. Plate the chicken fried steaks with mashed potatoes and vegetables and serve the gravy at the table to pour over the top.

## Gluten-free Nutty Chicken Fingers

Servings: 4
Cooking Time: 10 Minutes
**Ingredients:**
- ½ cup gluten-free flour
- ½ teaspoon garlic powder
- ¼ teaspoon onion powder
- ¼ teaspoon black pepper
- ¼ teaspoon salt
- 1 cup walnuts, pulsed into coarse flour
- ½ cup gluten-free breadcrumbs
- 2 large eggs
- 1 pound boneless, skinless chicken tenders

**Directions:**
1. Preheat the air fryer to 400°F (205°C).
2. In a medium bowl, mix the flour, garlic, onion, pepper, and salt. Set aside.
3. In a separate bowl, mix the walnut flour and breadcrumbs.
4. In a third bowl, whisk the eggs.
5. Liberally spray the air fryer basket with olive oil spray.
6. Pat the chicken tenders dry with a paper towel. Dredge the tenders one at a time in the flour, then dip them in the egg, and toss them in the breadcrumb coating. Repeat until all tenders are coated.
7. Set each tender in the air fryer, leaving room on each side of the tender to allow for flipping.
8. When the basket is full, cook 5 minutes, flip, and cook another 5 minutes. Check the internal temperature after cooking completes; it should read 165°F (75°C). If it does not, cook another 2 to 4 minutes.
9. Remove the tenders and let cool 5 minutes before serving. Repeat until all the tenders are cooked.

## Yummy Maple-mustard Chicken Kabobs

Servings: 4
Cooking Time: 35 Minutes+ Chilling Time
**Ingredients:**
- 1 lb boneless, skinless chicken thighs, cubed
- 1 green bell pepper, chopped
- ½ cup honey mustard
- ½ yellow onion, chopped
- 8 cherry tomatoes
- 2 tbsp chopped scallions

**Directions:**
1. Toss chicken cubes and honey mustard in a bowl and let chill covered in the fridge for 30 minutes. Preheat air fryer to 350ºF. Thread chicken cubes, onion, cherry tomatoes, and bell peppers, alternating, onto 8 skewers. Place them on a kebab rack. Place rack in the frying basket and Air Fry for 12 minutes. Top with scallions to serve.

## Saucy Chicken Thighs

Servings: 4
Cooking Time: 35 Minutes
**Ingredients:**
- 8 boneless, skinless chicken thighs
- 1 tbsp Italian seasoning
- Salt and pepper to taste
- 2 garlic cloves, minced
- ½ tsp apple cider vinegar
- ½ cup honey
- ¼ cup Dijon mustard

**Directions:**
1. Preheat air fryer to 400°F (205°C). Season the chicken with Italian seasoning, salt, and black pepper. Place in the greased frying basket and Bake for 15 minutes, flipping once halfway through cooking.
2. While the chicken is cooking, add garlic, honey, vinegar, and Dijon mustard in a saucepan and stir-fry over medium heat for 4 minutes or until the sauce has thickened and warmed through. Transfer the thighs to a serving dish and drizzle with honey-mustard sauce. Serve and enjoy!

## Chicken Nuggets

Servings: 20
Cooking Time: 14 Minutes Per Batch
**Ingredients:**
- 1 pound boneless, skinless chicken thighs, cut into 1-inch chunks
- ¾ teaspoon salt
- ½ teaspoon black pepper
- ½ teaspoon garlic powder
- ½ teaspoon onion powder
- ½ cup flour
- 2 eggs, beaten
- ½ cup panko breadcrumbs
- 3 tablespoons plain breadcrumbs
- oil for misting or cooking spray

**Directions:**
1. In the bowl of a food processor, combine chicken, ½ teaspoon salt, pepper, garlic powder, and onion powder. Process in short pulses until chicken is very finely chopped and well blended.
2. Place flour in one shallow dish and beaten eggs in another. In a third dish or plastic bag, mix together the panko crumbs, plain breadcrumbs, and ¼ teaspoon salt.
3. Shape chicken mixture into small nuggets. Dip nuggets in flour, then eggs, then panko crumb mixture.
4. Spray nuggets on both sides with oil or cooking spray and place in air fryer basket in a single layer, close but not overlapping.
5. Cook at 360°F (180°C) for 10minutes. Spray with oil and cook 4 minutes, until chicken is done and coating is golden brown.
6. Repeat step 5 to cook remaining nuggets.

## Chicken Cutlets With Broccoli Rabe And Roasted Peppers

Servings: 2
Cooking Time: 10 Minutes
**Ingredients:**
- ½ bunch broccoli rabe
- olive oil, in a spray bottle
- salt and freshly ground black pepper
- ⅔ cup roasted red pepper strips
- 2 (4-ounce) boneless, skinless chicken breasts
- 2 tablespoons all-purpose flour*
- 1 egg, beaten
- ⅓ cup seasoned breadcrumbs*
- 2 slices aged provolone cheese

**Directions:**
1. Bring a medium saucepot of salted water to a boil on the stovetop. Blanch the broccoli rabe for 3 minutes in the boiling water and then drain. When it has cooled a little, squeeze out as much water as possible, drizzle a little olive oil on top, season with salt and black pepper and set aside. Dry the roasted red peppers with a clean kitchen towel and set them aside as well.
2. Place each chicken breast between 2 pieces of plastic wrap. Use a meat pounder to flatten the chicken breasts to about ½-inch thick. Season the chicken on both sides with salt and pepper.
3. Preheat the air fryer to 400°F (205°C).
4. Set up a dredging station with three shallow dishes. Place the flour in one dish, the egg in a second dish and the breadcrumbs in a third dish. Coat the chicken on all sides with the flour. Shake off any excess flour and dip the chicken into the egg. Let the excess egg drip off and coat both sides of the chicken in the breadcrumbs. Spray the chicken with olive oil on both sides and transfer to the air fryer basket.
5. Air-fry the chicken at 400°F (205°C) for 5 minutes. Turn the chicken over and air-fry for another minute. Then, top the chicken breast with the broccoli rabe and roasted peppers. Place a slice of the provolone cheese on top and secure it with a toothpick or two.
6. Air-fry at 360° for 3 to 4 minutes to melt the cheese and warm everything together.

## Sticky Drumsticks

Servings: 4
Cooking Time: 45 Minutes
Ingredients:
- 1 lb chicken drumsticks
- 1 tbsp chicken seasoning
- 1 tsp dried chili flakes
- Salt and pepper to taste
- ¼ cup honey
- 1 cup barbecue sauce

Directions:
1. Preheat air fryer to 390°F (200°C). Season drumsticks with chicken seasoning, chili flakes, salt, and pepper. Place one batch of drumsticks in the greased frying basket and Air Fry for 18-20 minutes, flipping once until golden.
2. While the chicken is cooking, combine honey and barbecue sauce in a small bowl. Remove the drumsticks to a serving dish. Drizzle honey-barbecue sauce over and serve.

## Chicken Breasts Wrapped In Bacon

Servings: 4
Cooking Time: 35 Minutes
Ingredients:
- ¼ cup mayonnaise
- ¼ cup sour cream
- 3 tbsp ketchup
- 1 tbsp yellow mustard
- 1 tbsp light brown sugar
- 1 lb chicken tenders
- 1 tsp dried parsley
- 8 bacon slices

Directions:
1. Preheat the air fryer to 370°F (185°C). Combine the mayonnaise, sour cream, ketchup, mustard, and brown sugar in a bowl and mix well, then set aside. Sprinkle the chicken with the parsley and wrap each one in a slice of bacon. Put the wrapped chicken in the frying basket in a single layer and Air Fry for 18-20 minutes, flipping once until the bacon is crisp. Serve with sauce.

## Kale & Rice Chicken Rolls

Servings: 4
Cooking Time: 35 Minutes
Ingredients:
- 4 boneless, skinless chicken thighs
- ½ tsp ground fenugreek seeds
- 1 cup cooked wild rice
- 2 sundried tomatoes, diced
- ½ cup chopped kale
- 2 garlic cloves, minced
- 1 tsp salt
- 1 lemon, juiced
- ½ cup crumbled feta
- 1 tbsp olive oil

Directions:
1. Preheat air fryer to 380°F (195°C). Put the chicken thighs between two pieces of plastic wrap, and using a meat mallet or a rolling pin, pound them out to about ¼-inch thick. Combine the rice, tomatoes, kale, garlic, salt, fenugreek seeds and lemon juice in a bowl and mix well.
2. Divide the rice mixture among the chicken thighs and sprinkle with feta. Fold the sides of the chicken thigh over the filling, and then gently place each of them seam-side down into the greased air frying basket. Drizzle the stuffed chicken thighs with olive oil. Roast the stuffed chicken thighs for 12 minutes, then turn them over and cook for an additional 10 minutes. Serve and enjoy!

## Fancy Chicken Piccata

Servings: 4
Cooking Time: 30 Minutes
Ingredients:
- 1 lb chicken breasts, cut into cutlets
- Salt and pepper to taste
- 2 egg whites
- 2/3 cup bread crumbs
- 1 tsp Italian seasoning
- 1 tbsp whipped butter
- ½ cup chicken broth
- ½ onion powder
- ¼ cup fino sherry
- Juice of 1 lemon
- 1 tbsp capers, drained
- 1 lemon, sliced
- 2 tbsp chopped parsley

Directions:
1. Preheat air fryer to 370°F (185°C). Place the cutlets between two sheets of parchment paper. Pound to a ¼-inch thickness and season with salt and pepper. Beat egg whites with 1 tsp of water in a bowl. Put the bread crumbs, Parmesan cheese, onion powder, and Italian seasoning in a second bowl. Dip the cutlet in the egg bowl, and then in the crumb mix. Put the cutlets in the greased frying basket. Air Fry for 6 minutes, flipping once until crispy and golden.
2. Melt butter in a skillet. Stir in broth, sherry, lemon juice, lemon halves, and black pepper. Bring to a boil over high heat until the sauce is reduced by half, 4 minutes. Remove from heat. Pick out the lemon rinds and discard them. Stir in capers. Plate a cutlet, spoon some sauce over and garnish with lemon sleeves and parsley to serve.

## Japanese-style Turkey Meatballs

Servings: 4
Cooking Time: 25 Minutes
**Ingredients:**
- 1 1/3 lb ground turkey
- ¼ cup panko bread crumbs
- 4 chopped scallions
- ¼ cup chopped cilantro
- 1 egg
- 1 tbsp grated ginger
- 1 garlic clove, minced
- 3 tbsp shoyu
- 2 tsp toasted sesame oil
- ¾ tsp salt
- 2 tbsp oyster sauce sauce
- 2 tbsp fresh orange juice

**Directions:**
1. Add ground turkey, panko, 3 scallions, cilantro, egg, ginger, garlic, 1 tbsp of shoyu sauce, sesame oil, and salt in a bowl. Mix with hands until combined. Divide the mixture into 12 equal parts and roll into balls. Preheat air fryer to 380°F (195°C). Place the meatballs in the greased frying basket. Bake for about 9-11 minutes, flipping once until browned and cooked through. Repeat for all meatballs.
2. In a small saucepan over medium heat, add oyster sauce, orange juice and remaining shoyu sauce. Bring to a boil, then reduce the heat to low. Cook until the sauce is slightly reduced, 3 minutes. Serve the meatballs with the oyster sauce drizzled over them and topped with the remaining scallions.

## Jerk Turkey Meatballs

Servings: 7
Cooking Time: 8 Minutes
**Ingredients:**
- 1 pound lean ground turkey
- ¼ cup chopped onion
- 1 teaspoon minced garlic
- ½ teaspoon dried thyme
- ¼ teaspoon ground cinnamon
- 1 teaspoon cayenne pepper
- ½ teaspoon paprika
- ½ teaspoon salt
- ⅛ teaspoon black pepper
- ¼ teaspoon red pepper flakes
- 2 teaspoons brown sugar
- 1 large egg, whisked
- ⅓ cup panko breadcrumbs
- 2⅓ cups cooked brown Jasmine rice
- 2 green onions, chopped
- ¾ cup sweet onion dressing

**Directions:**
1. Preheat the air fryer to 350°F (175°C).
2. In a medium bowl, mix the ground turkey with the onion, garlic, thyme, cinnamon, cayenne pepper, paprika, salt, pepper, red pepper flakes, and brown sugar. Add the whisked egg and stir in the breadcrumbs until the turkey starts to hold together.
3. Using a 1-ounce scoop, portion the turkey into meatballs. You should get about 28 meatballs.
4. Spray the air fryer basket with olive oil spray.
5. Place the meatballs into the air fryer basket and cook for 5 minutes, shake the basket, and cook another 2 to 4 minutes (or until the internal temperature of the meatballs reaches 165°F (75°C)).
6. Remove the meatballs from the basket and repeat for the remaining meatballs.
7. Serve warm over a bed of rice with chopped green onions and spicy Caribbean jerk dressing.

## Cornflake Chicken Nuggets

Servings: 4
Cooking Time: 25 Minutes
**Ingredients:**
- 1 egg white
- 1 tbsp lemon juice
- ½ tsp dried basil
- ½ tsp ground paprika
- 1 lb chicken breast fingers
- ½ cup ground cornflakes
- 2 slices bread, crumbled

**Directions:**
1. Preheat air fryer to 400°F (205°C). Whisk the egg white, lemon juice, basil, and paprika, then add the chicken and stir. Combine the cornflakes and breadcrumbs on a plate, then put the chicken fingers in the mix to coat. Put the nuggets in the frying basket and Air Fry for 10-13 minutes, turning halfway through, until golden, crisp and cooked through. Serve hot!

## Chicken Cordon Bleu Patties

Servings: 4
Cooking Time: 30 Minutes
**Ingredients:**
- 1/3 cup grated Fontina cheese
- 3 tbsp milk
- 1/3 cup bread crumbs

- 1 egg, beaten
- ½ tsp dried parsley
- Salt and pepper to taste
- 1 ¼ lb ground chicken
- ¼ cup finely chopped ham

**Directions:**
1. Preheat air fryer to 350°F (175°C). Mix milk, breadcrumbs, egg, parsley, salt and pepper in a bowl. Using your hands, add the chicken and gently mix until just combined. Divide into 8 portions and shape into thin patties. Place on waxed paper. On 4 of the patties, top with ham and Fontina cheese, then place another patty on top of that. Gently pinch the edges together so that none of the ham or cheese is peeking out. Arrange the burgers in the greased frying basket and Air Fry until cooked through, for 14-16 minutes. Serve and enjoy!

## Simple Buttermilk Fried Chicken

Servings: 4
Cooking Time: 27 Minutes

**Ingredients:**
- 1 (4-pound) chicken, cut into 8 pieces
- 2 cups buttermilk
- hot sauce (optional)
- 1½ cups flour*
- 2 teaspoons paprika
- 1 teaspoon salt
- freshly ground black pepper
- 2 eggs, lightly beaten
- vegetable oil, in a spray bottle

**Directions:**
1. Cut the chicken into 8 pieces and submerge them in the buttermilk and hot sauce, if using. A zipper-sealable plastic bag works well for this. Let the chicken soak in the buttermilk for at least one hour or even overnight in the refrigerator.
2. Set up a dredging station. Mix the flour, paprika, salt and black pepper in a clean zipper-sealable plastic bag. Whisk the eggs and place them in a shallow dish. Remove four pieces of chicken from the buttermilk and transfer them to the bag with the flour. Shake them around to coat on all sides. Remove the chicken from the flour, shaking off any excess flour, and dip them into the beaten egg. Return the chicken to the bag of seasoned flour and shake again. Set the coated chicken aside and repeat with the remaining four pieces of chicken.
3. Preheat the air fryer to 370°F (185°C).
4. Spray the chicken on all sides with the vegetable oil and then transfer one batch to the air fryer basket. Air-fry the chicken at 370°F (185°C) for 20 minutes, flipping the pieces over halfway through the cooking process, taking care not to knock off the breading. Transfer the chicken to a plate, but do not cover. Repeat with the second batch of chicken.
5. Lower the temperature on the air fryer to 340°F (170°C). Flip the chicken back over and place the first batch of chicken on top of the second batch already in the basket. Air-fry for another 7 minutes and serve warm.

## Indian-inspired Chicken Skewers

Servings:4
Cooking Time: 40 Minutes + Chilling Time

**Ingredients:**
- 1 lb boneless, skinless chicken thighs, cubed
- 1 red onion, diced
- 1 tbsp grated ginger
- 2 tbsp lime juice
- 1 cup canned coconut milk
- 2 tbsp tomato paste
- 2 tbsp olive oil
- 1 tbsp ground cumin
- 1 tbsp ground coriander
- 1 tsp cayenne pepper
- 1 tsp ground turmeric
- ½ tsp red chili powder
- ¼ tsp curry powder
- 2 tsp salt
- 2 tbsp chopped cilantro

**Directions:**
1. Toss red onion, ginger, lime juice, coconut milk, tomato paste, olive oil, cumin, coriander, cayenne pepper, turmeric, chili powder, curry powder, salt, and chicken until fully coated. Let chill in the fridge for 2 hours.
2. Preheat air fryer to 350°F. Thread chicken onto 8 skewers and place them on a kebab rack. Place rack in the frying basket and Air Fry for 12 minutes. Discard marinade. Garnish with cilantro to serve.

## Buttery Chicken Legs

Servings:4
Cooking Time: 50 Minutes

**Ingredients:**
- 1 tsp baking powder
- 1 tsp dried mustard
- 1 tsp smoked paprika
- 1 tsp garlic powder
- 1 tsp dried thyme
- Salt and pepper to taste
- 1 ½ lb chicken legs

- 3 tbsp butter, melted

**Directions:**
1. Preheat air fryer to 370°F. Combine all ingredients, except for butter, in a bowl until coated. Place the chicken legs in the greased frying basket. Air Fry for 18 minutes, flipping once and brushing with melted butter on both sides. Let chill onto a serving plate for 5 minutes before serving.

## Easy Turkey Meatballs

Servings: 4
Cooking Time: 20 Minutes

**Ingredients:**
- 1 lb ground turkey
- ½ celery stalk, chopped
- 1 egg
- ¼ tsp red pepper flakes
- ¼ cup bread crumbs
- Salt and pepper to taste
- ½ tsp garlic powder
- ½ tsp onion powder
- ½ tsp cayenne pepper

**Directions:**
1. Preheat air fryer to 360°F (180°C). Add all of the ingredients to a bowl and mix well. Shape the mixture into 12 balls and arrange them on the greased frying basket. Air Fry for 10-12 minutes or until the meatballs are cooked through and browned. Serve and enjoy!

## Sesame Orange Chicken

Servings: 2
Cooking Time: 9 Minutes

**Ingredients:**
- 1 pound boneless, skinless chicken breasts, cut into cubes
- salt and freshly ground black pepper
- ¼ cup cornstarch
- 2 eggs, beaten
- 1½ cups panko breadcrumbs
- vegetable or peanut oil, in a spray bottle
- 12 ounces orange marmalade
- 1 tablespoon soy sauce
- 1 teaspoon minced ginger
- 2 tablespoons hoisin sauce
- 1 tablespoon sesame oil
- sesame seeds, toasted

**Directions:**
1. Season the chicken pieces with salt and pepper. Set up a dredging station. Put the cornstarch in a zipper-sealable plastic bag. Place the beaten eggs in a bowl and put the panko breadcrumbs in a shallow dish. Transfer the seasoned chicken to the bag with the cornstarch and shake well to completely coat the chicken on all sides. Remove the chicken from the bag, shaking off any excess cornstarch and dip the pieces into the egg. Let any excess egg drip from the chicken and transfer into the breadcrumbs, pressing the crumbs onto the chicken pieces with your hands. Spray the chicken pieces with vegetable or peanut oil.
2. Preheat the air fryer to 400°F (205°C).
3. Combine the orange marmalade, soy sauce, ginger, hoisin sauce and sesame oil in a saucepan. Bring the mixture to a boil on the stovetop, lower the heat and simmer for 10 minutes, until the sauce has thickened. Set aside and keep warm.
4. Transfer the coated chicken to the air fryer basket and air-fry at 400°F (205°C) for 9 minutes, shaking the basket a few times during the cooking process to help the chicken cook evenly.
5. Right before serving, toss the browned chicken pieces with the sesame orange sauce. Serve over white rice with steamed broccoli. Sprinkle the sesame seeds on top.

## Fiesta Chicken Plate

Servings: 4
Cooking Time: 15 Minutes

**Ingredients:**
- 1 pound boneless, skinless chicken breasts (2 large breasts)
- 2 tablespoons lime juice
- 1 teaspoon cumin
- ½ teaspoon salt
- ½ cup grated Pepper Jack cheese
- 1 16-ounce can refried beans
- ½ cup salsa
- 2 cups shredded lettuce
- 1 medium tomato, chopped
- 2 avocados, peeled and sliced
- 1 small onion, sliced into thin rings
- sour cream
- tortilla chips (optional)

**Directions:**
1. Split each chicken breast in half lengthwise.
2. Mix lime juice, cumin, and salt together and brush on all surfaces of chicken breasts.
3. Place in air fryer basket and cook at 390°F (200°C) for 15 minutes, until well done.
4. Divide the cheese evenly over chicken breasts and cook for an additional minute to melt cheese.

5. While chicken is cooking, heat refried beans on stovetop or in microwave.

6. When ready to serve, divide beans among 4 plates. Place chicken breasts on top of beans and spoon salsa over. Arrange the lettuce, tomatoes, and avocados artfully on each plate and scatter with the onion rings.

7. Pass sour cream at the table and serve with tortilla chips if desired.

## Indian Chicken Tandoori

Servings: 2
Cooking Time: 35 Minutes
**Ingredients:**
- 2 chicken breasts, cubed
- ½ cup hung curd
- 1 tsp turmeric powder
- 1 tsp red chili powder
- 1 tsp chaat masala powder
- Pinch of salt

**Directions:**
1. Preheat air fryer to 350°F (175°C). Mix the hung curd, turmeric, red chili powder, chaat masala powder, and salt in a mixing bowl. Stir until the mixture is free of lumps. Coat the chicken with the mixture, cover, and refrigerate for 30 minutes to marinate. Place the marinated chicken chunks in a baking pan and drizzle with the remaining marinade. Bake for 25 minutes until the chicken is juicy and spiced. Serve warm.

## Spinach & Turkey Meatballs

Servings: 4
Cooking Time: 45 Minutes
**Ingredients:**
- ¼ cup grated Parmesan cheese
- 2 scallions, chopped
- 1 garlic clove, minced
- 1 egg, beaten
- 1 cup baby spinach
- ¼ cup bread crumbs
- 1 tsp dried oregano
- Salt and pepper to taste
- 1 ¼ lb ground turkey

**Directions:**
1. Preheat the air fryer to 400°F (205°C) and preheat the oven to 250°F (120°C). Combine the scallions, garlic, egg, baby spinach, breadcrumbs, Parmesan, oregano, salt, and pepper in a bowl and mix well. Add the turkey and mix, then form into 1½-inch balls. Add as many meatballs as will fit in a single layer in the frying basket and Air Fry for 10-15 minutes, shaking once around minute 7. Put the cooked meatballs on a tray in the oven and cover with foil to keep warm. Repeat with the remaining balls.

## Spiced Mexican Stir-fried Chicken

Servings: 4
Cooking Time: 30 Minutes
**Ingredients:**
- 1 lb chicken breasts, cubed
- 2 green onions, chopped
- 1 red bell pepper, chopped
- 1 jalapeño pepper, minced
- 2 tsp olive oil
- 2/3 cup canned black beans
- ½ cup salsa
- 2 tsp Mexican chili powder

**Directions:**
1. Preheat air fryer to 400°F (205°C). Combine the chicken, green onions, bell pepper, jalapeño, and olive oil in a bowl. Transfer to a bowl to the frying basket and Air Fry for 10 minutes, stirring once during cooking. When done, stir in the black beans, salsa, and chili powder. Air Fry for 7-10 minutes or until cooked through. Serve.

## Enchilada Chicken Quesadillas

Servings: 4
Cooking Time: 35 Minutes
**Ingredients:**
- 2 cups cooked chicken breasts, shredded
- 1 can diced green chilies, including juice
- 2 cups grated Mexican cheese blend
- 3/4 cup sour cream
- 2 tsp chili powder
- 1 tsp cumin
- 1 tbsp chipotle sauce
- 1 tsp dried onion flakes
- ½ tsp salt
- 3 tbsp butter, melted
- 8 flour tortillas

**Directions:**
1. In a small bowl, whisk the sour cream, chipotle sauce and chili powder. Let chill in the fridge until ready to use.

2. Preheat air fryer at 350°F. Mix the chicken, green chilies, cumin, and salt in a bowl. Set aside. Brush on one side of a tortilla lightly with melted butter. Layer with ¼ cup of chicken, onion flakes and ¼ cup of Mexican cheese. Top with a second tortilla and lightly brush with butter on top. Repeat with the remaining ingredients. Place quesadillas, butter side down, in the frying basket and Bake for 3 minutes. Cut them into 6 sections and serve with cream sauce on the side.

## Mustardy Chicken Bites

Servings: 4
Cooking Time: 20 Minutes + Chilling Time
**Ingredients:**
- 2 tbsp horseradish mustard
- 1 tbsp mayonnaise
- 1 tbsp olive oil
- 2 chicken breasts, cubes
- 1 tbsp parsley

**Directions:**
1. Combine all ingredients, excluding parsley, in a bowl. Let marinate covered in the fridge for 30 minutes. Preheat air fryer at 350ºF. Place chicken cubes in the greased frying basket and Air Fry for 9 minutes, tossing once. Serve immediately sprinkled with parsley.

## Bacon & Chicken Flatbread

Servings: 2
Cooking Time: 35 Minutes
**Ingredients:**
- 1 flatbread dough
- 1 chicken breast, cubed
- 1 cup breadcrumbs
- 2 eggs, beaten
- Salt and pepper to taste
- 2 tsp dry rosemary
- 1 tsp fajita seasoning
- 1 tsp onion powder
- 3 bacon strips
- ½ tbsp ranch sauce

**Directions:**
1. Preheat air fryer to 360°F (180°C). Place the breadcrumbs, onion powder, rosemary, salt, and pepper in a mixing bowl. Coat the chicken with the mixture, dip into the beaten eggs, then roll again into the dry ingredients. Arrange the coated chicken pieces on one side of the greased frying basket. On the other side of the basket, lay the bacon strips. Air Fry for 6 minutes. Turn the bacon pieces over and flip the chicken and cook for another 6 minutes.
2. Roll the flatbread out and spread the ranch sauce all over the surface. Top with the bacon and chicken and sprinkle with fajita seasoning. Close the bread to contain the filling and place it in the air fryer. Cook for 10 minutes, flipping the flatbread once until golden brown. Let it cool for a few minutes. Then slice and serve.

## Creole Chicken Drumettes

Servings: 4
Cooking Time: 50 Minutes
**Ingredients:**
- 1 lb chicken drumettes
- ½ cup flour
- ½ cup heavy cream
- ½ cup sour cream
- ½ cup bread crumbs
- 1 tbsp Creole seasoning
- 2 tbsp melted butter

**Directions:**
1. Preheat air fryer to 370ºF. Combine chicken drumettes and flour in a bowl. Shake away excess flour and set aside. Mix the heavy cream and sour cream in a bowl. In another bowl, combine bread crumbs and Creole seasoning. Dip floured drumettes in cream mixture, then dredge them in crumbs. Place the chicken drumettes in the greased frying basket and Air Fry for 20 minutes, tossing once and brushing with melted butter. Let rest for a few minutes on a plate and serve.

## Thai Chicken Drumsticks

Servings: 4
Cooking Time: 20 Minutes
**Ingredients:**
- 2 tablespoons soy sauce
- ¼ cup rice wine vinegar
- 2 tablespoons chili garlic sauce
- 2 tablespoons sesame oil
- 1 teaspoon minced fresh ginger
- 2 teaspoons sugar
- ½ teaspoon ground coriander
- juice of 1 lime
- 8 chicken drumsticks (about 2½ pounds)
- ¼ cup chopped peanuts
- chopped fresh cilantro
- lime wedges

**Directions:**
1. Combine the soy sauce, rice wine vinegar, chili sauce, sesame oil, ginger, sugar, coriander and lime juice in a large bowl and mix together. Add the chicken drumsticks and marinate for 30 minutes.
2. Preheat the air fryer to 370°F (185°C).
3. Place the chicken in the air fryer basket. It's ok if the ends of the drumsticks overlap a little. Spoon half of the marinade over the chicken, and reserve the other half.
4. Air-fry for 10 minutes. Turn the chicken over and pour the rest of the marinade over the chicken. Air-fry for an additional 10 minutes.
5. Transfer the chicken to a plate to rest and cool to an edible temperature. Pour the marinade from the bottom of

the air fryer into a small saucepan and bring it to a simmer over medium-high heat. Simmer the liquid for 2 minutes so that it thickens enough to coat the back of a spoon.
6. Transfer the chicken to a serving platter, pour the sauce over the chicken and sprinkle the chopped peanuts on top. Garnish with chopped cilantro and lime wedges.

## Chicken Burgers With Blue Cheese Sauce

Servings: 4
Cooking Time: 40 Minutes
**Ingredients:**
- ¼ cup crumbled blue cheese
- ¼ cup sour cream
- 2 tbsp mayonnaise
- 1 tbsp red hot sauce
- Salt to taste
- 3 tbsp buffalo wing sauce
- 1 lb ground chicken
- 2 tbsp grated carrot
- 2 tbsp diced celery
- 1 egg white

**Directions:**
1. Whisk the blue cheese, sour cream, mayonnaise, red hot sauce, salt, and 1 tbsp of buffalo sauce in a bowl. Let sit covered in the fridge until ready to use.
2. Preheat air fryer at 350ºF. In another bowl, combine the remaining ingredients. Form mixture into 4 patties, making a slight indentation in the middle of each. Place patties in the greased frying basket and Air Fry for 13 minutes until you reach your desired doneness, flipping once. Serve with the blue cheese sauce.

## Southwest Gluten-free Turkey Meatloaf

Servings: 8
Cooking Time: 35 Minutes
**Ingredients:**
- 1 pound lean ground turkey
- ¼ cup corn grits
- ¼ cup diced onion
- 1 teaspoon minced garlic
- ½ teaspoon black pepper
- ½ teaspoon salt
- 1 large egg
- ½ cup ketchup
- 4 teaspoons chipotle hot sauce
- ⅓ cup shredded cheddar cheese

**Directions:**

1. Preheat the air fryer to 350°F (175°C).
2. In a large bowl, mix together the ground turkey, corn grits, onion, garlic, black pepper, and salt.
3. In a small bowl, whisk the egg. Add the egg to the turkey mixture and combine.
4. In a small bowl, mix the ketchup and hot sauce. Set aside.
5. Liberally spray a 9-x-4-inch loaf pan with olive oil spray. Depending on the size of your air fryer, you may need to use 2 or 3 mini loaf pans.
6. Spoon the ground turkey mixture into the loaf pan and evenly top with half of the ketchup mixture. Cover with foil and place the meatloaf into the air fryer. Cook for 30 minutes; remove the foil and discard. Check the internal temperature (it should be nearing 165°F (75°C)).
7. Coat the top of the meatloaf with the remaining ketchup mixture, and sprinkle the cheese over the top. Place the meatloaf back in the air fryer for the remaining 5 minutes (or until the internal temperature reaches 165°F (75°C)).
8. Remove from the oven and let cool 5 minutes before serving. Serve warm with desired sides.

## Satay Chicken Skewers

Servings: 4
Cooking Time: 35 Minutes
**Ingredients:**
- 2 chicken breasts, cut into strips
- 1 ½ tbsp Thai red curry paste
- ¼ cup peanut butter
- 1 tbsp maple syrup
- 1 tbsp tamari
- 1 tbsp lime juice
- 2 tsp chopped onions
- ¼ tsp minced ginger
- 1 clove garlic, minced
- 1 cup coconut milk
- 1 tsp fish sauce
- 1 tbsp chopped cilantro

**Directions:**
1. Mix the peanut butter, maple syrup, tamari, lime juice, ¼ tsp of sriracha, onions, ginger, garlic, and 2 tbsp of water in a bowl. Reserve 1 tbsp of the sauce. Set aside. Combine the reserved peanut sauce, fish sauce, coconut milk, Thai red curry paste, cilantro and chicken strips in a bowl and let marinate in the fridge for 15 minutes.
2. Preheat air fryer at 350ºF. Thread chicken strips onto skewers and place them on a kebab rack. Place rack in the frying basket and Air Fry for 12 minutes. Serve with previously prepared peanut sauce on the side.

## Teriyaki Chicken Bites

Servings: 4
Cooking Time: 30 Minutes
**Ingredients:**
- 1 lb boneless, skinless chicken thighs, cubed
- 1 green onion, sliced diagonally
- 1 large egg
- 1 tbsp teriyaki sauce
- 4 tbsp flour
- 1 tsp sesame oil
- 2 tsp balsamic vinegar
- 2 tbsp tamari
- 3 cloves garlic, minced
- 2 tsp grated fresh ginger
- 2 tsp chili garlic sauce
- 2 tsp granular honey
- Salt and pepper to taste

**Directions:**
1. Preheat air fryer to 400ºF. Beat the egg, teriyaki sauce, and flour in a bowl. Stir in chicken pieces until fully coated. In another bowl, combine the remaining ingredients, except for the green onion. Reserve. Place chicken pieces in the frying basket lightly greased with olive oil and Air Fry for 15 minutes, tossing every 5 minutes. Remove them to the bowl with the sauce and toss to coat. Scatter with green onions to serve. Enjoy!

## Moroccan-style Chicken Strips

Servings: 4
Cooking Time: 30 Minutes
**Ingredients:**
- 4 chicken breasts, cut into strips
- 2 tsp olive oil
- 2 tbsp cornstarch
- 3 garlic cloves, minced
- ½ cup chicken broth
- ¼ cup lemon juice
- 1 tbsp honey
- ½ tsp ras el hanout
- 1 cup cooked couscous

**Directions:**
1. Preheat air fryer to 400°F (205°C). Mix the chicken and olive oil in a bowl, then add the cornstarch. Stir to coat. Add the garlic and transfer to a baking pan. Put the pan in the fryer. Bake for 10 minutes. Stir at least once during cooking.
2. When done, pour in the chicken broth, lemon juice, honey, and ras el hanout. Bake for an additional 6-9 minutes or until the sauce is thick and the chicken cooked through with no pink showing. Serve with couscous.

## Italian-inspired Chicken Pizzadillas

Servings: 4
Cooking Time: 25 Minutes
**Ingredients:**
- 2 cups cooked boneless, skinless chicken, shredded
- 1 cup grated provolone cheese
- 8 basil and menta leaves, julienned
- ½ tsp salt
- 1 tsp garlic powder
- 3 tbsp butter, melted
- 8 flour tortillas
- 1 cup marinara sauce
- 1 cup grated cheddar cheese

**Directions:**
1. Preheat air fryer at 350ºF. Sprinkle chicken with salt and garlic powder. Brush on one side of a tortilla lightly with melted butter. Spread ¼ cup of marinara sauce, then top with ½ cup of chicken, ¼ cup of cheddar cheese, ¼ cup of provolone, and finally, ¼ of basil and menta leaves. Top with a second tortilla and lightly brush with butter on top. Repeat with the remaining ingredients. Place quesadillas, butter side down, in the frying basket and Bake for 3 minutes. Cut them into 6 sections and serve.

## Spinach And Feta Stuffed Chicken Breasts

Servings: 4
Cooking Time: 27 Minutes
**Ingredients:**
- 1 (10-ounce) package frozen spinach, thawed and drained well
- 1 cup feta cheese, crumbled
- ½ teaspoon freshly ground black pepper
- 4 boneless chicken breasts
- salt and freshly ground black pepper
- 1 tablespoon olive oil

**Directions:**
1. Prepare the filling. Squeeze out as much liquid as possible from the thawed spinach. Rough chop the spinach and transfer it to a mixing bowl with the feta cheese and the freshly ground black pepper.
2. Prepare the chicken breast. Place the chicken breast on a cutting board and press down on the chicken breast with one hand to keep it stabilized. Make an incision about 1-inch long in the fattest side of the breast. Move the knife up and down inside the chicken breast, without poking through

either the top or the bottom, or the other side of the breast. The inside pocket should be about 3-inches long, but the opening should only be about 1-inch wide. If this is too difficult, you can make the incision longer, but you will have to be more careful when cooking the chicken breast since this will expose more of the stuffing.

3. Once you have prepared the chicken breasts, use your fingers to stuff the filling into each pocket, spreading the mixture down as far as you can.

4. Preheat the air fryer to 380°F (195°C).

5. Lightly brush or spray the air fryer basket and the chicken breasts with olive oil. Transfer two of the stuffed chicken breasts to the air fryer. Air-fry for 12 minutes, turning the chicken breasts over halfway through the cooking time. Remove the chicken to a resting plate and air-fry the second two breasts for 12 minutes. Return the first batch of chicken to the air fryer with the second batch and air-fry for 3 more minutes. When the chicken is cooked, an instant read thermometer should register 165°F (75°C) in the thickest part of the chicken, as well as in the stuffing.

6. Remove the chicken breasts and let them rest on a cutting board for 2 to 3 minutes. Slice the chicken on the bias and serve with the slices fanned out.

## Farmer's Fried Chicken

Servings: 4
Cooking Time: 55 Minutes
**Ingredients:**
- 3 lb whole chicken, cut into breasts, drumsticks, and thighs
- 2 cups flour
- 4 tsp salt
- 4 tsp dried basil
- 4 tsp dried thyme
- 2 tsp dried shallot powder
- 2 tsp smoked paprika
- 1 tsp mustard powder
- 1 tsp celery salt
- 1 cup kefir
- ¼ cup honey

**Directions:**
1. Preheat the air fryer to 370°F (1805°C). Combine the flour, salt, basil, thyme, shallot, paprika, mustard powder, and celery salt in a bowl. Pour into a glass jar. Mix the kefir and honey in a large bowl and add the chicken, stir to coat. Marinate for 15 minutes at room temperature. Remove the chicken from the kefir mixture; discard the rest. Put 2/3 cup of the flour mix onto a plate and dip the chicken. Shake gently and put on a wire rack for 10 minutes. Line the frying basket with round parchment paper with holes punched in it. Place the chicken in a single layer and spray with cooking oil. Air Fry for 18-25 minutes, flipping once around minute 10. Serve hot.

## Harissa Chicken Wings

Servings: 4
Cooking Time: 25 Minutes
**Ingredients:**
- 8 whole chicken wings
- 1 tsp garlic powder
- ¼ tsp dried oregano
- 1 tbsp harissa seasoning

**Directions:**
1. Preheat air fryer to 400°F (205°C). Season the wings with garlic, harissa seasoning, and oregano. Place them in the greased frying basket and spray with cooking oil spray. Air Fry for 10 minutes, shake the basket, and cook for another 5-7 minutes until golden and crispy. Serve warm.

## Greek Chicken Wings

Servings: 4
Cooking Time: 30 Minutes
**Ingredients:**
- 8 whole chicken wings
- ½ lemon, juiced
- ½ tsp garlic powder
- 1 tsp shallot powder
- ½ tsp Greek seasoning
- Salt and pepper to taste
- ¼ cup buttermilk
- ½ cup all-purpose flour

**Directions:**
1. Preheat air fryer to 400°F (205°C). Put the wings in a resealable bag along with lemon juice, garlic, shallot, Greek seasoning, salt and pepper. Seal the bag and shake to coat. Set up bowls large enough to fit the wings.

2. In one bowl, pour the buttermilk. In the other, add flour. Using tongs, dip the wings into the buttermilk, then dredge in flour. Transfer the wings in the greased frying basket, spraying lightly with cooking oil. Air Fry for 25 minutes, shaking twice, until golden and cooked through. Allow to cool slightly, and serve.

# Chicken Skewers

Servings: 4
Cooking Time: 55 Minutes
**Ingredients:**
- 1 lb boneless skinless chicken thighs, cut into pieces
- 1 sweet onion, cut into 1-inch pieces
- 1 zucchini, cut into 1-inch pieces
- 1 red bell pepper, cut into 1-inch pieces
- ¼ cup olive oil
- 1 tsp garlic powder
- 1 tsp shallot powder
- 1 tsp ground cumin
- ½ tsp dried oregano
- ½ tsp dried thyme
- ¼ cup lemon juice
- 1 tbsp apple cider vinegar
- 12 grape tomatoes

**Directions:**
1. Combine the olive oil, garlic powder, shallot powder, cumin, oregano, thyme, lemon juice, and vinegar in a bowl; mix well. Alternate skewering the chicken, bell pepper, onion, zucchini, and tomatoes. Once all of the skewers are prepared, place them in a greased baking dish and pour the olive oil marinade over the top. Turn to coat. Cover with plastic wrap and refrigerate.
2. Preheat air fryer to 380°F (195°C). Remove the skewers from the marinade and arrange them in a single layer on the frying basket. Bake for 25 minutes, rotating once. Let the skewers sit for 5 minutes. Serve and enjoy!

# Tortilla Crusted Chicken Breast

Servings: 2
Cooking Time: 12 Minutes
**Ingredients:**
- ⅓ cup flour
- 1 teaspoon salt
- 1½ teaspoons chili powder
- 1 teaspoon ground cumin
- freshly ground black pepper
- 1 egg, beaten
- ¾ cup coarsely crushed yellow corn tortilla chips
- 2 (3- to 4-ounce) boneless chicken breasts
- vegetable oil
- ½ cup salsa
- ½ cup crumbled queso fresco
- fresh cilantro leaves
- sour cream or guacamole (optional)

**Directions:**
1. Set up a dredging station with three shallow dishes. Combine the flour, salt, chili powder, cumin and black pepper in the first shallow dish. Beat the egg in the second shallow dish. Place the crushed tortilla chips in the third shallow dish.
2. Dredge the chicken in the spiced flour, covering all sides of the breast. Then dip the chicken into the egg, coating the chicken completely. Finally, place the chicken into the tortilla chips and press the chips onto the chicken to make sure they adhere to all sides of the breast. Spray the coated chicken breasts on both sides with vegetable oil.
3. Preheat the air fryer to 380°F (195°C).
4. Air-fry the chicken for 6 minutes. Then turn the chicken breasts over and air-fry for another 6 minutes. (Increase the cooking time if you are using chicken breasts larger than 3 to 4 ounces.)
5. When the chicken has finished cooking, serve each breast with a little salsa, the crumbled queso fresco and cilantro as the finishing touch. Serve some sour cream and/or guacamole at the table, if desired.

# Fantasy Sweet Chili Chicken Strips

Servings: 2
Cooking Time: 20 Minutes
**Ingredients:**
- 1 lb chicken strips
- 1 cup sweet chili sauce
- ½ cup bread crumbs
- ½ cup cornmeal

**Directions:**
1. Preheat air fryer at 350°F. Combine chicken strips and sweet chili sauce in a bowl until fully coated. In another bowl, mix the remaining ingredients. Dredge strips in the mixture. Shake off any excess. Place chicken strips in the greased frying basket and Air Fry for 10 minutes, tossing once. Serve right away.

# Simple Salsa Chicken Thighs

Servings: 2
Cooking Time: 35 Minutes
**Ingredients:**
- 1 lb boneless, skinless chicken thighs
- 1 cup mild chunky salsa
- ½ tsp taco seasoning
- 2 lime wedges for serving

**Directions:**
1. Preheat air fryer to 350°F. Add chicken thighs into a baking pan and pour salsa and taco seasoning over. Place the pan in the frying basket and Air Fry for 30 minutes until golden brown. Serve with lime wedges.

# Guajillo Chile Chicken Meatballs

Servings: 4
Cooking Time: 30 Minutes

**Ingredients:**
- 1 lb ground chicken
- 1 large egg
- ½ cup bread crumbs
- 1 tbsp sour cream
- 2 tsp brown mustard
- 2 tbsp grated onion
- 2 tbsp tomato paste
- 1 tsp ground cumin
- 1 tsp guajillo chile powder
- 2 tbsp olive oil

**Directions:**
1. Preheat air fryer to 350°F. Mix the ground chicken, egg, bread crumbs, sour cream, mustard, onion, tomato paste, cumin, and chili powder in a bowl. Form into 16 meatballs. Place the meatballs in the greased frying basket and Air Fry for 8-10 minutes, shaking once until browned and cooked through. Serve immediately.

# Parmesan Crusted Chicken Cordon Bleu

Servings: 2
Cooking Time: 14 Minutes

**Ingredients:**
- 2 (6-ounce) boneless, skinless chicken breasts
- salt and freshly ground black pepper
- 1 tablespoon Dijon mustard
- 4 slices Swiss cheese
- 4 slices deli-sliced ham
- ¼ cup all-purpose flour*
- 1 egg, beaten
- ¾ cup panko breadcrumbs*
- ⅓ cup grated Parmesan cheese
- olive oil, in a spray bottle

**Directions:**
1. Butterfly the chicken breasts. Place the chicken breast on a cutting board and press down on the breast with the palm of your hand. Slice into the long side of the chicken breast, parallel to the cutting board, but not all the way through to the other side. Open the chicken breast like a "book". Place a piece of plastic wrap over the chicken breast and gently pound it with a meat mallet to make it evenly thick.
2. Season the chicken with salt and pepper. Spread the Dijon mustard on the inside of each chicken breast. Layer one slice of cheese on top of the mustard, then top with the 2 slices of ham and the other slice of cheese.
3. Starting with the long edge of the chicken breast, roll the chicken up to the other side. Secure it shut with 1 or 2 toothpicks.
4. Preheat the air fryer to 350°F (175°C).
5. Set up a dredging station with three shallow dishes. Place the flour in the first dish. Place the beaten egg in the second shallow dish. Combine the panko breadcrumbs and Parmesan cheese together in the third shallow dish. Dip the stuffed and rolled chicken breasts in the flour, then the beaten egg and then roll in the breadcrumb-cheese mixture to cover on all sides. Press the crumbs onto the chicken breasts with your hands to make sure they are well adhered. Spray the chicken breasts with olive oil and transfer to the air fryer basket.
6. Air-fry at 350°F (175°C) for 14 minutes, flipping the breasts over halfway through the cooking time. Let the chicken rest for a few minutes before removing the toothpicks, slicing and serving.

# Crispy Chicken Tenders

Servings: 4
Cooking Time: 20 Minutes

**Ingredients:**
- 1 egg
- ¼ cup almond milk
- ¼ cup almond flour
- ¼ cup bread crumbs
- Salt and pepper to taste
- ½ tsp dried thyme
- ½ tsp dried sage
- ½ tsp garlic powder
- ½ tsp chili powder
- 1 lb chicken tenderloins
- 1 lemon, quartered

**Directions:**
1. Preheat air fryer to 360°F (180°C). Whisk together the egg and almond milk in a bowl until frothy. Mix the flour, bread crumbs, salt, pepper, thyme, sage, chili powder and garlic powder in a separate bowl. Dip each chicken tenderloin into the egg mixture, then coat with the bread crumb mixture. Put the breaded chicken tenderloins into the frying basket in a single layer. Air Fry for 12 minutes, turning once. Serve with lemon slices.

# Chicken Wellington

Servings: 2
Cooking Time: 31 Minutes
**Ingredients:**
- 2 (5-ounce) boneless, skinless chicken breasts
- ½ cup White Worcestershire sauce
- 3 tablespoons butter
- ½ cup finely diced onion (about ½ onion)
- 8 ounces button mushrooms, finely chopped
- ¼ cup chicken stock
- 2 tablespoons White Worcestershire sauce (or white wine)
- salt and freshly ground black pepper
- 1 tablespoon chopped fresh tarragon
- 2 sheets puff pastry, thawed
- 1 egg, beaten
- vegetable oil

**Directions:**
1. Place the chicken breasts in a shallow dish. Pour the White Worcestershire sauce over the chicken coating both sides and marinate for 30 minutes.
2. While the chicken is marinating, melt the butter in a large skillet over medium-high heat on the stovetop. Add the onion and sauté for a few minutes, until it starts to soften. Add the mushrooms and sauté for 5 minutes until the vegetables are brown and soft. Deglaze the skillet with the chicken stock, scraping up any bits from the bottom of the pan. Add the White Worcestershire sauce and simmer for 3 minutes until the mixture reduces and starts to thicken. Season with salt and freshly ground black pepper. Remove the mushroom mixture from the heat and stir in the fresh tarragon. Let the mushroom mixture cool.
3. Preheat the air fryer to 360°F (180°C).
4. Remove the chicken from the marinade and transfer it to the air fryer basket. Tuck the small end of the chicken breast under the thicker part to shape it into a circle rather than an oval. Pour the marinade over the chicken and air-fry for 10 minutes.
5. Roll out the puff pastry and cut out two 6-inch squares. Brush the perimeter of each square with the egg wash. Place half of the mushroom mixture in the center of each puff pastry square. Place the chicken breasts, top side down on the mushroom mixture. Starting with one corner of puff pastry and working in one direction, pull the pastry up over the chicken to enclose it and press the ends of the pastry together in the middle. Brush the pastry with the egg wash to seal the edges. Turn the Wellingtons over and set aside.
6. To make a decorative design with the remaining puff pastry, cut out four 10-inch strips. For each Wellington, twist two of the strips together, place them over the chicken breast wrapped in puff pastry, and tuck the ends underneath to seal it. Brush the entire top and sides of the Wellingtons with the egg wash.
7. Preheat the air fryer to 350°F (175°C).
8. Spray or brush the air fryer basket with vegetable oil. Air-fry the chicken Wellingtons for 13 minutes. Carefully turn the Wellingtons over. Air-fry for another 8 minutes. Transfer to serving plates, light a candle and enjoy!

# Ranch Chicken Tortillas

Servings: 4
Cooking Time: 35 Minutes
**Ingredients:**
- 2 chicken breasts
- 1 tbsp Ranch seasoning
- 1 tbsp taco seasoning
- 1 cup flour
- 1 egg
- ½ cup bread crumbs
- 4 flour tortillas
- 1 ½ cups shredded lettuce
- 3 tbsp ranch dressing
- 2 tbsp cilantro, chopped

**Directions:**
1. Preheat air fryer to 370°F (185°C). Slice the chicken breasts into cutlets by cutting in half horizontally on a cutting board. Rub with ranch and taco seasonings. In one shallow bowl, add flour. In another shallow bowl, beat the egg. In the third shallow bowl, add bread crumbs.
2. Lightly spray the air fryer basket with cooking oil. First, dip the cutlet in the flour, dredge in egg, and then finish by coating with bread crumbs. Place the cutlets in the fryer and Bake for 6-8 minutes. Flip them and cook further for 4 minutes until crisp. Allow the chicken to cook for a few minutes, then cut into strips. Divide into 4 equal portions along with shredded lettuce, ranch dressing, cilantro and tortillas. Serve and enjoy!

# Chicken Salad With White Dressing

Servings: 2
Cooking Time: 20 Minutes
**Ingredients:**
- 2 chicken breasts, cut into strips
- ¼ cup diced peeled red onion
- ½ peeled English cucumber, diced
- 1 tbsp crushed red pepper flakes
- 1 cup Greek yogurt
- 3 tbsp light mayonnaise

- 1 tbsp mustard
- 1 tsp chopped dill
- 1 tsp chopped mint
- 1 tsp lemon juice
- 2 cloves garlic, minced
- Salt and pepper to taste
- 3 cups mixed greens
- 10 Kalamata olives, halved
- 1 tomato, diced
- ¼ cup feta cheese crumbles

**Directions:**
1. Preheat air fryer at 350ºF. In a small bowl, whisk the Greek yogurt, mayonnaise, mustard, cucumber, dill, mint, salt, lemon juice, and garlic, and let chill the resulting dressing covered in the fridge until ready to use. Sprinkle the chicken strips with salt and pepper. Place them in the frying basket and Air Fry for 10 minutes, tossing once. Place the mixed greens and pepper flakes in a salad bowl. Top each with red onion, olives, tomato, feta cheese, and grilled chicken. Drizzle with the dressing and serve.

# Fish And Seafood Recipes

## Crispy Sweet-and-sour Cod Fillets

Servings:3
Cooking Time: 12 Minutes
**Ingredients:**
- 1½ cups Plain panko bread crumbs (gluten-free, if a concern)
- 2 tablespoons Regular or low-fat mayonnaise (not fat-free; gluten-free, if a concern)
- ¼ cup Sweet pickle relish
- 3 4- to 5-ounce skinless cod fillets

**Directions:**
1. Preheat the air fryer to 400°F (205°C).
2. Pour the bread crumbs into a shallow soup plate or a small pie plate. Mix the mayonnaise and relish in a small bowl until well combined. Smear this mixture all over the cod fillets. Set them in the crumbs and turn until evenly coated on all sides, even on the ends.
3. Set the coated cod fillets in the basket with as much air space between them as possible. They should not touch. Air-fry undisturbed for 12 minutes, or until browned and crisp.
4. Use a nonstick-safe spatula to transfer the cod pieces to a wire rack. Cool for only a minute or two before serving hot.

## Miso-rubbed Salmon Fillets

Servings:3
Cooking Time: 5 Minutes
**Ingredients:**
- ¼ cup White (shiro) miso paste (usually made from rice and soy beans)
- 1½ tablespoons Mirin or a substitute (see here)
- 2½ teaspoons Unseasoned rice vinegar (see here)
- Vegetable oil spray
- 3 6-ounce skin-on salmon fillets (for more information, see here)

**Directions:**
1. Preheat the air fryer to 400°F (205°C).
2. Mix the miso, mirin, and vinegar in a small bowl until uniform.
3. Remove the basket from the machine. Generously spray the skin side of each fillet. Pick them up one by one with a nonstick-safe spatula and set them in the basket skin side down with as much air space between them as possible. Coat the top of each fillet with the miso mixture, dividing it evenly between them.
4. Return the basket to the machine. Air-fry undisturbed for 5 minutes, or until lightly browned and firm.
5. Use a nonstick-safe spatula to transfer the fillets to serving plates. Cool for only a minute or so before serving.

# Herb-crusted Sole

Servings: 4
Cooking Time: 20 Minutes
**Ingredients:**
- ½ lemon, juiced and zested
- 4 sole fillets
- ½ tsp dried thyme
- ½ tsp dried marjoram
- ½ tsp dried parsley
- Black pepper to taste
- 1 bread slice, crumbled
- 2 tsp olive oil

**Directions:**
1. Preheat air fryer to 320°F (160°C). In a bowl, combine the lemon zest, thyme, marjoram, parsley, pepper, breadcrumbs, and olive oil and stir. Arrange the sole fillets on a lined baking pan, skin-side down. Pour the lemon juice over the fillets, then press them firmly into the breadcrumb mixture to coat. Air Fry for 8-11 minutes, until the breadcrumbs are crisp and golden brown. Serve warm.

# Sweet & Spicy Swordfish Kebabs

Servings: 4
Cooking Time: 30 Minutes
**Ingredients:**
- ½ cup canned pineapple chunks, drained, juice reserved
- 1 lb swordfish steaks, cubed
- ½ cup large red grapes
- 1 tbsp honey
- 2 tsp grated fresh ginger
- 1 tsp olive oil
- Pinch cayenne pepper

**Directions:**
1. Preheat air fryer to 370°F (185°C). Poke 8 bamboo skewers through the swordfish, pineapple, and grapes. Mix the honey, 1 tbsp of pineapple juice, ginger, olive oil, and cayenne in a bowl, then use a brush to rub the mix on the kebabs. Allow the marinate to sit on the kebab for 10 minutes. Grill the kebabs for 8-12 minutes until the fish is cooked through and the fruit is soft and glazed. Brush the kebabs again with the mix, then toss the rest of the marinade. Serve warm and enjoy!

# Stuffed Shrimp

Servings: 4
Cooking Time: 12 Minutes Per Batch
**Ingredients:**
- 16 tail-on shrimp, peeled and deveined (last tail section intact)
- ¾ cup crushed panko breadcrumbs
- oil for misting or cooking spray
- Stuffing
- 2 6-ounce cans lump crabmeat
- 2 tablespoons chopped shallots
- 2 tablespoons chopped green onions
- 2 tablespoons chopped celery
- 2 tablespoons chopped green bell pepper
- ½ cup crushed saltine crackers
- 1 teaspoon Old Bay Seasoning
- 1 teaspoon garlic powder
- ¼ teaspoon ground thyme
- 2 teaspoons dried parsley flakes
- 2 teaspoons fresh lemon juice
- 2 teaspoons Worcestershire sauce
- 1 egg, beaten

**Directions:**
1. Rinse shrimp. Remove tail section (shell) from 4 shrimp, discard, and chop the meat finely.
2. To prepare the remaining 12 shrimp, cut a deep slit down the back side so that the meat lies open flat. Do not cut all the way through.
3. Preheat air fryer to 360°F (180°C).
4. Place chopped shrimp in a large bowl with all of the stuffing ingredients and stir to combine.
5. Divide stuffing into 12 portions, about 2 tablespoons each.
6. Place one stuffing portion onto the back of each shrimp and form into a ball or oblong shape. Press firmly so that stuffing sticks together and adheres to shrimp.
7. Gently roll each stuffed shrimp in panko crumbs and mist with oil or cooking spray.
8. Place 6 shrimp in air fryer basket and cook at 360°F (180°C) for 10minutes. Mist with oil or spray and cook 2 minutes longer or until stuffing cooks through inside and is crispy outside.
9. Repeat step 8 to cook remaining shrimp.

# Almond-crusted Fish

Servings: 4
Cooking Time: 10 Minutes
**Ingredients:**
- 4 4-ounce fish fillets
- ¾ cup breadcrumbs
- ¼ cup sliced almonds, crushed
- 2 tablespoons lemon juice
- ⅛ teaspoon cayenne
- salt and pepper

- ¾ cup flour
- 1 egg, beaten with 1 tablespoon water
- oil for misting or cooking spray

**Directions:**
1. Split fish fillets lengthwise down the center to create 8 pieces.
2. Mix breadcrumbs and almonds together and set aside.
3. Mix the lemon juice and cayenne together. Brush on all sides of fish.
4. Season fish to taste with salt and pepper.
5. Place the flour on a sheet of wax paper.
6. Roll fillets in flour, dip in egg wash, and roll in the crumb mixture.
7. Mist both sides of fish with oil or cooking spray.
8. Spray air fryer basket and lay fillets inside.
9. Cook at 390°F (200°C) for 5minutes, turn fish over, and cook for an additional 5minutes or until fish is done and flakes easily.

## Tex-mex Fish Tacos

Servings:3
Cooking Time: 7 Minutes
**Ingredients:**
- ¾ teaspoon Chile powder
- ¼ teaspoon Ground cumin
- ¼ teaspoon Dried oregano
- 3 5-ounce skinless mahi-mahi fillets
- Vegetable oil spray
- 3 Corn or flour tortillas
- 6 tablespoons Diced tomatoes
- 3 tablespoons Regular, low-fat, or fat-free sour cream

**Directions:**
1. Preheat the air fryer to 400°F (205°C).
2. Stir the chile powder, cumin, and oregano in a small bowl until well combined.
3. Coat each piece of fish all over (even the sides and ends) with vegetable oil spray. Sprinkle the spice mixture evenly over all sides of the fillets. Lightly spray them again.
4. When the machine is at temperature, set the fillets in the basket with as much air space between them as possible. Air-fry undisturbed for 7 minutes, until lightly browned and firm but not hard.
5. Use a nonstick-safe spatula to transfer the fillets to a wire rack. Microwave the tortillas on high for a few seconds, until supple. Put a fillet in each tortilla and top each with 2 tablespoons diced tomatoes and 1 tablespoon sour cream.

## Easy Asian-style Tuna

Servings: 4
Cooking Time: 25 Minutes
**Ingredients:**
- 1 jalapeño pepper, minced
- ½ tsp Chinese five-spice
- 4 tuna steaks
- ½ tsp toasted sesame oil
- 2 garlic cloves, grated
- 1 tbsp grated fresh ginger
- Black pepper to taste
- 2 tbsp lemon juice

**Directions:**
1. Preheat air fryer to 380°F (195°C). Pour sesame oil over the tuna steaks and let them sit while you make the marinade. Combine the jalapeño, garlic, ginger, five-spice powder, black pepper, and lemon juice in a bowl, then brush the mix on the fish. Let it sit for 10 minutes. Air Fry the tuna in the fryer for 6-11 minutes until it is cooked through and flakes easily when pressed with a fork. Serve warm.

## Fish Sticks For Grown-ups

Servings: 4
Cooking Time: 6 Minutes
**Ingredients:**
- 1 pound fish fillets
- ½ teaspoon hot sauce
- 1 tablespoon coarse brown mustard
- 1 teaspoon Worcestershire sauce
- salt
- Crumb Coating
- ¾ cup panko breadcrumbs
- ¼ cup stone-ground cornmeal
- ¼ teaspoon salt
- oil for misting or cooking spray

**Directions:**
1. Cut fish fillets crosswise into slices 1-inch wide.
2. Mix the hot sauce, mustard, and Worcestershire sauce together to make a paste and rub on all sides of the fish. Season to taste with salt.
3. Mix crumb coating ingredients together and spread on a sheet of wax paper.
4. Roll the fish fillets in the crumb mixture.
5. Spray all sides with olive oil or cooking spray and place in air fryer basket in a single layer.
6. Cook at 390°F (200°C) for 6 minutes, until fish flakes easily.

## Crunchy And Buttery Cod With Ritz® Cracker Crust

Servings: 2
Cooking Time: 10 Minutes
**Ingredients:**
- 4 tablespoons butter, melted
- 8 to 10 RITZ® crackers, crushed into crumbs
- 2 (6-ounce) cod fillets
- salt and freshly ground black pepper
- 1 lemon

**Directions:**
1. Preheat the air fryer to 380°F (195°C).
2. Melt the butter in a small saucepan on the stovetop or in a microwavable dish in the microwave, and then transfer the butter to a shallow dish. Place the crushed RITZ® crackers into a second shallow dish.
3. Season the fish fillets with salt and freshly ground black pepper. Dip them into the butter and then coat both sides with the RITZ® crackers.
4. Place the fish into the air fryer basket and air-fry at 380°F (195°C) for 10 minutes, flipping the fish over halfway through the cooking time.
5. Serve with a wedge of lemon to squeeze over the top.

## Lightened-up Breaded Fish Filets

Servings: 4
Cooking Time: 10 Minutes
**Ingredients:**
- ½ cup all-purpose flour
- ½ teaspoon cayenne pepper
- 1 teaspoon garlic powder
- ½ teaspoon black pepper
- ¼ teaspoon salt
- 2 eggs, whisked
- 1½ cups panko breadcrumbs
- 1 pound boneless white fish filets
- 1 cup tartar sauce
- 1 lemon, sliced into wedges

**Directions:**
1. In a medium bowl, mix the flour, cayenne pepper, garlic powder, pepper, and salt.
2. In a shallow dish, place the eggs.
3. In a third dish, place the breadcrumbs.
4. Cover the fish in the flour, dip them in the egg, and coat them with panko. Repeat until all fish are covered in the breading.
5. Liberally spray the metal trivet that fits inside the air fryer basket with olive oil mist. Place the fish onto the trivet, leaving space between the filets to flip. Cook for 5 minutes, flip the fish, and cook another 5 minutes. Repeat until all the fish is cooked.
6. Serve warm with tartar sauce and lemon wedges.

## Mediterranean Sea Scallops

Servings: 2
Cooking Time: 20 Minutes
**Ingredients:**
- 1 tbsp olive oil
- 1 shallot, minced
- 2 tbsp capers
- 2 cloves garlic, minced
- ½ cup heavy cream
- 3 tbsp butter
- 1 tbsp lemon juice
- Salt and pepper to taste
- ¼ tbsp cumin powder
- ¼ tbsp curry powder
- 1 lb jumbo sea scallops
- 2 tbsp chopped parsley
- 1 tbsp chopped cilantro

**Directions:**
1. Warm the olive oil in a saucepan over medium heat. Add shallot and stir-fry for 2 minutes until translucent. Stir in capers, cumin, curry, garlic, heavy cream, 1 tbsp of butter, lemon juice, salt, and pepper and cook for 2 minutes until rolling a boil. Low the heat and simmer for 3 minutes until the caper sauce thickens. Turn the heat off.
2. Preheat air fryer at 400ºF. In a bowl, add the remaining butter and scallops and toss to coat on all sides. Place scallops in the greased frying basket and Air Fry for 8 minutes, flipping once. Drizzle caper sauce over, scatter with parsley, cilantro and serve.

## Hot Calamari Rings

Servings: 4
Cooking Time: 25 Minutes
**Ingredients:**
- ½ cup all-purpose flour
- 2 tsp hot chili powder
- 2 eggs
- 1 tbsp milk
- 1 cup bread crumbs
- Salt and pepper to taste
- 1 lb calamari rings
- 1 lime, quartered
- ½ cup aioli sauce

**Directions:**

1. Preheat air fryer at 400°F. In a shallow bowl, add flour and hot chili powder. In another bowl, mix the eggs and milk. In a third bowl, mix the breadcrumbs, salt and pepper. Dip calamari rings in flour mix first, then in eggs mix and shake off excess. Then, roll ring through breadcrumb mixture. Place calamari rings in the greased frying basket and Air Fry for 4 minutes, tossing once. Squeeze lime quarters over calamari. Serve with aioli sauce.

## Piña Colada Shrimp

Servings: 4
Cooking Time: 25 Minutes
**Ingredients:**
- 1 lb large shrimp, deveined and shelled
- 1 can crushed pineapple
- ½ cup sour cream
- ¼ cup pineapple preserves
- 2 egg whites
- 1 tbsp dark rum
- 2/3 cup cornstarch
- 2/3 cup sweetened coconut
- 1 cup panko bread crumbs

**Directions:**
1. Preheat air fryer to 400°F (205°C). Drain the crushed pineapple and reserve the juice. Next, transfer the pineapple to a small bowl and mix with sour cream and preserves. Set aside. In a shallow bowl, beat egg whites with 1 tbsp of the reserved pineapple juice and rum. On a separate plate, add the cornstarch. On another plate, stir together coconut and bread crumbs. Coat the shrimp with the cornstarch. Then, dip the shrimp into the egg white mixture. Shake off drips and then coat with the coconut mixture. Place the shrimp in the greased frying basket. Air Fry until crispy and golden, 7 minutes. Serve warm.

## Tuna Patties With Dill Sauce

Servings: 6
Cooking Time: 10 Minutes
**Ingredients:**
- Two 5-ounce cans albacore tuna, drained
- ½ teaspoon garlic powder
- 2 teaspoons dried dill, divided
- ½ teaspoon black pepper
- ½ teaspoon salt, divided
- ¼ cup minced onion
- 1 large egg
- 7 tablespoons mayonnaise, divided
- ¼ cup panko breadcrumbs
- 1 teaspoon fresh lemon juice
- ¼ teaspoon fresh lemon zest
- 6 pieces butterleaf lettuce
- 1 cup diced tomatoes

**Directions:**
1. In a large bowl, mix the tuna with the garlic powder, 1 teaspoon of the dried dill, the black pepper, ¼ teaspoon of the salt, and the onion. Make sure to use the back of a fork to really break up the tuna so there are no large chunks.
2. Mix in the egg and 1 tablespoon of the mayonnaise; then fold in the breadcrumbs so the tuna begins to form a thick batter that holds together.
3. Portion the tuna mixture into 6 equal patties and place on a plate lined with parchment paper in the refrigerator for at least 30 minutes. This will help the patties hold together in the air fryer.
4. When ready to cook, preheat the air fryer to 350°F (175°C).
5. Liberally spray the metal trivet that sits inside the air fryer basket with olive oil mist and place the patties onto the trivet.
6. Cook for 5 minutes, flip, and cook another 5 minutes.
7. While the patties are cooking, make the dill sauce by combining the remaining 6 tablespoons of mayonnaise with the remaining 1 teaspoon of dill, the lemon juice, the lemon zest, and the remaining ¼ teaspoon of salt. Set aside.
8. Remove the patties from the air fryer.
9. Place 1 slice of lettuce on a plate and top with the tuna patty and a tomato slice. Repeat to form the remaining servings. Drizzle the dill dressing over the top. Serve immediately.

## Shrimp

Servings: 4
Cooking Time: 8 Minutes
**Ingredients:**
- 1 pound (26–30 count) shrimp, peeled, deveined, and butterflied (last tail section of shell intact)
- Marinade
- 1 5-ounce can evaporated milk
- 2 eggs, beaten
- 2 tablespoons white vinegar
- 1 tablespoon baking powder
- Coating
- 1 cup crushed panko breadcrumbs
- ½ teaspoon paprika
- ½ teaspoon Old Bay Seasoning
- ¼ teaspoon garlic powder
- oil for misting or cooking spray

**Directions:**

1. Stir together all marinade ingredients until well mixed. Add shrimp and stir to coat. Refrigerate for 1 hour.
2. When ready to cook, preheat air fryer to 390°F (200°C).
3. Combine coating ingredients in shallow dish.
4. Remove shrimp from marinade, roll in crumb mixture, and spray with olive oil or cooking spray.
5. Cooking in two batches, place shrimp in air fryer basket in single layer, close but not overlapping. Cook at 390°F (200°C) for 8 minutes, until light golden brown and crispy.
6. Repeat step 5 to cook remaining shrimp.

## Halibut Quesadillas

Servings: 2
Cooking Time: 30 Minutes
**Ingredients:**
- ¼ cup shredded cheddar
- ¼ cup shredded mozzarella
- 1 tsp olive oil
- 2 tortilla shells
- 1 halibut fillet
- ½ peeled avocado, sliced
- 1 garlic clove, minced
- Salt and pepper to taste
- ½ tsp lemon juice

**Directions:**
1. Preheat air fryer to 350°F (175°C). Brush the halibut fillet with olive oil and sprinkle with salt and pepper. Bake in the air fryer for 12-14 minutes, flipping once until cooked through. Combine the avocado, garlic, salt, pepper, and lemon juice in a bowl and, using a fork, mash lightly until the avocado is slightly chunky. Add and spread the resulting guacamole on one tortilla. Top with the cooked fish and cheeses, and cover with the second tortilla. Bake in the air fryer 6-8, flipping once until the cheese is melted. Serve immediately.

## Honey Pecan Shrimp

Servings: 4
Cooking Time: 10 Minutes
**Ingredients:**
- ¼ cup cornstarch
- ¾ teaspoon sea salt, divided
- ¼ teaspoon pepper
- 2 egg whites
- ⅔ cup finely chopped pecans
- 1 pound raw, peeled, and deveined shrimp
- ¼ cup honey
- 2 tablespoons mayonnaise

**Directions:**
1. In a small bowl, whisk together the cornstarch, ½ teaspoon of the salt, and the pepper.
2. In a second bowl, whisk together the egg whites until soft and foamy. (They don't need to be whipped to peaks or even soft peaks, just frothy.)
3. In a third bowl, mix together the pecans and the remaining ¼ teaspoon of sea salt.
4. Pat the shrimp dry with paper towels. Working in small batches, dip the shrimp into the cornstarch, then into the egg whites, and then into the pecans until all the shrimp are coated with pecans.
5. Preheat the air fryer to 330°F (165°C).
6. Place the coated shrimp inside the air fryer basket and spray with cooking spray. Cook for 5 minutes, toss the shrimp, and cook another 5 minutes.
7. Meanwhile, place the honey in a microwave-safe bowl and microwave for 30 seconds. Whisk in the mayonnaise until smooth and creamy. Pour the honey sauce into a serving bowl. Add the cooked shrimp to the serving bowl while hot and toss to coat. Serve immediately.

## Saucy Shrimp

Servings: 4
Cooking Time: 30 Minutes
**Ingredients:**
- 1 lb peeled shrimp, deveined
- ½ cup grated coconut
- ¼ cup bread crumbs
- ¼ cup flour
- ¼ tsp smoked paprika
- Salt and pepper to taste
- 1 egg
- 2 tbsp maple syrup
- ½ tsp rice vinegar
- 1 tbsp hot sauce
- ⅛ tsp red pepper flakes
- ¼ cup orange juice
- 1 tsp cornstarch
- ½ cup banana ketchup
- 1 lemon, sliced

**Directions:**
1. Preheat air fryer to 350°F (175°C). Combine coconut, bread crumbs, flour, paprika, black pepper, and salt in a bowl. In a separate bowl, whisk egg and 1 teaspoon water. Dip one shrimp into the egg bowl and shake off excess drips. Dip the shrimp in the bread crumb mixture and coat it completely. Continue the process for all of the shrimp. Arrange the shrimp on the greased frying basket. Air Fry for

5 minutes, then use tongs to flip the shrimp. Cook for another 2-3 minutes.

2. To make the sauce, add maple syrup, banana ketchup, hot sauce, vinegar, and red pepper flakes in a small saucepan over medium heat. Make a slurry in a small bowl with orange juice and cornstarch. Stir in slurry and continue stirring. Bring the sauce to a boil and cook for 5 minutes. When the sauce begins to thicken, remove from heat and allow to sit for 5 minutes. Serve shrimp warm along with sauce and lemon slices on the side.

## Mom´s Tuna Melt Toastie

Servings: 4
Cooking Time: 30 Minutes
**Ingredients:**
- 4 white bread slices
- 2 oz canned tuna
- 2 tbsp mayonnaise
- ½ lemon, zested and juiced
- Salt and pepper to taste
- ½ red onion, finely sliced
- 1 red tomato, sliced
- 4 cheddar cheese slices
- 2 tbsp butter, melted

**Directions:**
1. Preheat air fryer to 360°F (180°C). Put the butter-greased bread slices in the frying basket. Toast for 6 minutes. Meanwhile, mix the tuna, lemon juice and zest, salt, pepper, and mayonnaise in a small bowl. When the time is over, slide the frying basket out, flip the bread slices, and spread the tuna mixture evenly all over them. Cover with tomato slices, red onion, and cheddar cheese. Toast for 10 minutes or until the cheese is melted and lightly bubbling. Serve and enjoy!

## Mahi-mahi "burrito" Fillets

Servings:3
Cooking Time: 10 Minutes
**Ingredients:**
- 1 Large egg white
- 1½ cups (6 ounces) Crushed corn tortilla chips (gluten-free, if a concern)
- 1 tablespoon Chile powder
- 3 5-ounce skinless mahi-mahi fillets
- 6 tablespoons Canned refried beans
- Vegetable oil spray

**Directions:**
1. Preheat the air fryer to 400°F (205°C).

2. Set up and fill two shallow soup plates or small pie plates on your counter: one with the egg white, beaten until foamy; and one with the crushed tortilla chips.

3. Gently rub ½ teaspoon chile powder on each side of each fillet.

4. Spread (or maybe smear) 1 tablespoon refried beans over both sides and the edges of a fillet. Dip the fillet in the egg white, turning to coat it on both sides. Let any excess egg white slip back into the rest, then set the fillet in the crushed tortilla chips. Turn several times, pressing gently to coat it evenly. Coat the fillet on all sides with the vegetable oil spray, then set it aside. Prepare the remaining fillet(s) in the same way.

5. When the machine is at temperature, set the fillets in the basket with as much air space between them as possible. Air-fry undisturbed for 10 minutes, or until crisp and browned.

6. Use a nonstick-safe spatula to transfer the fillets to a serving platter or plates. Cool for only a minute or so, then serve hot.

## Yummy Salmon Burgers With Salsa Rosa

Servings: 4
Cooking Time: 35 Minutes + Chilling Time
**Ingredients:**
- ¼ cup minced red onion
- ¼ cup slivered onions
- ½ cup mayonnaise
- 2 tsp ketchup
- 1 tsp brandy
- 2 tsp orange juice
- 1 lb salmon fillets
- 5 tbsp panko bread crumbs
- 1 garlic clove, minced
- 1 large egg, lightly beaten
- 1 tbsp Dijon mustard
- 1 tsp fresh lemon juice
- 1 tbsp chopped parsley
- Salt to taste
- 4 buns
- 8 Boston lettuce leaves

**Directions:**
1. Mix the mayonnaise, ketchup, brandy, and orange juice in a bowl until blended. Set aside the resulting salsa rosa until ready to serve. Cut a 4-oz section of salmon and place in a food processor. Pulse until it turns into a paste. Chop the remaining salmon into cubes and transfer to a bowl along

with the salmon paste. Add the panko, minced onion, garlic, egg, mustard, lemon juice, parsley, and salt. Toss to combine. Divide into 5 patties about ¾-inch thick. Refrigerate for 30 minutes.

2. Preheat air fryer to 400°F (205°C). Place the patties in the greased frying basket. Air Fry for 12-14 minutes, flipping once until golden. Serve each patty on a bun, 2 lettuce leaves, 2 tbsp of salsa rosa, and slivered onions. Enjoy!

## Mediterranean Salmon Burgers

Servings: 4
Cooking Time: 30 Minutes
**Ingredients:**
- 1 lb salmon fillets
- 1 scallion, diced
- 4 tbsp mayonnaise
- 1 egg
- 1 tsp capers, drained
- Salt and pepper to taste
- ¼ tsp paprika
- 1 lemon, zested
- 1 lemon, sliced
- 1 tbsp chopped dill
- ¼ cup bread crumbs
- 4 buns, toasted
- 4 tsp whole-grain mustard
- 4 lettuce leaves
- 1 small tomato, sliced

**Directions:**
1. Preheat air fryer to 400°F (205°C). Divide salmon in half. Cut one of the halves into chunks and transfer the chunks to the food processor. Also, add scallion, 2 tablespoons mayonnaise, egg, capers, dill, salt, pepper, paprika, and lemon zest. Pulse to puree. Dice the rest of the salmon into ¼-inch chunks. Combine chunks and puree along with bread crumbs in a large bowl. Shape the fish into 4 patties and transfer to the frying basket. Air Fry for 5 minutes, then flip the patties. Air Fry for another 5 to 7 minutes. Place the patties each on a bun along with 1 teaspoon mustard, mayonnaise, lettuce, lemon slices, and a slice of tomato. Serve and enjoy.

## The Best Oysters Rockefeller

Servings: 2
Cooking Time: 30 Minutes
**Ingredients:**
- 4 tsp grated Parmesan
- 2 tbsp butter
- 1 sweet onion, minced
- 1 clove garlic, minced
- 1 cup baby spinach
- ⅛ tsp Tabasco hot sauce
- ½ tsp lemon juice
- ½ tsp lemon zest
- ¼ cup bread crumbs
- 12 oysters, on the half shell

**Directions:**
1. Melt butter in a skillet over medium heat. Stir in onion, garlic, and spinach and stir-fry for 3 minutes until the onion is translucent. Mix in Parmesan cheese, hot sauce, lemon juice, lemon zest, and bread crumbs. Divide this mixture between the tops of oysters.

2. Preheat air fryer to 400°F. Place oysters in the frying basket and Air Fry for 6 minutes. Serve immediately.

## Baltimore Crab Cakes

Servings: 4
Cooking Time: 35 Minutes
**Ingredients:**
- ½ lb lump crabmeat, shells discarded
- 2 tbsp mayonnaise
- ½ tsp yellow mustard
- ½ tsp lemon juice
- ½ tbsp minced shallot
- ¼ cup bread crumbs
- 1 egg
- Salt and pepper to taste
- 4 poached eggs
- ½ cup bechamel sauce
- 2 tsp chopped chives
- 1 lemon, cut into wedges

**Directions:**
1. Preheat air fryer at 400°F. Combine all ingredients, except eggs, sauce, and chives, in a bowl. Form mixture into 4 patties. Place crab cakes in the greased frying basket and Air Fry for 10 minutes, flipping once. Transfer them to a serving dish. Top each crab cake with 1 poached egg, drizzle with Bechamel sauce and scatter with chives and lemon wedges. Serve and enjoy!

# Fish Cakes

Servings: 4
Cooking Time: 10 Minutes
**Ingredients:**
- ¾ cup mashed potatoes (about 1 large russet potato)
- 12 ounces cod or other white fish
- salt and pepper
- oil for misting or cooking spray
- 1 large egg
- ¼ cup potato starch
- ½ cup panko breadcrumbs
- 1 tablespoon fresh chopped chives
- 2 tablespoons minced onion

**Directions:**
1. Peel potatoes, cut into cubes, and cook on stovetop till soft.
2. Salt and pepper raw fish to taste. Mist with oil or cooking spray, and cook in air fryer at 360°F (180°C) for 6 to 8minutes, until fish flakes easily. If fish is crowded, rearrange halfway through cooking to ensure all pieces cook evenly.
3. Transfer fish to a plate and break apart to cool.
4. Beat egg in a shallow dish.
5. Place potato starch in another shallow dish, and panko crumbs in a third dish.
6. When potatoes are done, drain in colander and rinse with cold water.
7. In a large bowl, mash the potatoes and stir in the chives and onion. Add salt and pepper to taste, then stir in the fish.
8. If needed, stir in a tablespoon of the beaten egg to help bind the mixture.
9. Shape into 8 small, fat patties. Dust lightly with potato starch, dip in egg, and roll in panko crumbs. Spray both sides with oil or cooking spray.
10. Cook at 360°F (180°C) for 10 minutes, until golden brown and crispy.

# Breaded Parmesan Perch

Servings: 5
Cooking Time: 15 Minutes
**Ingredients:**
- ¼ cup grated Parmesan
- ½ tsp salt
- ¼ tsp paprika
- 1 tbsp chopped dill
- 1 tsp dried thyme
- 2 tsp Dijon mustard
- 2 tbsp bread crumbs
- 4 ocean perch fillets
- 1 lemon, quartered
- 2 tbsp chopped cilantro

**Directions:**
1. Preheat air fryer to 400°F (205°C). Combine salt, paprika, pepper, dill, mustard, thyme, Parmesan, and bread crumbs in a wide bowl. Coat all sides of the fillets in the breading, then transfer to the greased frying basket. Air Fry for 8 minutes until outside is golden and the inside is cooked through. Garnish with lemon wedges and sprinkle with cilantro. Serve and enjoy!

# Fish-in-chips

Servings: 4
Cooking Time: 11 Minutes
**Ingredients:**
- 1 cup All-purpose flour or potato starch
- 2 Large egg(s), well beaten
- 1½ cups (6 ounces) Crushed plain potato chips, preferably thick-cut or ruffled (gluten-free, if a concern)
- 4 4-ounce skinless cod fillets

**Directions:**
1. Preheat the air fryer to 400°F (205°C).
2. Set up and fill three shallow soup plates or small pie plates on your counter: one for the flour, one for the beaten egg(s), and one for the crushed potato chips.
3. Dip a piece of cod in the flour, turning it to coat on all sides, even the ends and sides. Gently shake off any excess flour, then dip it in the beaten egg(s). Gently turn to coat it on all sides, then let any excess egg slip back into the rest. Set the fillet in the crushed potato chips and turn several times and onto all sides, pressing gently to coat the fish. Dip it back in the egg(s), coating all sides but taking care that the coating doesn't slip off; then dip it back in the potato chips for a thick, even coating. Set it aside and coat more fillets in the same way.
4. When the machine is at temperature, set the fillets in the basket with as much air space between them as possible. Air-fry undisturbed for 11 minutes, until golden brown and firm but not hard.
5. Use kitchen tongs to transfer the fillets to a wire rack. Cool for just a minute or two before serving.

## Teriyaki Salmon

Servings: 4
Cooking Time: 20 Minutes
**Ingredients:**
- ¼ cup raw honey
- 4 garlic cloves, minced
- 1 tbsp olive oil
- ½ tsp salt
- ½ tsp soy sauce
- ¼ tsp blackening seasoning
- 4 salmon fillets

**Directions:**
1. Preheat air fryer to 380°F (195°C). Combine together the honey, garlic, olive oil, soy sauce, blackening seasoning and salt in a bowl. Put the salmon in a single layer on the greased frying basket. Brush the top of each fillet with the honey-garlic mixture. Roast for 10-12 minutes. Serve and enjoy!

## Feta & Shrimp Pita

Servings: 4
Cooking Time: 15 Minutes
**Ingredients:**
- 1 lb peeled shrimp, deveined
- 2 tbsp olive oil
- 1 tsp dried oregano
- ½ tsp dried thyme
- ½ tsp garlic powder
- ¼ tsp shallot powder
- ¼ tsp tarragon powder
- Salt and pepper to taste
- 4 whole-wheat pitas
- 4 oz feta cheese, crumbled
- 1 cup grated lettuce
- 1 tomato, diced
- ¼ cup black olives, sliced
- 1 lemon

**Directions:**
1. Preheat the oven to 380°F (195°C). Mix the shrimp with olive oil, oregano, thyme, garlic powder, shallot powder, tarragon powder salt, and pepper in a bowl. Pour shrimp in a single layer in the frying basket and Bake for 6-8 minutes or until no longer pink and cooked through. Divide the shrimp into warmed pitas with feta, lettuce, tomato, olives, and a squeeze of lemon. Serve and enjoy!

## Catfish Nuggets

Servings: 4
Cooking Time: 7 Minutes Per Batch
**Ingredients:**
- 2 medium catfish fillets, cut in chunks (approximately 1 x 2 inch)
- salt and pepper
- 2 eggs
- 2 tablespoons skim milk
- ½ cup cornstarch
- 1 cup panko breadcrumbs, crushed
- oil for misting or cooking spray

**Directions:**
1. Season catfish chunks with salt and pepper to your liking.
2. Beat together eggs and milk in a small bowl.
3. Place cornstarch in a second small bowl.
4. Place breadcrumbs in a third small bowl.
5. Dip catfish chunks in cornstarch, dip in egg wash, shake off excess, then roll in breadcrumbs.
6. Spray all sides of catfish chunks with oil or cooking spray.
7. Place chunks in air fryer basket in a single layer, leaving space between for air circulation.
8. Cook at 390°F (200°C) for 4minutes, turn, and cook an additional 3 minutes, until fish flakes easily and outside is crispy brown.
9. Repeat steps 7 and 8 to cook remaining catfish nuggets.

## Restaurant-style Breaded Shrimp

Servings: 2
Cooking Time: 35 Minutes
**Ingredients:**
- ½ lb fresh shrimp, peeled
- 2 eggs, beaten
- ½ cup breadcrumbs
- ½ onion, finely chopped
- ½ tsp ground ginger
- ½ tsp garlic powder
- ½ tsp turmeric
- ½ tsp red chili powder
- Salt and pepper to taste
- ½ tsp amchur powder

**Directions:**
1. Preheat air fryer to 350°F (175°C). Place the beaten eggs in a bowl and dip in the shrimp. Blend the bread crumbs with all the dry ingredients in another bowl. Add in the shrimp and toss to coat. Place the coated shrimp in the greased frying basket. Air Fry for 12-14 minutes until the breaded crust of the shrimp is golden brown. Toss the basket two or three times during the cooking time. Serve.

# Crab Stuffed Salmon Roast

Servings: 4
Cooking Time: 20 Minutes
**Ingredients:**
- 1 (1½-pound) salmon fillet
- salt and freshly ground black pepper
- 6 ounces crabmeat
- 1 teaspoon finely chopped lemon zest
- 1 teaspoon Dijon mustard
- 1 tablespoon chopped fresh parsley, plus more for garnish
- 1 scallion, chopped
- ¼ teaspoon salt
- olive oil

**Directions:**
1. Prepare the salmon fillet by butterflying it. Slice into the thickest side of the salmon, parallel to the countertop and along the length of the fillet. Don't slice all the way through to the other side – stop about an inch from the edge. Open the salmon up like a book. Season the salmon with salt and freshly ground black pepper.
2. Make the crab filling by combining the crabmeat, lemon zest, mustard, parsley, scallion, salt and freshly ground black pepper in a bowl. Spread this filling in the center of the salmon. Fold one side of the salmon over the filling. Then fold the other side over on top.
3. Transfer the rolled salmon to the center of a piece of parchment paper that is roughly 6- to 7-inches wide and about 12-inches long. The parchment paper will act as a sling, making it easier to put the salmon into the air fryer. Preheat the air fryer to 370°F (185°C). Use the parchment paper to transfer the salmon roast to the air fryer basket and tuck the ends of the paper down beside the salmon. Drizzle a little olive oil on top and season with salt and pepper.
4. Air-fry the salmon at 370°F (185°C) for 20 minutes.
5. Remove the roast from the air fryer and let it rest for a few minutes. Then, slice it, sprinkle some more lemon zest and parsley (or fresh chives) on top and serve.

# Shrimp Al Pesto

Servings: 4
Cooking Time: 10 Minutes
**Ingredients:**
- 1 lb peeled shrimp, deveined
- ¼ cup pesto sauce
- 1 lime, sliced
- 2 cups cooked farro

**Directions:**
1. Preheat air fryer to 360°F. Coat the shrimp with the pesto sauce in a bowl. Put the shrimp in a single layer in the frying basket. Put the lime slices over the shrimp and Roast for 5 minutes. Remove lime and discard. Serve the shrimp over a bed of farro pilaf. Enjoy!

# Korean-style Fried Calamari

Servings: 4
Cooking Time: 25 Minutes
**Ingredients:**
- 2 tbsp tomato paste
- 1 tbsp gochujang
- 1 tbsp lime juice
- 1 tsp lime zest
- 1 tsp smoked paprika
- ½ tsp salt
- 1 cup bread crumbs
- 1/3 lb calamari rings

**Directions:**
1. Preheat air fryer to 400°F. Whisk tomato paste, gochujang, lime juice and zest, paprika, and salt in a bowl. In another bowl, add in the bread crumbs. Dredge calamari rings in the tomato mixture, shake off excess, then roll through the crumbs. Place calamari rings in the greased frying basket and Air Fry for 4-5 minutes, flipping once. Serve.

# Family Fish Nuggets With Tartar Sauce

Servings: 4
Cooking Time: 30 Minutes
**Ingredients:**
- ½ cup mayonnaise
- 1 tbsp yellow mustard
- ½ cup diced dill pickles
- Salt and pepper to taste
- 1 egg, beaten
- ¼ cup cornstarch
- ¼ cup flour
- 1 lb cod, cut into sticks

**Directions:**
1. In a bowl, whisk the mayonnaise, mustard, pickles, salt, and pepper. Set aside the resulting tarter sauce.
2. Preheat air fryer to 350°F. Add the beaten egg to a bowl. In another bowl, combine cornstarch, flour, salt, and pepper. Dip fish nuggets in the egg and roll them in the flour mixture. Place fish nuggets in the lightly greased frying basket and Air Fry for 10 minutes, flipping once. Serve with the sauce on the side.

## Lime Flaming Halibut

Servings: 2
Cooking Time: 20 Minutes
**Ingredients:**
- 2 tbsp butter, melted
- ½ tsp chili powder
- ½ cup bread crumbs
- 2 halibut fillets

**Directions:**
1. Preheat air fryer to 350ºF. In a bowl, mix the butter, chili powder and bread crumbs. Press mixture onto tops of halibut fillets. Place halibut in the greased frying basket and Air Fry for 10 minutes or until the fish is opaque and flake easily with a fork. Serve right away.

## Maple Balsamic Glazed Salmon

Servings: 4
Cooking Time: 10 Minutes
**Ingredients:**
- 4 (6-ounce) fillets of salmon
- salt and freshly ground black pepper
- vegetable oil
- ¼ cup pure maple syrup
- 3 tablespoons balsamic vinegar
- 1 teaspoon Dijon mustard

**Directions:**
1. Preheat the air fryer to 400°F (205°C).
2. Season the salmon well with salt and freshly ground black pepper. Spray or brush the bottom of the air fryer basket with vegetable oil and place the salmon fillets inside. Air-fry the salmon for 5 minutes.
3. While the salmon is air-frying, combine the maple syrup, balsamic vinegar and Dijon mustard in a small saucepan over medium heat and stir to blend well. Let the mixture simmer while the fish is cooking. It should start to thicken slightly, but keep your eye on it so it doesn't burn.
4. Brush the glaze on the salmon fillets and air-fry for an additional 5 minutes. The salmon should feel firm to the touch when finished and the glaze should be nicely browned on top. Brush a little more glaze on top before removing and serving with rice and vegetables, or a nice green salad.

## Pecan-crusted Tilapia

Servings: 4
Cooking Time: 8 Minutes
**Ingredients:**
- 1 pound skinless, boneless tilapia filets
- ¼ cup butter, melted
- 1 teaspoon minced fresh or dried rosemary
- 1 cup finely chopped pecans
- 1 teaspoon sea salt
- ¼ teaspoon paprika
- 2 tablespoons chopped parsley
- 1 lemon, cut into wedges

**Directions:**
1. Pat the tilapia filets dry with paper towels.
2. Pour the melted butter over the filets and flip the filets to coat them completely.
3. In a medium bowl, mix together the rosemary, pecans, salt, and paprika.
4. Preheat the air fryer to 350°F (175°C).
5. Place the tilapia filets into the air fryer basket and top with the pecan coating. Cook for 6 to 8 minutes. The fish should be firm to the touch and flake easily when fully cooked.
6. Remove the fish from the air fryer. Top the fish with chopped parsley and serve with lemon wedges.

## Curried Sweet-and-spicy Scallops

Servings: 3
Cooking Time: 5 Minutes
**Ingredients:**
- 6 tablespoons Thai sweet chili sauce
- 2 cups (from about 5 cups cereal) Crushed Rice Krispies or other rice-puff cereal
- 2 teaspoons Yellow curry powder, purchased or homemade (see here)
- 1 pound Sea scallops
- Vegetable oil spray

**Directions:**
1. Preheat the air fryer to 400°F (205°C).
2. Set up and fill two shallow soup plates or small pie plates on your counter: one for the chili sauce and one for crumbs, mixed with the curry powder.
3. Dip a scallop into the chili sauce, coating it on all sides. Set it in the cereal mixture and turn several times to coat evenly. Gently shake off any excess and set the scallop on a cutting board. Continue dipping and coating the remaining scallops. Coat them all on all sides with the vegetable oil spray.
4. Set the scallops in the basket with as much air space between them as possible. Air-fry undisturbed for 5 minutes, or until lightly browned and crunchy.
5. Remove the basket. Set aside for 2 minutes to let the coating set up. Then gently pour the contents of the basket onto a platter and serve at once.

# Home-style Fish Sticks

Servings: 4
Cooking Time: 30 Minutes
**Ingredients:**
- 1 lb cod fillets, cut into sticks
- 1 cup flour
- 1 egg
- ¼ cup cornmeal
- Salt and pepper to taste
- ¼ tsp smoked paprika
- 1 lemon

**Directions:**
1. Preheat air fryer at 350ºF. In a bowl, add ½ cup of flour. In another bowl, beat the egg and in a third bowl, combine the remaining flour, cornmeal, salt, black pepper and paprika. Roll the sticks in the flour, shake off excess flour. Then, dip them in the egg, shake off excess egg. Finally, dredge them in the cornmeal mixture. Place fish fingers in the greased frying basket and Air Fry for 10 minutes, flipping once. Serve with squeezed lemon.

# Chinese Firecracker Shrimp

Servings: 4
Cooking Time: 20 Minutes
**Ingredients:**
- 1 lb peeled shrimp, deveined
- 2 green onions, chopped
- 2 tbsp sesame seeds
- Salt and pepper to taste
- 1 egg
- ½ cup all-purpose flour
- ¾ cup panko bread crumbs
- 1/3 cup sour cream
- 2 tbsp Sriracha sauce
- ¼ cup sweet chili sauce

**Directions:**
1. Preheat air fryer to 400°F (205°C). Set out three small bowls. In the first, add flour. In the second, beat the egg. In the third, add the crumbs. Season the shrimp with salt and pepper. Dip the shrimp in the flour, then dredge in the egg, and finally in the bread crumbs. Place the shrimp in the greased frying basket and Air Fry for 8 minutes, flipping once until crispy. Combine sour cream, Sriracha, and sweet chili sauce in a bowl. Top the shrimp with sesame seeds and green onions and serve with the chili sauce.

# Coconut Jerk Shrimp

Servings: 3
Cooking Time: 8 Minutes
**Ingredients:**
- 1 Large egg white(s)
- 1 teaspoon Purchased or homemade jerk dried seasoning blend (see the headnote)
- ¾ cup Plain panko bread crumbs (gluten-free, if a concern)
- ¾ cup Unsweetened shredded coconut
- 12 Large shrimp (20–25 per pound), peeled and deveined
- Coconut oil spray

**Directions:**
1. Preheat the air fryer to 375°F (190°C).
2. Whisk the egg white(s) and seasoning blend in a bowl until foamy. Add the shrimp and toss well to coat evenly.
3. Mix the bread crumbs and coconut on a dinner plate until well combined. Use kitchen tongs to pick up a shrimp, letting the excess egg white mixture slip back into the rest. Set the shrimp in the bread-crumb mixture. Turn several times to coat evenly and thoroughly. Set on a cutting board and continue coating the remainder of the shrimp.
4. Lightly coat all the shrimp on both sides with the coconut oil spray. Set them in the basket in one layer with as much space between them as possible. (You can even stand some up along the basket's wall in some models.) Air-fry undisturbed for 6 minutes, or until the coating is lightly browned. If the air fryer is at 360°F (180°C), you may need to add 2 minutes to the cooking time.
5. Use clean kitchen tongs to transfer the shrimp to a wire rack. Cool for only a minute or two before serving.

# Garlic-butter Lobster Tails

Servings: 2
Cooking Time: 20 Minutes
**Ingredients:**
- 2 lobster tails
- 1 tbsp butter, melted
- ½ tsp Old Bay Seasoning
- ½ tsp garlic powder
- 1 tbsp chopped parsley
- 2 lemon wedges

**Directions:**
1. Preheat air fryer to 400ºF. Using kitchen shears, cut down the middle of each lobster tail on the softer side. Carefully run your finger between the lobster meat and the shell to loosen the meat. Place lobster tails in the frying basket, cut sides up, and Air Fry for 4 minutes. Rub with butter, garlic powder and Old Bay seasoning and cook for 4 more minutes. Garnish with parsley and lemon wedges. Serve and enjoy!

## Mojito Fish Tacos

Servings: 4
Cooking Time: 30 Minutes
**Ingredients:**
- 1 ½ cups chopped red cabbage
- 1 lb cod fillets
- 2 tsp olive oil
- 3 tbsp lemon juice
- 1 large carrot, grated
- 1 tbsp white rum
- ½ cup salsa
- 1/3 cup Greek yogurt
- 4 soft tortillas

**Directions:**
1. Preheat air fryer to 390°F (200°C). Rub the fish with olive oil, then a splash with a tablespoon of lemon juice. Place in the fryer and Air Fry for 9-12 minutes. The fish should flake when done. Mix the remaining lemon juice, red cabbage, carrots, salsa, rum, and yogurt in a bowl. Take the fish out of the fryer and tear into large pieces. Serve with tortillas and cabbage mixture. Enjoy!

## Rich Salmon Burgers With Broccoli Slaw

Servings: 4
Cooking Time: 25 Minutes
**Ingredients:**
- 1 lb salmon fillets
- 1 egg
- ¼ cup dill, chopped
- 1 cup bread crumbs
- Salt to taste
- ½ tsp cayenne pepper
- 1 lime, zested
- 1 tsp fish sauce
- 4 buns
- 3 cups chopped broccoli
- ½ cup shredded carrots
- ¼ cup sunflower seeds
- 2 garlic cloves, minced
- 1 cup Greek yogurt

**Directions:**
1. Preheat air fryer to 360°F (180°C). Blitz the salmon fillets in your food processor until they are finely chopped. Remove to a large bowl and add egg, dill, bread crumbs, salt, and cayenne. Stir to combine. Form the mixture into 4 patties. Put them into the frying basket and Bake for 10 minutes, flipping once. Combine broccoli, carrots, sunflower seeds, garlic, salt, lime, fish sauce, and Greek yogurt in a bowl. Serve the salmon burgers onto buns with broccoli slaw. Enjoy!

## Tuna Nuggets In Hoisin Sauce

Servings: 4
Cooking Time: 7 Minutes
**Ingredients:**
- ½ cup hoisin sauce
- 2 tablespoons rice wine vinegar
- 2 teaspoons sesame oil
- 1 teaspoon garlic powder
- 2 teaspoons dried lemongrass
- ¼ teaspoon red pepper flakes
- ½ small onion, quartered and thinly sliced
- 8 ounces fresh tuna, cut into 1-inch cubes
- cooking spray
- 3 cups cooked jasmine rice

**Directions:**
1. Mix the hoisin sauce, vinegar, sesame oil, and seasonings together.
2. Stir in the onions and tuna nuggets.
3. Spray air fryer baking pan with nonstick spray and pour in tuna mixture.
4. Cook at 390°F (200°C) for 3minutes. Stir gently.
5. Cook 2minutes and stir again, checking for doneness. Tuna should be barely cooked through, just beginning to flake and still very moist. If necessary, continue cooking and stirring in 1-minute intervals until done.
6. Serve warm over hot jasmine rice.

## Peppery Tilapia Roulade

Servings: 4
Cooking Time: 25 Minutes
**Ingredients:**
- 4 jarred roasted red pepper slices
- 1 egg
- ½ cup breadcrumbs
- Salt and pepper to taste
- 4 tilapia fillets
- 2 tbsp butter, melted
- 4 lime wedges
- 1 tsp dill

**Directions:**
1. Preheat air fryer at 350°F. Beat the egg and 2 tbsp of water in a bowl. In another bowl, mix the breadcrumbs, salt, and pepper. Place a red pepper slice and sprinkle with dill on each fish fillet. Tightly roll tilapia fillets from one short end

to the other. Secure with toothpicks. Roll each fillet in the egg mixture, then dredge them in the breadcrumbs. Place fish rolls in the greased frying basket and drizzle the tops with melted butter. Roast for 6 minutes. Let rest in a serving dish for 5 minutes before removing the toothpicks. Serve with lime wedges. Enjoy!

## Cheesy Tuna Tower

Servings:2
Cooking Time: 15 Minutes
**Ingredients:**
- ½ cup grated mozzarella
- 1 can tuna in water
- ¼ cup mayonnaise
- 2 tsp yellow mustard
- 1 tbsp minced dill pickle
- 1 tbsp minced celery
- 1 tbsp minced green onion
- Salt and pepper to taste
- 4 tomato slices
- 8 avocado slices

**Directions:**
1. Preheat air fryer to 350ºF. In a bowl, combine tuna, mayonnaise, mustard, pickle, celery, green onion, salt, and pepper. Cut a piece of parchment paper to fit the bottom of the frying basket. Place tomato slices on paper in a single layer and top with 2 avocado slices. Share tuna salad over avocado slices and top with mozzarella cheese. Place the towers in the frying basket and Bake for 4 minutes until the cheese starts to brown. Serve warm.

## Coconut Shrimp With Plum Sauce

Servings: 2
Cooking Time: 30 Minutes
**Ingredients:**
- ½ lb raw shrimp, peeled
- 2 eggs
- ½ cup breadcrumbs
- 1 tsp red chili powder
- 2 tbsp dried coconut flakes
- Salt and pepper to taste
- ½ cup plum sauce

**Directions:**
1. Preheat air fryer to 350°F (175°C). Whisk the eggs with salt and pepper in a bowl. Dip in the shrimp, fully submerging. Combine the bread crumbs, coconut flakes, chili powder, salt, and pepper in another bowl until evenly blended. Coat the shrimp in the crumb mixture and place them in the foil-lined frying basket. Air Fry for 14-16 minutes. Halfway through the cooking time, shake the basket. Serve with plum sauce for dipping and enjoy!

# Beef , pork & Lamb Recipes

## Pork Cutlets With Almond-lemon Crust

Servings: 3
Cooking Time: 14 Minutes
**Ingredients:**
- ¾ cup Almond flour
- ¾ cup Plain dried bread crumbs (gluten-free, if a concern)
- 1½ teaspoons Finely grated lemon zest
- 1¼ teaspoons Table salt
- ¾ teaspoon Garlic powder
- ¾ teaspoon Dried oregano
- 1 Large egg white(s)
- 2 tablespoons Water
- 3 6-ounce center-cut boneless pork loin chops (about ¾ inch thick)
- Olive oil spray

**Directions:**
1. Preheat the air fryer to 375°F (190°C) .

2. Mix the almond flour, bread crumbs, lemon zest, salt, garlic powder, and dried oregano in a large bowl until well combined.

3. Whisk the egg white(s) and water in a shallow soup plate or small pie plate until uniform.

4. Dip a chop in the egg white mixture, turning it to coat all sides, even the ends. Let any excess egg white mixture slip back into the rest, then set it in the almond flour mixture. Turn it several times, pressing gently to coat it evenly. Generously coat the chop with olive oil spray, then set aside to dip and coat the remaining chop(s).

5. Set the chops in the basket with as much air space between them as possible. Air-fry undisturbed for 12 minutes, or until browned and crunchy. You may need to add 2 minutes to the cooking time if the machine is at 360°F (180°C).

6. Use kitchen tongs to transfer the chops to a wire rack. Cool for a few minutes before serving.

## Boneless Ribeyes

Servings: 2
Cooking Time: 10-15 Minutes
**Ingredients:**
- 2 8-ounce boneless ribeye steaks
- 4 teaspoons Worcestershire sauce
- ½ teaspoon garlic powder
- pepper
- 4 teaspoons extra virgin olive oil
- salt

**Directions:**
1. Season steaks on both sides with Worcestershire sauce. Use the back of a spoon to spread evenly.
2. Sprinkle both sides of steaks with garlic powder and coarsely ground black pepper to taste.
3. Drizzle both sides of steaks with olive oil, again using the back of a spoon to spread evenly over surfaces.
4. Allow steaks to marinate for 30minutes.
5. Place both steaks in air fryer basket and cook at 390°F (200°C) for 5minutes.
6. Turn steaks over and cook until done:
7. Medium rare: additional 5 minutes
8. Medium: additional 7 minutes
9. Well done: additional 10 minutes
10. Remove steaks from air fryer basket and let sit 5minutes. Salt to taste and serve.

## Kielbasa Sausage With Pierogies And Caramelized Onions

Servings: 3
Cooking Time: 30 Minutes
**Ingredients:**
- 1 Vidalia or sweet onion, sliced
- olive oil
- salt and freshly ground black pepper
- 2 tablespoons butter, cut into small cubes
- 1 teaspoon sugar
- 1 pound light Polish kielbasa sausage, cut into 2-inch chunks
- 1 (13-ounce) package frozen mini pierogies
- 2 teaspoons vegetable or olive oil
- chopped scallions

**Directions:**
1. Preheat the air fryer to 400°F (205°C).
2. Toss the sliced onions with a little olive oil, salt and pepper and transfer them to the air fryer basket. Dot the onions with pieces of butter and air-fry at 400°F (205°C) for 2 minutes. Then sprinkle the sugar over the onions and stir. Pour any melted butter from the bottom of the air fryer drawer over the onions (do this over the sink – some of the butter will spill through the basket). Continue to air-fry for another 13 minutes, stirring or shaking the basket every few minutes to cook the onions evenly.
3. Add the kielbasa chunks to the onions and toss. Air-fry for another 5 minutes, shaking the basket halfway through the cooking time. Transfer the kielbasa and onions to a bowl and cover with aluminum foil to keep warm.
4. Toss the frozen pierogies with the vegetable or olive oil and transfer them to the air fryer basket. Air-fry at 400°F (205°C) for 8 minutes, shaking the basket twice during the cooking time.
5. When the pierogies have finished cooking, return the kielbasa and onions to the air fryer and gently toss with the pierogies. Air-fry for 2 more minutes and then transfer everything to a serving platter. Garnish with the chopped scallions and serve hot with the spicy sour cream sauce below.
6. Kielbasa Sausage with Pierogies and Caramelized Onions

## Almond And Sun-dried Tomato Crusted Pork Chops

Servings: 4
Cooking Time: 10 Minutes
**Ingredients:**
- ½ cup oil-packed sun-dried tomatoes
- ½ cup toasted almonds
- ¼ cup grated Parmesan cheese
- ½ cup olive oil
- 2 tablespoons water
- ½ teaspoon salt

- freshly ground black pepper
- 4 center-cut boneless pork chops (about 1¼ pounds)

**Directions:**
1. Place the sun-dried tomatoes into a food processor and pulse them until they are coarsely chopped. Add the almonds, Parmesan cheese, olive oil, water, salt and pepper. Process all the ingredients into a smooth paste. Spread most of the paste (leave a little in reserve) onto both sides of the pork chops and then pierce the meat several times with a needle-style meat tenderizer or a fork. Let the pork chops sit and marinate for at least 1 hour (refrigerate if marinating for longer than 1 hour).
2. Preheat the air fryer to 370°F (185°C).
3. Brush a little olive oil on the bottom of the air fryer basket. Transfer the pork chops into the air fryer basket, spooning a little more of the sun-dried tomato paste onto the pork chops if there are any gaps where the paste may have been rubbed off. Air-fry the pork chops at 370°F (18°C) for 10 minutes, turning the chops over halfway through the cooking process.
4. When the pork chops have finished cooking, transfer them to a serving plate and serve with mashed potatoes and vegetables for a hearty meal.

## Premium Steakhouse Salad

Servings: 2
Cooking Time: 20 Minutes
**Ingredients:**
- 1 head iceberg lettuce, cut into thin strips
- 2 tbsp olive oil
- 1 tbsp white wine vinegar
- 1 tbsp Greek yogurt
- 1 tsp Dijon mustard
- 1 (¾-lb) strip steak
- Salt and pepper to taste
- 2 tbsp chopped walnuts
- ¼ cup blue cheese crumbles
- 4 cherry tomatoes, halved
- 4 fig wedges

**Directions:**
1. In a bowl, whisk the olive oil, vinegar, Greek yogurt, and mustard. Let chill covered in the fridge until ready to use. Preheat air fryer to 400°F. Sprinkle the steak with salt and pepper. Place it in the greased frying basket and Air Fry for 9 minutes or until you reach your desired doneness, flipping once. Let sit onto a cutting board for 5 minutes.
2. Combine lettuce and mustard dressing in a large bowl, then divide between 2 medium bowls. Thinly slice steak and add to salads. Scatter with walnuts, blue cheese, cherry tomatoes, and fig wedges. Serve immediately.

## Mongolian Beef

Servings: 4
Cooking Time: 15 Minutes
**Ingredients:**
- 1½ pounds flank steak, thinly sliced on the bias into ¼-inch strips
- Marinade
- 2 tablespoons soy sauce*
- 1 clove garlic, smashed
- big pinch crushed red pepper flakes
- Sauce
- 1 tablespoon vegetable oil
- 2 cloves garlic, minced
- 1 tablespoon finely grated fresh ginger
- 3 dried red chili peppers
- ¾ cup soy sauce*
- ¾ cup chicken stock
- 5 to 6 tablespoons brown sugar (depending on how sweet you want the sauce)
- ½ cup cornstarch, divided
- 1 bunch scallions, sliced into 2-inch pieces

**Directions:**
1. Marinate the beef in the soy sauce, garlic and red pepper flakes for one hour.
2. In the meantime, make the sauce. Preheat a small saucepan over medium heat on the stovetop. Add the oil, garlic, ginger and dried chili peppers and sauté for just a minute or two. Add the soy sauce, chicken stock and brown sugar and continue to simmer for a few minutes. Dissolve 3 tablespoons of cornstarch in 3 tablespoons of water and stir this into the saucepan. Stir the sauce over medium heat until it thickens. Set this aside.
3. Preheat the air fryer to 400°F (205°C).
4. Remove the beef from the marinade and transfer it to a zipper sealable plastic bag with the remaining cornstarch. Shake it around to completely coat the beef and transfer the coated strips of beef to a baking sheet or plate, shaking off any excess cornstarch. Spray the strips with vegetable oil on all sides and transfer them to the air fryer basket.
5. Air-fry at 400°F (205°C) for 15 minutes, shaking the basket to toss and rotate the beef strips throughout the cooking process. Add the scallions for the last 4 minutes of the cooking. Transfer the hot beef strips and scallions to a bowl and toss with the sauce (warmed on the stovetop if necessary), coating all the beef strips with the sauce. Serve warm over white rice.

# Cinnamon-stick Kofta Skewers

Servings: 8
Cooking Time: 15 Minutes
**Ingredients:**
- 1 pound Lean ground beef
- ½ teaspoon Ground cumin
- ½ teaspoon Onion powder
- ½ teaspoon Ground dried turmeric
- ½ teaspoon Ground cinnamon
- ½ teaspoon Table salt
- Up to a ⅛ teaspoon Cayenne
- 8 3½- to 4-inch-long cinnamon sticks (see the headnote)
- Vegetable oil spray

**Directions:**
1. Preheat the air fryer to 375°F (190°C).
2. Gently mix the ground beef, cumin, onion powder, turmeric, cinnamon, salt, and cayenne in a bowl until the meat is evenly mixed with the spices. (Clean, dry hands work best!) Divide this mixture into 2-ounce portions, each about the size of a golf ball.
3. Wrap one portion of the meat mixture around a cinnamon stick, using about three-quarters of the length of the stick, covering one end but leaving a little "handle" of cinnamon stick protruding from the other end. Set aside and continue making more kofta skewers.
4. Generously coat the formed kofta skewers on all sides with vegetable oil spray. Set them in the basket with as much air space between them as possible. Air-fry undisturbed for 13 minutes, or until browned and cooked through. If the machine is at 360°F (180°C), you may need to add 2 minutes to the cooking time.
5. Use a nonstick-safe spatula, and perhaps kitchen tongs for balance, to gently transfer the kofta skewers to a wire rack. Cool for at least 5 minutes or up to 20 minutes before serving.

# Indian Fry Bread Tacos

Servings: 4
Cooking Time: 20 Minutes
**Ingredients:**
- 1 cup all-purpose flour
- 1½ teaspoons salt, divided
- 1½ teaspoons baking powder
- ¼ cup milk
- ¼ cup warm water
- ½ pound lean ground beef
- One 14.5-ounce can pinto beans, drained and rinsed
- 1 tablespoon taco seasoning
- ½ cup shredded cheddar cheese
- 2 cups shredded lettuce
- ¼ cup black olives, chopped
- 1 Roma tomato, diced
- 1 avocado, diced
- 1 lime

**Directions:**
1. In a large bowl, whisk together the flour, 1 teaspoon of the salt, and baking powder. Make a well in the center and add in the milk and water. Form a ball and gently knead the dough four times. Cover the bowl with a damp towel, and set aside.
2. Preheat the air fryer to 380°F (195°C).
3. In a medium bowl, mix together the ground beef, beans, and taco seasoning. Crumble the meat mixture into the air fryer basket and cook for 5 minutes; toss the meat and cook an additional 2 to 3 minutes, or until cooked fully. Place the cooked meat in a bowl for taco assembly; season with the remaining ½ teaspoon salt as desired.
4. On a floured surface, place the dough. Cut the dough into 4 equal parts. Using a rolling pin, roll out each piece of dough to 5 inches in diameter. Spray the dough with cooking spray and place in the air fryer basket, working in batches as needed. Cook for 3 minutes, flip over, spray with cooking spray, and cook for an additional 1 to 3 minutes, until golden and puffy.
5. To assemble, place the fry breads on a serving platter. Equally divide the meat and bean mixture on top of the fry bread. Divide the cheese, lettuce, olives, tomatoes, and avocado among the four tacos. Squeeze lime over the top prior to serving.

# Pork & Beef Egg Rolls

Servings: 8
Cooking Time: 8 Minutes
**Ingredients:**
- ¼ pound very lean ground beef
- ¼ pound lean ground pork
- 1 tablespoon soy sauce
- 1 teaspoon olive oil
- ½ cup grated carrots
- 2 green onions, chopped
- 2 cups grated Napa cabbage
- ¼ cup chopped water chestnuts
- ¼ teaspoon salt
- ¼ teaspoon garlic powder
- ¼ teaspoon black pepper
- 1 egg
- 1 tablespoon water

- 8 egg roll wraps
- oil for misting or cooking spray

**Directions:**
1. In a large skillet, brown beef and pork with soy sauce. Remove cooked meat from skillet, drain, and set aside.
2. Pour off any excess grease from skillet. Add olive oil, carrots, and onions. Sauté until barely tender, about 1 minute.
3. Stir in cabbage, cover, and cook for 1 minute or just until cabbage slightly wilts. Remove from heat.
4. In a large bowl, combine the cooked meats and vegetables, water chestnuts, salt, garlic powder, and pepper. Stir well. If needed, add more salt to taste.
5. Beat together egg and water in a small bowl.
6. Fill egg roll wrappers, using about ¼ cup of filling for each wrap. Roll up and brush all over with egg wash to seal. Spray very lightly with olive oil or cooking spray.
7. Place 4 egg rolls in air fryer basket and cook at 390°F (200°C) for 4minutes. Turn over and cook 4 more minutes, until golden brown and crispy.
8. Repeat to cook remaining egg rolls.

## Aromatic Pork Tenderloin

Servings: 6
Cooking Time: 65 Minutes
**Ingredients:**
- 1 pork tenderloin
- 2 tbsp olive oil
- 2 garlic cloves, minced
- 1 tsp dried sage
- 1 tsp dried marjoram
- 1 tsp dried thyme
- 1 tsp paprika
- Salt and pepper to taste

**Directions:**
1. Preheat air fryer to 360°F (180°C). Drizzle oil over the tenderloin, then rub garlic, sage, marjoram, thyme, paprika, salt and pepper all over. Place the tenderloin in the greased frying basket and Bake for 45 minutes. Flip the pork and cook for another 15 minutes. Check the temperature for doneness. Let the cooked tenderloin rest for 10 minutes before slicing. Serve and enjoy!

## Corned Beef Hash

Servings: 6
Cooking Time: 15 Minutes
**Ingredients:**
- 3 cups (about 14 ounces) Frozen unseasoned hash brown cubes (no need to thaw)
- 9 ounces Deli corned beef, cut into ¾-inch-thick slices, then cubed
- ¾ cup Roughly chopped yellow or white onion
- ¾ cup Stemmed, cored, and roughly chopped red bell pepper
- 2½ tablespoons Olive oil
- ¼ teaspoon Dried thyme
- ¼ teaspoon Dried sage leaves
- Up to a ⅛ teaspoon Cayenne

**Directions:**
1. Preheat the air fryer to 400°F (205°C).
2. Mix all the ingredients in a large or very large bowl until the potato cubes and corned beef are coated in the spices.
3. Spread the mixture in the basket in as close to an even layer as you can. Air-fry for 15 minutes, tossing and rearranging the pieces at the 5- and 10-minute marks to expose covered bits, until the potatoes are browned, even crisp, and the mixture is very fragrant.
4. Pour the contents of the basket onto a serving platter or divide between serving plates. Cool for a couple of minutes before serving.

## Paprika Fried Beef

Servings: 4
Cooking Time: 30 Minutes
**Ingredients:**
- Celery salt to taste
- 4 beef cube steaks
- ½ cup milk
- 1 cup flour
- 2 tsp paprika
- 1 egg
- 1 cup bread crumbs
- 2 tbsp olive oil

**Directions:**
1. Preheat air fryer to 350°F (175°C). Place the cube steaks in a zipper sealed bag or between two sheets of cling wrap. Gently pound the steaks until they are slightly thinner. Set aside. In a bowl, mix together milk, flour, paprika, celery salt, and egg until just combined. In a separate bowl, mix together the crumbs and olive oil. Take the steaks and dip them into the buttermilk batter, shake off some of the excess, and return to a plate for 5 minutes. Next, dip the steaks in the bread crumbs, patting the crumbs into both sides. Air Fry the steaks until the crust is crispy and brown, 12-16 minutes. Serve warm.

## Beef & Barley Stuffed Bell Peppers

Servings: 4
Cooking Time: 30 Minutes
**Ingredients:**
- 1 cup pulled cooked roast beef
- 4 bell peppers, tops removed
- 1 onion, chopped
- ½ cup grated carrot
- 2 tsp olive oil
- 2 tomatoes, chopped
- 1 cup cooked barley
- 1 tsp dried marjoram

**Directions:**
1. Preheat air fryer to 400°F (205°C). Cut the tops of the bell peppers, then remove the stems. Put the onion, carrots, and olive oil in a baking pan and cook for 2-4 minutes. The veggies should be crispy but soft. Put the veggies in a bowl, toss in the tomatoes, barley, roast beef, and marjoram, and mix to combine. Spoon the veggie mix into the cleaned bell peppers and put them in the frying basket. Bake for 12-16 minutes or until the peppers are tender. Serve warm.

## Herby Lamb Chops

Servings: 2
Cooking Time: 25 Minutes
**Ingredients:**
- 3 lamb chops
- 1 cup breadcrumbs
- 2 eggs, beaten
- Salt and pepper to taste
- ½ tbsp thyme
- ½ tbsp mint, chopped
- ½ tsp garlic powder
- ½ tsp ground rosemary
- ½ tsp cayenne powder
- ½ tsp ras el hanout

**Directions:**
1. Preheat air fryer to 320°F (160°C). Mix the breadcrumbs, thyme, mint, garlic, rosemary, cayenne, ras el hanout, salt, and pepper in a bowl. Dip the lamb chops in the beaten eggs, then coat with the crumb mixture. Air Fry for 14-16 minutes, turning once. Serve and enjoy!

## Red Curry Flank Steak

Servings: 4
Cooking Time: 18 Minutes
**Ingredients:**
- 3 tablespoons red curry paste
- ¼ cup olive oil
- 2 teaspoons grated fresh ginger
- 2 tablespoons soy sauce
- 2 tablespoons rice wine vinegar
- 3 scallions, minced
- 1½ pounds flank steak
- fresh cilantro (or parsley) leaves

**Directions:**
1. Mix the red curry paste, olive oil, ginger, soy sauce, rice vinegar and scallions together in a bowl. Place the flank steak in a shallow glass dish and pour half the marinade over the steak. Pierce the steak several times with a fork or meat tenderizer to let the marinade penetrate the meat. Turn the steak over, pour the remaining marinade over the top and pierce the steak several times again. Cover and marinate the steak in the refrigerator for 6 to 8 hours.
2. When you are ready to cook, remove the steak from the refrigerator and let it sit at room temperature for 30 minutes.
3. Preheat the air fryer to 400°F (205°C).
4. Cut the flank steak in half so that it fits more easily into the air fryer and transfer both pieces to the air fryer basket. Pour the marinade over the steak. Air-fry for 18 minutes, depending on your preferred degree of doneness of the steak (12 minutes = medium rare). Flip the steak over halfway through the cooking time.
5. When your desired degree of doneness has been reached, remove the steak to a cutting board and let it rest for 5 minutes before slicing. Thinly slice the flank steak against the grain of the meat. Transfer the slices to a serving platter, pour any juice from the bottom of the air fryer over the sliced flank steak and sprinkle the fresh cilantro on top.

## Lamb Chops In Currant Sauce

Servings: 4
Cooking Time: 30 Minutes
**Ingredients:**
- ½ cup chicken broth
- 2 tbsp red currant jelly
- 2 tbsp Dijon mustard
- 1 tbsp lemon juice
- ½ tsp dried thyme
- ½ tsp dried mint
- 8 lamb chops
- Salt and pepper to taste

**Directions:**
1. Preheat the air fryer to 375°F (190°C). Combine the broth, jelly, mustard, lemon juice, mint, and thyme and mix with a whisk until smooth. Sprinkle the chops with salt and pepper and brush with some of the broth mixture.
2. Set 4 chops in the frying basket in a single layer, then add a raised rack and lay the rest of the chops on top. Bake for 15-20 minutes. Then, lay them in a cake pan and add the chicken broth mix. Put in the fryer and Bake for 3-5 more minutes or until the sauce is bubbling and the chops are tender.

## Italian Meatballs

Servings: 4
Cooking Time: 12 Minutes
**Ingredients:**
- 12 ounces lean ground beef
- 4 ounces Italian sausage, casing removed
- ½ cup breadcrumbs
- 1 cup grated Parmesan cheese
- 1 egg
- 2 tablespoons milk
- 2 teaspoons Italian seasoning
- ½ teaspoon onion powder
- ½ teaspoon garlic powder
- Pinch of red pepper flakes

**Directions:**
1. In a large bowl, place all the ingredients and mix well. Roll out 24 meatballs.
2. Preheat the air fryer to 360°F (180°C).
3. Place the meatballs in the air fryer basket and cook for 12 minutes, tossing every 4 minutes. Using a food thermometer, check to ensure the internal temperature of the meatballs is 165°F (75°C).

## Stuffed Pork Chops

Servings: 4
Cooking Time: 12 Minutes
**Ingredients:**
- 4 boneless pork chops
- ½ teaspoon salt
- ½ teaspoon black pepper
- ¼ teaspoon paprika
- 1 cup frozen spinach, defrosted and squeezed dry
- 2 cloves garlic, minced
- 2 ounces cream cheese
- ¼ cup grated Parmesan cheese
- 1 tablespoon extra-virgin olive oil

**Directions:**
1. Pat the pork chops with a paper towel. Make a slit in the side of each pork chop to create a pouch.
2. Season the pork chops with the salt, pepper, and paprika.
3. In a small bowl, mix together the spinach, garlic, cream cheese, and Parmesan cheese.
4. Divide the mixture into fourths and stuff the pork chop pouches. Secure the pouches with toothpicks.
5. Preheat the air fryer to 400°F (205°C).
6. Place the stuffed pork chops in the air fryer basket and spray liberally with cooking spray. Cook for 6 minutes, flip and coat with more cooking spray, and cook another 6 minutes. Check to make sure the meat is cooked to an internal temperature of 145°F (65°C). Cook the pork chops in batches, as needed.

## Calzones South Of The Border

Servings: 8
Cooking Time: 8 Minutes
**Ingredients:**
- Filling
- ¼ pound ground pork sausage
- ½ teaspoon chile powder
- ¼ teaspoon ground cumin
- ⅛ teaspoon garlic powder
- ⅛ teaspoon onion powder
- ⅛ teaspoon oregano
- ½ cup ricotta cheese
- 1 ounce sharp Cheddar cheese, shredded
- 2 ounces Pepper Jack cheese, shredded
- 1 4-ounce can chopped green chiles, drained
- oil for misting or cooking spray
- salsa, sour cream, or guacamole
- Crust
- 2 cups white wheat flour, plus more for kneading and rolling
- 1 package (¼ ounce) RapidRise yeast
- 1 teaspoon salt
- ½ teaspoon chile powder
- ½ teaspoon ground cumin
- 1 cup warm water (115°F (45°C) to 125°F (50°C))
- 2 teaspoons olive oil

**Directions:**
1. Crumble sausage into air fryer baking pan and stir in the filling seasonings: chile powder, cumin, garlic powder, onion powder, and oregano. Cook at 390°F (200°C) for 2minutes. Stir, breaking apart, and cook for 3 to 4minutes, until well done. Remove and set aside on paper towels to drain.
2. To make dough, combine flour, yeast, salt, chile powder, and cumin. Stir in warm water and oil until soft dough forms. Turn out onto lightly floured board and knead for 3 or 4minutes. Let dough rest for 10minutes.
3. Place the three cheeses in a medium bowl. Add cooked sausage and chiles and stir until well mixed.
4. Cut dough into 8 pieces.
5. Working with 4 pieces of the dough, press each into a circle about 5 inches in diameter. Top each dough circle with 2 heaping tablespoons of filling. Fold over into a half-moon shape and press edges together. Seal edges firmly to prevent leakage. Spray both sides with oil or cooking spray.

6. Place 4 calzones in air fryer basket and cook at 360°F (180°C) for 5minutes. Mist with oil or spray and cook for 3minutes, until crust is done and nicely browned.
7. While the first batch is cooking, press out the remaining dough, fill, and shape into calzones.
8. Spray both sides with oil or cooking spray and cook for 5minutes. If needed, mist with oil and continue cooking for 3 minutes longer. This second batch will cook a little faster than the first because your air fryer is already hot.
9. Serve plain or with salsa, sour cream, or guacamole.

## Indonesian Pork Satay

Servings: 4
Cooking Time: 30 Minutes
**Ingredients:**
- 1 lb pork tenderloin, cubed
- ¼ cup minced onion
- 2 garlic cloves, minced
- 1 jalapeño pepper, minced
- 2 tbsp lime juice
- 2 tbsp coconut milk
- ½ tbsp ground coriander
- ½ tsp ground cumin
- 2 tbsp peanut butter
- 2 tsp curry powder

**Directions:**
1. Combine the pork, onion, garlic, jalapeño, lime juice, coconut milk, peanut butter, ground coriander, cumin, and curry powder in a bowl. Stir well and allow to marinate for 10 minutes.
2. Preheat air fryer to 380°F (195°C). Use a holey spoon and take the pork out of the marinade and set the marinade aside. Poke 8 bamboo skewers through the meat, then place the skewers in the air fryer. Use a cooking brush to rub the marinade on each skewer, then Grill for 10-14 minutes, adding more marinade if necessary. The pork should be golden and cooked through when finished. Serve warm.

## Tonkatsu

Servings: 3
Cooking Time: 10 Minutes
**Ingredients:**
- ½ cup All-purpose flour or tapioca flour
- 1 Large egg white(s), well beaten
- ¾ cup Plain panko bread crumbs (gluten-free, if a concern)
- 3 4-ounce center-cut boneless pork loin chops (about ½ inch thick)
- Vegetable oil spray

**Directions:**
1. Preheat the air fryer to 375°F (190°C).
2. Set up and fill three shallow soup plates or small pie plates on your counter: one for the flour, one for the beaten egg white(s), and one for the bread crumbs.
3. Set a chop in the flour and roll it to coat all sides, even the ends. Gently shake off any excess flour and set it in the egg white(s). Gently roll and turn it to coat all sides. Let any excess egg white slip back into the rest, then set the chop in the bread crumbs. Turn it several times, pressing gently to get an even coating on all sides and the ends. Generously coat the breaded chop with vegetable oil spray, then set it aside so you can dredge, coat, and spray the remaining chop(s).
4. Set the chops in the basket with as much air space between them as possible. Air-fry undisturbed for 10 minutes, or until golden brown and crisp.
5. Use kitchen tongs to transfer the chops to a wire rack and cool for a couple of minutes before serving.

## Traditional Moo Shu Pork Lettuce Wraps

Servings: 4
Cooking Time: 40 Minutes
**Ingredients:**
- ½ cup sliced shiitake mushrooms
- 1 lb boneless pork loin, cubed
- 3 tbsp cornstarch
- 2 tbsp rice vinegar
- 3 tbsp hoisin sauce
- 1 tsp oyster sauce
- 3 tsp sesame oil
- 1 tsp sesame seeds
- ¼ tsp ground ginger
- 1 egg
- 2 tbsp flour
- 1 bag coleslaw mix
- 1 cup chopped baby spinach
- 3 green onions, sliced
- 8 iceberg lettuce leaves

**Directions:**
1. Preheat air fryer at 350ºF. Make a slurry by whisking 1 tbsp of cornstarch and 1 tbsp of water in a bowl. Set aside. Warm a saucepan over heat, add in rice vinegar, hoisin sauce, oyster sauce, 1 tsp of sesame oil, and ginger, and cook for 3 minutes, stirring often. Add in cornstarch slurry and cook for 1 minute. Set aside and let the mixture thicken. Beat the egg, flour, and the remaining cornstarch in a bowl. Set aside.

2. Dredge pork cubes in the egg mixture. Shake off any excess. Place them in the greased frying basket and Air Fry for 8 minutes, shaking once. Warm the remaining sesame oil in a skillet over medium heat. Add in coleslaw mix, baby spinach, green onions, and mushrooms and cook for 5 minutes until the coleslaw wilts. Turn the heat off. Add in cooked pork, pour in oyster sauce mixture, and toss until coated. Divide mixture between lettuce leaves, sprinkle with sesame seed, roll them up, and serve.

## Pepper Steak

Servings: 4
Cooking Time: 30 Minutes
**Ingredients:**
- 2 tablespoons cornstarch
- 1 tablespoon sugar
- ¾ cup beef broth
- ¼ cup hoisin sauce
- 3 tablespoons soy sauce
- 1 teaspoon sesame oil
- ½ teaspoon freshly ground black pepper
- 1½ pounds boneless New York strip steaks, sliced into ½-inch strips
- 1 onion, sliced
- 3 small bell peppers, red, yellow and green, sliced

**Directions:**
1. Whisk the cornstarch and sugar together in a large bowl to break up any lumps in the cornstarch. Add the beef broth and whisk until combined and smooth. Stir in the hoisin sauce, soy sauce, sesame oil and freshly ground black pepper. Add the beef, onion and peppers, and toss to coat. Marinate the beef and vegetables at room temperature for 30 minutes, stirring a few times to keep meat and vegetables coated.
2. Preheat the air fryer to 350°F (175°C).
3. Transfer the beef, onion, and peppers to the air fryer basket with tongs, reserving the marinade. Air-fry the beef and vegetables for 30 minutes, stirring well two or three times during the cooking process.
4. While the beef is air-frying, bring the reserved marinade to a simmer in a small saucepan over medium heat on the stovetop. Simmer for 5 minutes until the sauce thickens.
5. When the steak and vegetables have finished cooking, transfer them to a serving platter. Pour the hot sauce over the pepper steak and serve with white rice.

## Blackberry Bbq Glazed Country-style Ribs

Servings: 2
Cooking Time: 40 Minutes
**Ingredients:**
- ½ cup + 2 tablespoons sherry or Madeira wine, divided
- 1 pound boneless country-style pork ribs
- salt and freshly ground black pepper
- 1 tablespoon Chinese 5-spice powder
- ¼ cup blackberry preserves
- ¼ cup hoisin sauce*
- 1 clove garlic, minced
- 1 generous tablespoon grated fresh ginger
- 2 scallions, chopped
- 1 tablespoon sesame seeds, toasted

**Directions:**
1. Preheat the air fryer to 330°F (165°C) and pour ½ cup of the sherry into the bottom of the air fryer drawer.
2. Season the ribs with salt, pepper and the 5-spice powder.
3. Air-fry the ribs at 330°F (165°C) for 20 minutes, turning them over halfway through the cooking time.
4. While the ribs are cooking, make the sauce. Combine the remaining sherry, blackberry preserves, hoisin sauce, garlic and ginger in a small saucepan. Bring to a simmer on the stovetop for a few minutes, until the sauce thickens.
5. When the time is up on the air fryer, turn the ribs over, pour a little sauce on the ribs and air-fry for another 10 minutes at 330°F (165°C). Turn the ribs over again, pour on more of the sauce and air-fry at 330°F (165°C) for a final 10 minutes.
6. Let the ribs rest for at least 5 minutes before serving them warm with a little more glaze brushed on and the scallions and sesame seeds sprinkled on top.

## Exotic Pork Skewers

Servings: 4
Cooking Time: 30 Minutes
**Ingredients:**
- 1/3 cup apricot jam
- 2 tbsp lemon juice
- 2 tsp olive oil
- ½ tsp dried tarragon
- 1 lb pork tenderloin, cubed
- 4 pitted cherries, halved
- 4 pitted apricots, halved

**Directions:**
1. Preheat air fryer to 380°F (195°C). Toss the jam, lemon juice, olive oil, and tarragon in a big bowl and mix well. Place the pork in the bowl, then stir well to coat. Allow marinating for 10 minutes. Poke 4 metal skewers through the pork, cherries, and apricots, alternating ingredients. Use a cooking brush to rub the marinade on the skewers, then place them in the air fryer. Toss the rest of the marinade. Air Fry the kebabs for 4-6 minutes on each side until the pork is cooked through and the fruit is soft. Serve!

## Kochukaru Pork Lettuce Cups

Servings: 4
Cooking Time: 25 Minutes
**Ingredients:**
- 1 tsp kochukaru (chili pepper flakes)
- 12 baby romaine lettuce leaves
- 1 lb pork tenderloin, sliced
- Salt and pepper to taste
- 3 scallions, chopped
- 3 garlic cloves, crushed
- ¼ cup soy sauce
- 2 tbsp gochujang
- ½ tbsp light brown sugar
- ½ tbsp honey
- 1 tbsp grated fresh ginger
- 2 tbsp rice vinegar
- 1 tsp toasted sesame oil
- 2 ¼ cups cooked brown rice
- ½ tbsp sesame seeds
- 2 spring onions, sliced

**Directions:**
1. Mix the scallions, garlic, soy sauce, kochukaru, honey, brown sugar, and ginger in a small bowl. Mix well. Place the pork in a large bowl. Season with salt and pepper. Pour the marinade over the pork, tossing the meat in the marinade until coated. Cover the bowl with plastic wrap and allow to marinate overnight. When ready to cook,
2. Preheat air fryer to 400°F (205°C). Remove the pork from the bowl and discard the marinade. Place the pork in the greased frying basket and Air Fry for 10 minutes, flipping once until browned and cooked through. Meanwhile, prepare the gochujang sauce. Mix the gochujang, rice vinegar, and sesame oil until smooth. To make the cup, add 3 tbsp of brown rice on the lettuce leaf. Place a slice of pork on top, drizzle a tsp of gochujang sauce and sprinkle with some sesame seeds and spring onions. Wrap the lettuce over the mixture similar to a burrito. Serve warm.

## Skirt Steak With Horseradish Cream

Servings: 2
Cooking Time: 20 Minutes
**Ingredients:**
- 1 cup heavy cream
- 3 tbsp horseradish sauce
- 1 lemon, zested
- 1 skirt steak, halved
- 2 tbsp olive oil
- Salt and pepper to taste

**Directions:**
1. Mix together the heavy cream, horseradish sauce, and lemon zest in a small bowl. Let chill in the fridge.
2. Preheat air fryer to 400°F. Brush steak halves with olive oil and sprinkle with salt and pepper. Place steaks in the frying basket and Air Fry for 10 minutes or until you reach your desired doneness, flipping once. Let sit onto a cutting board for 5 minutes. Thinly slice against the grain and divide between 2 plates. Drizzle with the horseradish sauce over. Serve and enjoy!

## Greek Pork Chops

Servings: 4
Cooking Time: 30 Minutes
**Ingredients:**
- 3 tbsp grated Halloumi cheese
- 4 pork chops
- 1 tsp Greek seasoning
- Salt and pepper to taste
- ¼ cup all-purpose flour
- 2 tbsp bread crumbs

**Directions:**
1. Preheat air fryer to 380°F (195°C). Season the pork chops with Greek seasoning, salt and pepper. In a shallow bowl, add flour. In another shallow bowl, combine the crumbs and Halloumi. Dip the chops in the flour, then in the bread crumbs. Place them in the fryer and spray with cooking oil. Bake for 12-14 minutes, flipping once. Serve warm.

## Santorini Steak Bowls

Servings: 2
Cooking Time: 15 Minutes
**Ingredients:**
- 5 pitted Kalamata olives, halved
- 1 cucumber, diced
- 2 tomatoes, diced
- 1 tbsp apple cider vinegar
- 2 tsp olive oil
- ¼ cup feta cheese crumbles
- ½ tsp Greek oregano
- ½ tsp dried dill
- ¼ tsp garlic powder
- ⅛ tsp ground nutmeg
- Salt and pepper to taste
- 1 (¾-lb) strip steak

**Directions:**
1. In a large bowl, combine cucumber, tomatoes, vinegar, olive oil, olives, and feta cheese. Let chill covered in the

fridge until ready to use. Preheat air fryer to 400°F. Combine all spices in a bowl, then coat strip steak with this mixture. Add steak in the lightly greased frying basket and Air Fry for 10 minutes or until you reach your desired doneness, flipping once. Let sit onto a cutting board for 5 minutes. Thinly slice against the grain and divide between 2 bowls. Top with the cucumber mixture. Serve.

## Meatloaf With Tangy Tomato Glaze

Servings: 6
Cooking Time: 50 Minutes
**Ingredients:**
- 1 pound ground beef
- ½ pound ground pork
- ½ pound ground veal (or turkey)
- 1 medium onion, diced
- 1 small clove of garlic, minced
- 2 egg yolks, lightly beaten
- ½ cup tomato ketchup
- 1 tablespoon Worcestershire sauce
- ½ cup plain breadcrumbs*
- 2 teaspoons salt
- freshly ground black pepper
- ½ cup chopped fresh parsley, plus more for garnish
- 6 tablespoons ketchup
- 1 tablespoon balsamic vinegar
- 2 tablespoons brown sugar

**Directions:**
1. Combine the meats, onion, garlic, egg yolks, ketchup, Worcestershire sauce, breadcrumbs, salt, pepper and fresh parsley in a large bowl and mix well.
2. Preheat the air fryer to 350°F (175°C) and pour a little water into the bottom of the air fryer drawer. (This will help prevent the grease that drips into the bottom drawer from burning and smoking.)
3. Transfer the meatloaf mixture to the air fryer basket, packing it down gently. Run a spatula around the meatloaf to create a space about ½-inch wide between the meat and the side of the air fryer basket.
4. Air-fry at 350°F (175°C) for 20 minutes. Carefully invert the meatloaf onto a plate (remember to remove the basket from the air fryer drawer so you don't pour all the grease out) and slide it back into the air fryer basket to turn it over. Re-shape the meatloaf with a spatula if necessary. Air-fry for another 20 minutes at 350°F (175°C).
5. Combine the ketchup, balsamic vinegar and brown sugar in a bowl and spread the mixture over the meatloaf. Air-fry for another 10 minutes, until an instant read thermometer inserted into the center of the meatloaf registers 160°F (70°C).
6. Allow the meatloaf to rest for a few more minutes and then transfer it to a serving platter using a spatula. Slice the meatloaf, sprinkle a little chopped parsley on top if desired, and serve.

## Grilled Pork & Bell Pepper Salad

Servings: 4
Cooking Time: 25 Minutes
**Ingredients:**
- 1 cup sautéed button mushrooms, sliced
- 2 lb pork tenderloin, sliced
- 1 tsp olive oil
- 1 tsp dried marjoram
- 6 tomato wedges
- 6 green olives
- 6 cups mixed salad greens
- 1 red bell pepper, sliced
- 1/3 cup vinaigrette dressing

**Directions:**
1. Preheat air fryer to 400°F (205°C). Combine the pork and olive oil, making sure the pork is well-coated. Season with marjoram. Lay the pork in the air fryer. Grill for 4-6 minutes, turning once until the pork is cooked through.
2. While the pork is cooking, toss the salad greens, red bell pepper, tomatoes, olives, and mushrooms into a bowl. Lay the pork slices on top of the salad, season with vinaigrette, and toss. Serve while the pork is still warm.

## Cheesy Mushroom-stuffed Pork Loins

Servings: 3
Cooking Time: 30 Minutes
**Ingredients:**
- ¾ cup diced mushrooms
- 2 tsp olive oil
- 1 shallot, diced
- Salt and pepper to taste
- 3 center-cut pork loins
- 6 Gruyère cheese slices

**Directions:**
1. Warm the olive oil in a skillet over medium heat. Add in shallot and mushrooms and stir-fry for 3 minutes. Sprinkle with salt and pepper and cook for 1 minute.
2. Preheat air fryer to 350°F. Cut a pocket into each pork loin and set aside. Stuff an even amount of mushroom mixture into each chop pocket and top with 2 Gruyere cheese slices into each pocket. Place the pork in the lightly greased frying basket and Air Fry for 11 minutes cooked through and the cheese has melted. Let sit onto a cutting board for 5 minutes before serving.

# Kawaii Pork Roast

Servings: 6
Cooking Time: 50 Minutes
**Ingredients:**
- Salt and white pepper to taste
- 2 tbsp soy sauce
- 2 tbsp honey
- 1 tbsp sesame oil
- ¼ tsp ground ginger
- 1 tsp oregano
- 2 cloves garlic, minced
- 1 boneless pork loin

**Directions:**
1. Preheat air fryer at 350°F. Mix all ingredients in a bowl. Massage mixture into all sides of pork loin. Place pork loin in the greased frying basket and Roast for 40 minutes, flipping once. Let rest onto a cutting board for 5 minutes before slicing. Serve right away.

# Lamb Chops

Servings: 2
Cooking Time: 20 Minutes
**Ingredients:**
- 2 teaspoons oil
- ½ teaspoon ground rosemary
- ½ teaspoon lemon juice
- 1 pound lamb chops, approximately 1-inch thick
- salt and pepper
- cooking spray

**Directions:**
1. Mix the oil, rosemary, and lemon juice together and rub into all sides of the lamb chops. Season to taste with salt and pepper.
2. For best flavor, cover lamb chops and allow them to rest in the fridge for 20 minutes.
3. Spray air fryer basket with nonstick spray and place lamb chops in it.
4. Cook at 360°F (180°C) for approximately 20minutes. This will cook chops to medium. The meat will be juicy but have no remaining pink. Cook for a minute or two longer for well done chops. For rare chops, stop cooking after about 12minutes and check for doneness.

# Honey Mesquite Pork Chops

Servings: 2
Cooking Time: 10 Minutes
**Ingredients:**
- 2 tablespoons mesquite seasoning
- ¼ cup honey
- 1 tablespoon olive oil
- 1 tablespoon water
- freshly ground black pepper
- 2 bone-in center cut pork chops (about 1 pound)

**Directions:**
1. Whisk the mesquite seasoning, honey, olive oil, water and freshly ground black pepper together in a shallow glass dish. Pierce the chops all over and on both sides with a fork or meat tenderizer. Add the pork chops to the marinade and massage the marinade into the chops. Cover and marinate for 30 minutes.
2. Preheat the air fryer to 330°F (165°C).
3. Transfer the pork chops to the air fryer basket and pour half of the marinade over the chops, reserving the remaining marinade. Air-fry the pork chops for 6 minutes. Flip the pork chops over and pour the remaining marinade on top. Air-fry for an additional 3 minutes at 330°F (165°C). Then, increase the air fryer temperature to 400°F (205°C) and air-fry the pork chops for an additional minute.
4. Transfer the pork chops to a serving plate, and let them rest for 5 minutes before serving. If you'd like a sauce for these chops, pour the cooked marinade from the bottom of the air fryer over the top.

# Crispy Lamb Shoulder Chops

Servings: 3
Cooking Time: 28 Minutes
**Ingredients:**
- ¾ cup All-purpose flour or gluten-free all-purpose flour
- 2 teaspoons Mild paprika
- 2 teaspoons Table salt
- 1½ teaspoons Garlic powder
- 1½ teaspoons Dried sage leaves
- 3 6-ounce bone-in lamb shoulder chops, any excess fat trimmed
- Olive oil spray

**Directions:**
1. Whisk the flour, paprika, salt, garlic powder, and sage in a large bowl until the mixture is of a uniform color. Add the chops and toss well to coat. Transfer them to a cutting board.
2. Preheat the air fryer to 375°F (190°C).
3. When the machine is at temperature, again dredge the chops one by one in the flour mixture. Lightly coat both sides of each chop with olive oil spray before putting it in the basket. Continue on with the remaining chop(s), leaving air space between them in the basket.
4. Air-fry, turning once, for 25 minutes, or until the chops are well browned and tender when pierced with the point of a paring knife. If the machine is at 360°F (180°C), you may need to add up to 3 minutes to the cooking time.
5. Use kitchen tongs to transfer the chops to a wire rack. Cool for 5 minutes before serving.

## Horseradish Mustard Pork Chops

Servings: 2
Cooking Time: 20 Minutes
**Ingredients:**
- ½ cup grated Pecorino cheese
- 1 egg white
- 1 tbsp horseradish mustard
- ¼ tsp black pepper
- 2 pork chops
- ¼ cup chopped cilantro

**Directions:**
1. Preheat air fryer to 350ºF. Whisk egg white and horseradish mustard in a bowl. In another bowl, combine Pecorino cheese and black pepper. Dip pork chops in the mustard mixture, then dredge them in the Parmesan mixture. Place pork chops in the frying basket lightly greased with olive oil and Air Fry for 12-14 minutes until cooked through and tender, flipping twice. Transfer the chops to a cutting board and let sit for 5 minutes. Scatter with cilantro to serve.

## Citrus Pork Lettuce Wraps

Servings: 4
Cooking Time: 35 Minutes
**Ingredients:**
- Salt and white pepper to taste
- 1 tbsp cornstarch
- 1 tbsp red wine vinegar
- 2 tbsp orange marmalade
- 1 tsp pulp-free orange juice
- 2 tsp olive oil
- ¼ tsp chili pepper
- ¼ tsp ground ginger
- 1 lb pork loin, cubed
- 8 iceberg lettuce leaves

**Directions:**
1. Create a slurry by whisking cornstarch and 1 tbsp of water in a bowl. Set aside. Place a small saucepan over medium heat. Add the red wine vinegar, orange marmalade, orange juice, olive oil, chili pepper, and ginger and cook for 3 minutes, stirring continuously. Mix in the slurry and simmer for 1 more minute. Turn the heat off and let it thicken, about 3 minutes.
2. Preheat air fryer to 350ºF. Sprinkle the pork with salt and white pepper. Place them in the greased frying basket and Air Fry for 8-10 minutes until cooked through and browned, turning once. Transfer pork cubes to a bowl with the sauce and toss to coat. Serve in lettuce leaves.

## Easy Tex-mex Chimichangas

Servings: 2
Cooking Time: 8 Minutes
**Ingredients:**
- ¼ pound Thinly sliced deli roast beef, chopped
- ½ cup (about 2 ounces) Shredded Cheddar cheese or shredded Tex-Mex cheese blend
- ¼ cup Jarred salsa verde or salsa rojo
- ½ teaspoon Ground cumin
- ½ teaspoon Dried oregano
- 2 Burrito-size (12-inch) flour tortilla(s), not corn tortillas (gluten-free, if a concern)
- ⅔ cup Canned refried beans
- Vegetable oil spray

**Directions:**
1. Preheat the air fryer to 375°F (190°C).
2. Stir the roast beef, cheese, salsa, cumin, and oregano in a bowl until well mixed.
3. Lay a tortilla on a clean, dry work surface. Spread ⅓ cup of the refried beans in the center lower third of the tortilla(s), leaving an inch on either side of the spread beans.
4. For one chimichanga, spread all of the roast beef mixture on top of the beans. For two, spread half of the roast beef mixture on each tortilla.
5. At either "end" of the filling mixture, fold the sides of the tortilla up and over the filling, partially covering it. Starting with the unfolded side of the tortilla just below the filling, roll the tortilla closed. Fold and roll the second filled tortilla, as necessary.
6. Coat the exterior of the tortilla(s) with vegetable oil spray. Set the chimichanga(s) seam side down in the basket, with at least ½ inch air space between them if you're working with two. Air-fry undisturbed for 8 minutes, or until the tortilla is lightly browned and crisp.
7. Use kitchen tongs to gently transfer the chimichanga(s) to a wire rack. Cool for at last 5 minutes or up to 20 minutes before serving.

## Lollipop Lamb Chops With Mint Pesto

Servings: 4
Cooking Time: 7 Minutes
**Ingredients:**
- Mint Pesto
- ½ small clove garlic
- ¼ cup packed fresh parsley
- ¾ cup packed fresh mint
- ½ teaspoon lemon juice

- ¼ cup grated Parmesan cheese
- ⅓ cup shelled pistachios
- ¼ teaspoon salt
- ½ cup olive oil
- 8 "frenched" lamb chops (1 rack)
- olive oil
- salt and freshly ground black pepper
- 1 tablespoon dried rosemary, chopped
- 1 tablespoon dried thyme

**Directions:**
1. Make the pesto by combining the garlic, parsley and mint in a food processor and process until finely chopped. Add the lemon juice, Parmesan cheese, pistachios and salt. Process until all the ingredients have turned into a paste. With the processor running, slowly pour the olive oil in through the feed tube. Scrape the sides of the processor with a spatula and process for another 30 seconds.
2. Preheat the air fryer to 400°F (205°C).
3. Rub both sides of the lamb chops with olive oil and season with salt, pepper, rosemary and thyme, pressing the herbs into the meat gently with your fingers. Transfer the lamb chops to the air fryer basket.
4. Air-fry the lamb chops at 400°F (205°C) for 5 minutes. Flip the chops over and air-fry for an additional 2 minutes. This should bring the chops to a medium-rare doneness, depending on their thickness. Adjust the cooking time up or down a minute or two accordingly for different degrees of doneness.
5. Serve the lamb chops with mint pesto drizzled on top.

## Homemade Pork Gyoza

Servings: 4
Cooking Time: 50 Minutes
**Ingredients:**
- 8 wonton wrappers
- 4 oz ground pork, browned
- 1 green apple
- 1 tsp rice vinegar
- 1 tbsp vegetable oil
- ½ tbsp oyster sauce
- 1 tbsp soy sauce
- A pinch of white pepper

**Directions:**
1. Preheat air fryer to 350°F (175°C). Combine the oyster sauce, soy sauce, rice vinegar, and white pepper in a small bowl. Add in the pork and stir thoroughly. Peel and core the apple, and slice into small cubes. Add the apples to the meat mixture, and combine thoroughly. Divide the filling between the wonton wrappers. Wrap the wontons into triangles and seal with a bit of water. Brush the wrappers with vegetable oil. Place them in the greased frying basket. Bake for 25 minutes until crispy golden brown on the outside and juicy and delicious on the inside. Serve.

## Fried Spam

Servings: 2
Cooking Time: 12 Minutes
**Ingredients:**
- ½ cup All-purpose flour or gluten-free all-purpose flour
- 1 Large egg(s)
- 1 tablespoon Wasabi paste
- 1⅓ cups Plain panko bread crumbs (gluten-free, if a concern)
- 4 ½-inch-thick Spam slices
- Vegetable oil spray

**Directions:**
1. Preheat the air fryer to 400°F (205°C).
2. Set up and fill three shallow soup plates or small pie plates on your counter: one for the flour; one for the egg(s), whisked with the wasabi paste until uniform; and one for the bread crumbs.
3. Dip a slice of Spam in the flour, coating both sides. Slip it into the egg mixture and turn to coat on both sides, even along the edges. Let any excess egg mixture slip back into the rest, then set the slice in the bread crumbs. Turn it several times, pressing gently to make an even coating on both sides. Generously coat both sides of the slice with vegetable oil spray. Set aside so you can dip, coat, and spray the remaining slice(s).
4. Set the slices in the basket in a single layer so that they don't touch (even if they're close together). Air-fry undisturbed for 12 minutes, or until very brown and quite crunchy.
5. Use kitchen tongs to transfer the slices to a wire rack. Cool for a minute or two before serving.

## Peppered Steak Bites

Servings: 4
Cooking Time: 14 Minutes
**Ingredients:**
- 1 pound sirloin steak, cut into 1-inch cubes
- ½ teaspoon coarse sea salt
- 1 teaspoon coarse black pepper
- 2 teaspoons Worcestershire sauce
- ½ teaspoon garlic powder
- ¼ teaspoon red pepper flakes
- ¼ cup chopped parsley

**Directions:**

1. Preheat the air fryer to 390°F (200°C).
2. In a large bowl, place the steak cubes and toss with the salt, pepper, Worcestershire sauce, garlic powder, and red pepper flakes.
3. Pour the steak into the air fryer basket and cook for 10 to 14 minutes, depending on how well done you prefer your bites. Starting at the 8-minute mark, toss the steak bites every 2 minutes to check for doneness.
4. When the steak is cooked, remove it from the basket to a serving bowl and top with the chopped parsley. Allow the steak to rest for 5 minutes before serving.

## **Crunchy Fried Pork Loin Chops**

Servings: 3
Cooking Time: 12 Minutes
**Ingredients:**
- 1 cup All-purpose flour or tapioca flour
- 1 Large egg(s), well beaten
- 1½ cups Seasoned Italian-style dried bread crumbs (gluten-free, if a concern)
- 3 4- to 5-ounce boneless center-cut pork loin chops
- Vegetable oil spray

**Directions:**
1. Preheat the air fryer to 350°F (175°C).
2. Set up and fill three shallow soup plates or small pie plates on your counter: one for the flour, one for the beaten egg(s), and one for the bread crumbs.
3. Dredge a pork chop in the flour, coating both sides as well as around the edge. Gently shake off any excess, then dip the chop in the egg(s), again coating both sides and the edge. Let any excess egg slip back into the rest, then set the chop in the bread crumbs, turning it and pressing gently to coat well on both sides and the edge. Coat the pork chop all over with vegetable oil spray and set aside so you can dredge, coat, and spray the additional chop(s).
4. Set the chops in the basket with as much air space between them as possible. Air-fry undisturbed for 12 minutes, or until brown and crunchy and an instant-read meat thermometer inserted into the center of a chop registers 145°F (65°C).
5. Use kitchen tongs to transfer the chops to a wire rack. Cool for 5 minutes before serving.

## **German-style Pork Patties**

Servings: 6
Cooking Time: 35 Minutes
**Ingredients:**
- 1 lb ground pork
- ¼ cup diced fresh pear
- 1 tbsp minced sage leaves
- 1 garlic clove, minced
- 2 tbsp chopped chives
- Salt and pepper to taste

**Directions:**
1. Preheat the air fryer to 375°F (190°C). Combine the pork, pear, sage, chives, garlic, salt, and pepper in a bowl and mix gently but thoroughly with your hands, then make 8 patties about ½ inch thick. Lay the patties in the frying basket in a single layer and Air Fry for 15-20 minutes, flipping once halfway through. Remove and drain on paper towels, then serve. Serve and enjoy!

## **Chile Con Carne Galette**

Servings: 4
Cooking Time: 30 Minutes
**Ingredients:**
- 1 can chili beans in chili sauce
- ½ cup canned fire-roasted diced tomatoes, drained
- ½ cup grated Mexican cheese blend
- 2 tsp olive oil
- ½ lb ground beef
- ½ cup dark beer
- ½ onion, diced
- 1 carrot, peeled and diced
- 1 celery stalk, diced
- ½ tsp ground cumin
- ½ tsp chili powder
- ¼ tsp salt
- 1 cup corn chips
- 3 tbsp beef broth
- 2 tsp corn masa

**Directions:**
1. Warm the olive oil in a skillet over -high heat for 30 seconds. Add in ground beef, onion, carrot, and celery and cook for 5 minutes until the beef is no longer pink. Drain the fat. Mix 3 tbsp beef broth and 2 tsp corn mass until smooth and then toss it in beans, chili sauce, dark beer, tomatoes, cumin, chili powder, and salt. Cook until thickened. Turn the heat off.
2. Preheat air fryer at 350ºF. Spoon beef mixture into a cake pan, then top with corn chips, followed by cheese blend. Place cake pan in the frying basket and Bake for 6 minutes. Let rest for 10 minutes before serving.

## Fusion Tender Flank Steak

Servings: 4
Cooking Time: 25 Minutes
**Ingredients:**
- 2 tbsp cilantro, chopped
- 2 tbsp chives, chopped
- ¼ tsp red pepper flakes
- 1 jalapeño pepper, minced
- 1 lime, juiced
- 3 tbsp olive oil
- Salt and pepper to taste
- 2 tbsp sesame oil
- 5 tbsp tamari sauce
- 3 tsp honey
- 1 tbsp grated fresh ginger
- 2 green onions, minced
- 2 garlic cloves, minced
- 1 ¼ pounds flank steak

**Directions:**
1. Combine the jalapeño pepper, cilantro, chives, lime juice, olive oil, salt, and pepper in a bowl. Set aside. Mix the sesame oil, tamari sauce, honey, ginger, green onions, garlic, and pepper flakes in another bowl. Stir until the honey is dissolved. Put the steak into the bowl and massage the marinade onto the meat. Marinate for 2 hours in the fridge. Preheat air fryer to 390 F.
2. Remove the steak from the marinade and place it in the greased frying basket. Air Fry for about 6 minutes, flip, and continue cooking for 6-8 more minutes. Allow to rest for a few minutes, slice thinly against the grain and top with the prepared dressing. Serve and enjoy!

## Mustard-crusted Rib-eye

Servings: 2
Cooking Time: 9 Minutes
**Ingredients:**
- Two 6-ounce rib-eye steaks, about 1-inch thick
- 1 teaspoon coarse salt
- ½ teaspoon coarse black pepper
- 2 tablespoons Dijon mustard

**Directions:**
1. Rub the steaks with the salt and pepper. Then spread the mustard on both sides of the steaks. Cover with foil and let the steaks sit at room temperature for 30 minutes.
2. Preheat the air fryer to 390°F (200°C).
3. Cook the steaks for 9 minutes. Check for an internal temperature of 140°F (60°C) and immediately remove the steaks and let them rest for 5 minutes before slicing.

## Stuffed Cabbage Rolls

Servings: 4
Cooking Time: 50 Minutes
**Ingredients:**
- ½ cup long-grain brown rice
- 12 green cabbage leaves
- 1 lb ground beef
- 4 garlic cloves, minced
- Salt and pepper to taste
- 1 tsp ground cinnamon
- ½ tsp ground cumin
- 2 tbsp chopped mint
- 1 lemon, juiced and zested
- ½ cup beef broth
- 1 tbsp olive oil
- 2 tbsp parsley, chopped

**Directions:**
1. Place a large pot of salted water over medium heat and bring to a boil. Add the cabbage leaves and boil them for 3 minutes. Remove from the water and set aside. Combine the ground beef, rice, garlic, salt, pepper, cinnamon, cumin, mint, lemon juice and zest in a bowl.
2. Preheat air fryer to 360°F (180°C). Divide the beef mixture between the cabbage leaves and roll them up. Place the finished rolls into a greased baking dish. Pour the beef broth over the cabbage rolls and then brush the tops with olive oil. Put the casserole dish into the frying basket and Bake for 30 minutes. Top with parsley and enjoy!

## Meat Loaves

Servings: 4
Cooking Time: 19 Minutes
**Ingredients:**
- Sauce
- ¼ cup white vinegar
- ¼ cup brown sugar
- 2 tablespoons Worcestershire sauce
- ½ cup ketchup
- Meat Loaves
- 1 pound very lean ground beef
- ⅔ cup dry bread (approx. 1 slice torn into small pieces)
- 1 egg
- ⅓ cup minced onion
- 1 teaspoon salt
- 2 tablespoons ketchup

**Directions:**

1. In a small saucepan, combine all sauce ingredients and bring to a boil. Remove from heat and stir to ensure that brown sugar dissolves completely.
2. In a large bowl, combine the beef, bread, egg, onion, salt, and ketchup. Mix well.
3. Divide meat mixture into 4 portions and shape each into a thick, round patty. Patties will be about 3 to 3½ inches in diameter, and all four should fit easily into the air fryer basket at once.
4. Cook at 360°F (180°C) for 18 minutes, until meat is well done. Baste tops of mini loaves with a small amount of sauce, and cook 1 minute.
5. Serve hot with additional sauce on the side.

## Pork Tenderloin With Apples & Celery

Servings: 4
Cooking Time: 30 Minutes
**Ingredients:**
- 1 lb pork tenderloin, cut into 4 pieces
- 2 Granny Smith apples, sliced
- 1 tbsp butter, melted
- 2 tsp olive oil
- 3 celery stalks, sliced
- 1 onion, sliced
- 2 tsp dried thyme
- 1/3 cup apple juice

**Directions:**
1. Preheat air fryer to 400°F (205°C). Brush olive oil and butter all over the pork, then toss the pork, apples, celery, onion, thyme, and apple juice in a bowl and mix well. Put the bowl in the air fryer and Roast for 15-19 minutes until the pork is cooked through and the apples and veggies are soft, stirring once during cooking. Serve warm.

## Bbq Back Ribs

Servings: 4
Cooking Time: 40 Minutes
**Ingredients:**
- 2 tbsp light brown sugar
- Salt and pepper to taste
- 2 tsp onion powder
- 1 tsp garlic powder
- 1 tsp mustard powder
- 1 tsp dried marjoram
- ½ tsp smoked paprika
- 1 tsp cayenne pepper
- 1 ½ pounds baby back ribs
- 2 tbsp barbecue sauce

**Directions:**
1. Preheat the air fryer to 375°F (190°C). Combine the brown sugar, salt, pepper, onion and garlic powder, mustard, paprika, cayenne, and marjoram in a bowl and mix. Pour into a small glass jar. Brush the ribs with barbecue sauce and sprinkle 1 tbsp of the seasoning mix. Rub the seasoning all over the meat. Set the ribs in the greased frying basket. Bake for 25 minutes until nicely browned, flipping them once halfway through cooking. Serve hot!

## Mini Meatloaves With Pancetta

Servings: 4
Cooking Time: 40 Minutes
**Ingredients:**
- ¼ cup grated Parmesan
- 1/3 cup quick-cooking oats
- 2 tbsp milk
- 3 tbsp ketchup
- 3 tbsp Dijon mustard
- 1 egg
- 1 tsp dried oregano
- Salt and pepper to taste
- 1 lb lean ground beef
- 4 pancetta slices, uncooked

**Directions:**
1. Preheat the air fryer to 375°F (190°C). Combine the oats, milk, 1 tbsp of ketchup, 1 tbsp of mustard, the egg, oregano, Parmesan cheese, salt, and pepper, and mix. Add the beef and mix with your hands, then form 4 mini loaves. Wrap each mini loaf with pancetta, covering the meat.
2. Combine the remaining ketchup and mustard and set aside. Line the frying basket with foil and poke holes in it, then set the loaves in the basket. Brush with the ketchup/mustard mix. Bake for 17-22 minutes or until cooked and golden. Serve and enjoy!

## Suwon Pork Meatballs

Servings: 4
Cooking Time: 30 Minutes
**Ingredients:**
- 1 lb ground pork
- 1 egg
- 1 tsp cumin
- 1 tbsp gochujang
- 1 tsp tamari
- ¼ tsp ground ginger
- ¼ cup bread crumbs
- 1 scallion, sliced

- 4 tbsp plum jam
- 1 tsp toasted sesame seeds

**Directions:**

1. Preheat air fryer at 350°F. In a bowl, combine all ingredients, except scallion greens, sesame seeds and plum jam. Form mixture into meatballs. Place meatballs in the greased frying basket and Air Fry for 8 minutes, flipping once. Garnish with scallion greens, plum jam and toasted sesame seeds to serve.

## Minted Lamb Chops

Servings: 4
Cooking Time: 20 Minutes
**Ingredients:**

- 8 lamb chops
- 2 tsp olive oil
- 1 ½ tsp chopped mint leaves
- 1 tsp ground coriander
- 1 lemon, zested
- ½ tsp baharat seasoning
- 1 garlic clove, minced
- Salt and pepper to taste

**Directions:**

1. Preheat air fryer to 390°F (200°C). Coat the lamb chops with olive oil. Set aside. Mix mint, coriander, baharat, zest, garlic, salt and pepper in a bowl. Rub the seasoning onto both sides of the chops. Place the chops in the greased frying basket and Air Fry for 10 minutes. Flip the lamb chops and cook for another 5 minutes. Let the lamb chops rest for a few minutes. Serve right away.

# Vegetarians Recipes

## Egg Rolls

Servings: 4
Cooking Time: 8 Minutes
**Ingredients:**

- 1 clove garlic, minced
- 1 teaspoon sesame oil
- 1 teaspoon olive oil
- ½ cup chopped celery
- ½ cup grated carrots
- 2 green onions, chopped
- 2 ounces mushrooms, chopped
- 2 cups shredded Napa cabbage
- 1 teaspoon low-sodium soy sauce
- 1 teaspoon cornstarch
- salt
- 1 egg
- 1 tablespoon water
- 4 egg roll wraps
- olive oil for misting or cooking spray

**Directions:**

1. In a large skillet, sauté garlic in sesame and olive oils over medium heat for 1 minute.
2. Add celery, carrots, onions, and mushrooms to skillet. Cook 1 minute, stirring.
3. Stir in cabbage, cover, and cook for 1 minute or just until cabbage slightly wilts.
4. In a small bowl, mix soy sauce and cornstarch. Stir into vegetables to thicken. Remove from heat. Salt to taste if needed.
5. Beat together egg and water in a small bowl.
6. Divide filling into 4 portions and roll up in egg roll wraps. Brush all over with egg wash to seal.
7. Mist egg rolls very lightly with olive oil or cooking spray and place in air fryer basket.
8. Cook at 390°F (200°C) for 4minutes. Turn over and cook 4 more minutes, until golden brown and crispy.

## Cheddar Stuffed Portobellos With Salsa

Servings: 4
Cooking Time: 20 Minutes
**Ingredients:**

- 8 portobello mushrooms
- 1/3 cup salsa
- ½ cup shredded cheddar
- 2 tbsp cilantro, chopped

**Directions:**
1. Preheat air fryer to 370°F (185°C). Remove the mushroom stems. Divide the salsa between the caps. Top with cheese and sprinkle with cilantro. Place the mushrooms in the greased frying basket and Bake for 8-10 minutes. Let cool slightly, then serve.

# Crunchy Rice Paper Samosas

Servings: 2
Cooking Time: 20 Minutes
**Ingredients:**
- 1 boiled potato, mashed
- ¼ cup green peas
- 1 tsp garam masala powder
- ½ tsp ginger garlic paste
- ½ tsp cayenne pepper
- ½ tsp turmeric powder
- Salt and pepper to taste
- 3 rice paper wrappers

**Directions:**
1. Preheat air fryer to 350°F (175°C). Place the mashed potatoes in a bowl. Add the peas, garam masala powder, ginger garlic paste, cayenne pepper, turmeric powder, salt, and pepper and stir until ingredients are evenly blended.
2. Lay the rice paper wrappers out on a lightly floured surface. Divide the potato mixture between the wrappers and fold the top edges over to seal. Transfer the samosas to the greased frying basket and Air Fry for 12 minutes, flipping once until the samosas are crispy and flaky. Remove and leave to cool for 5 minutes. Serve and enjoy!

# Grilled Cheese Sandwich

Servings: 1
Cooking Time: 15 Minutes
**Ingredients:**
- 2 sprouted bread slices
- 1 tsp sunflower oil
- 2 Halloumi cheese slices
- 1 tsp mellow white miso
- 1 garlic clove, minced
- 2 tbsp kimchi
- 1 cup Iceberg lettuce, torn

**Directions:**
1. Preheat air fryer to 390°F (200°C). Brush the outside of the bread with sunflower oil. Put the sliced cheese, buttered sides facing out inside and close the sandwich. Put the sandwich in the frying basket and Air Fry for 12 minutes, flipping once until golden and crispy on the outside.
2. On a plate, open the sandwich and spread the miso and garlic clove over the inside of one slice. Top with kimchi and lettuce, close the sandwich, cut in half, and serve.

# Quinoa Green Pizza

Servings: 2
Cooking Time: 25 Minutes
**Ingredients:**
- ¾ cup quinoa flour
- ½ tsp dried basil
- ½ tsp dried oregano
- 1 tbsp apple cider vinegar
- 1/3 cup ricotta cheese
- 2/3 cup chopped broccoli
- ½ tsp garlic powder

**Directions:**
1. Preheat air fryer to 350°F (175°C). Whisk quinoa flour, basil, oregano, apple cider vinegar, and ½ cup of water until smooth. Set aside. Cut 2 pieces of parchment paper. Place the quinoa mixture on one paper, top with another piece, and flatten to create a crust. Discard the top piece of paper. Bake for 5 minutes, turn and discard the other piece of paper. Spread the ricotta cheese over the crust, scatter with broccoli, and sprinkle with garlic. Grill at 400°F for 5 minutes until golden brown. Serve warm.

# Sweet Corn Bread

Servings: 6
Cooking Time: 35 Minutes
**Ingredients:**
- 2 eggs, beaten
- ½ cup cornmeal
- ½ cup pastry flour
- 1/3 cup sugar
- 1 tsp lemon zest
- ½ tbsp baking powder
- ¼ tsp salt
- ¼ tsp baking soda
- ½ tbsp lemon juice
- ½ cup milk
- ¼ cup sunflower oil

**Directions:**
1. Preheat air fryer to 350°F (175°C). Add the cornmeal, flour, sugar, lemon zest, baking powder, salt, and baking soda in a bowl. Stir with a whisk until combined. Add the eggs, lemon juice, milk, and oil to another bowl and stir well. Add the wet mixture to the dry mixture and stir gently until combined. Spray a baking pan with oil. Pour the batter in and Bake in the fryer for 25 minutes or until golden and a knife inserted in the center comes out clean. Cut into wedges and serve.

# Cheesy Eggplant Lasagna

Servings: 4
Cooking Time: 40 Minutes
**Ingredients:**
- ¾ cup chickpea flour
- ½ cup milk
- 3 tbsp lemon juice
- 1 tbsp chili sauce
- 2 tsp allspice
- 2 cups panko bread crumbs
- 1 eggplant, sliced
- 2 cups jarred tomato sauce
- ½ cup ricotta cheese
- 1/3 cup mozzarella cheese

**Directions:**
1. Preheat air fryer to 400°F (205°C). Whisk chickpea flour, milk, lemon juice, chili sauce, and allspice until smooth. Set aside. On a plate, put the breadcrumbs. Submerge each eggplant slice into the batter, shaking off any excess, and dip into the breadcrumbs until well coated. Bake for 10 minutes, turning once. Let cool slightly.
2. Spread 2 tbsp of tomato sauce at the bottom of a baking pan. Lay a single layer of eggplant slices, scatter with ricotta cheese and top with tomato sauce. Repeat the process until no ingredients are left. Scatter with mozzarella cheese on top and Bake at 350°F for 10 minutes until the eggplants are cooked and the cheese golden brown. Serve immediately.

# Tex-mex Potatoes With Avocado Dressing

Servings: 2
Cooking Time: 60 Minutes
**Ingredients:**
- ¼ cup chopped parsley, dill, cilantro, chives
- ¼ cup yogurt
- ½ avocado, diced
- 2 tbsp milk
- 2 tsp lemon juice
- ½ tsp lemon zest
- 1 green onion, chopped
- 2 cloves garlic, quartered
- Salt and pepper to taste
- 2 tsp olive oil
- 2 russet potatoes, scrubbed and perforated with a fork
- 1 cup steamed broccoli florets
- ½ cup canned white beans

**Directions:**
1. In a food processor, blend the yogurt, avocado, milk, lemon juice, lemon zest, green onion, garlic, parsley, dill, cilantro, chives, salt and pepper until smooth. Transfer it to a small bowl and let chill the dressing covered in the fridge until ready to use.
2. Preheat air fryer at 400ºF. Rub olive oil over both potatoes and sprinkle with salt and pepper. Place them in the frying basket and Bake for 45 minutes, flipping at 30 minutes mark. Let cool onto a cutting board for 5 minutes until cool enough to handle. Cut each potato lengthwise into slices and pinch ends together to open up each slice. Stuff broccoli and beans into potatoes and put them back into the basket, and cook for 3 more minutes. Drizzle avocado dressing over and serve.

# Vegetable Couscous

Servings: 4
Cooking Time: 10 Minutes
**Ingredients:**
- 4 ounces white mushrooms, sliced
- ½ medium green bell pepper, julienned
- 1 cup cubed zucchini
- ¼ small onion, slivered
- 1 stalk celery, thinly sliced
- ¼ teaspoon ground coriander
- ¼ teaspoon ground cumin
- salt and pepper
- 1 tablespoon olive oil
- Couscous
- ¾ cup uncooked couscous
- 1 cup vegetable broth or water
- ½ teaspoon salt (omit if using salted broth)

**Directions:**
1. Combine all vegetables in large bowl. Sprinkle with coriander, cumin, and salt and pepper to taste. Stir well, add olive oil, and stir again to coat vegetables evenly.
2. Place vegetables in air fryer basket and cook at 390°F (200°C) for 5minutes. Stir and cook for 5 more minutes, until tender.
3. While vegetables are cooking, prepare the couscous: Place broth or water and salt in large saucepan. Heat to boiling, stir in couscous, cover, and remove from heat.
4. Let couscous sit for 5minutes, stir in cooked vegetables, and serve hot.

## Easy Cheese & Spinach Lasagna

Servings: 6
Cooking Time: 50 Minutes
**Ingredients:**
- 1 zucchini, cut into strips
- 1 tbsp butter
- 4 garlic cloves, minced
- ½ yellow onion, diced
- 1 tsp dried oregano
- ¼ tsp red pepper flakes
- 1 can diced tomatoes
- 4 oz ricotta
- 3 tbsp grated mozzarella
- ½ cup grated cheddar
- 3 tsp grated Parmesan cheese
- ⅛ cup chopped basil
- 2 tbsp chopped parsley
- Salt and pepper to taste
- ¼ tsp ground nutmeg

**Directions:**
1. Preheat air fryer to 375°F (190°C). Melt butter in a medium skillet over medium heat. Stir in half of the garlic and onion and cook for 2 minutes. Stir in oregano and red pepper flakes and cook for 1 minute. Reduce the heat to medium-low and pour in crushed tomatoes and their juices. Cover the skillet and simmer for 5 minutes.
2. Mix ricotta, mozzarella, cheddar cheese, rest of the garlic, basil, black pepper, and nutmeg in a large bowl. Arrange a layer of zucchini strips in the baking dish. Scoop 1/3 of the cheese mixture and spread evenly over the zucchini. Spread 1/3 of the tomato sauce over the cheese. Repeat the steps two more times, then top the lasagna with Parmesan cheese. Bake in the frying basket for 25 minutes until the mixture is bubbling and the mozzarella is melted. Allow sitting for 10 minutes before cutting. Serve warm sprinkled with parsley and enjoy!

## Mushroom, Zucchini And Black Bean Burgers

Servings: 4
Cooking Time: 18 Minutes
**Ingredients:**
- 1 cup diced zucchini, (about ½ medium zucchini)
- 1 tablespoon olive oil
- salt and freshly ground black pepper
- 1 cup chopped brown mushrooms (about 3 ounces)
- 1 small clove garlic
- 1 (15-ounce) can black beans, drained and rinsed
- 1 teaspoon lemon zest
- 1 tablespoon chopped fresh cilantro
- ½ cup plain breadcrumbs
- 1 egg, beaten
- ½ teaspoon salt
- freshly ground black pepper
- whole-wheat pita bread, burger buns or brioche buns
- mayonnaise, tomato, avocado and lettuce, for serving

**Directions:**
1. Preheat the air fryer to 400°F (205°C).
2. Toss the zucchini with the olive oil, season with salt and freshly ground black pepper and air-fry for 6 minutes, shaking the basket once or twice while it cooks.
3. Transfer the zucchini to a food processor with the mushrooms, garlic and black beans and process until still a little chunky but broken down and pasty. Transfer the mixture to a bowl. Add the lemon zest, cilantro, breadcrumbs and egg and mix well. Season again with salt and freshly ground black pepper. Shape the mixture into four burger patties and refrigerate for at least 15 minutes.
4. Preheat the air fryer to 370°F (185°C). Transfer two of the veggie burgers to the air fryer basket and air-fry for 12 minutes, flipping the burgers gently halfway through the cooking time. Keep the burgers warm by loosely tenting them with foil while you cook the remaining two burgers. Return the first batch of burgers back into the air fryer with the second batch for the last two minutes of cooking to re-heat.
5. Serve on toasted whole-wheat pita bread, burger buns or brioche buns with some mayonnaise, tomato, avocado and lettuce.

## Balsamic Caprese Hasselback

Servings: 4
Cooking Time: 15 Minutes
**Ingredients:**
- 4 tomatoes
- 12 fresh basil leaves
- 1 ball fresh mozzarella
- Salt and pepper to taste
- 1 tbsp olive oil
- 2 tsp balsamic vinegar
- 1 tbsp basil, torn

**Directions:**
1. Preheat air fryer to 325°F. Remove the bottoms from the tomatoes to create a flat surface. Make 4 even slices on each tomato, 3/4 of the way down. Slice the mozzarella and the cut into 12 pieces. Stuff 1 basil leaf and a piece of mozzarella into each slice. Sprinkle with salt and pepper. Place the stuffed tomatoes in the frying basket and Air Fry for 3 minutes. Transfer to a large serving plate. Drizzle with olive oil and balsamic vinegar and scatter the basil over. Serve and enjoy!

## Creamy Broccoli & Mushroom Casserole

Servings: 4
Cooking Time: 30 Minutes
**Ingredients:**
- 4 cups broccoli florets, chopped
- 1 cup crushed cheddar cheese crisps
- ¼ cup diced onion
- ¼ tsp dried thyme
- ¼ tsp dried marjoram
- ¼ tsp dried oregano
- ½ cup diced mushrooms
- 1 egg
- 2 tbsp sour cream
- ¼ cup mayonnaise
- Salt and pepper to taste

**Directions:**
1. Preheat air fryer to 350ºF. Combine all ingredients, except for the cheese crisps, in a bowl. Spoon mixture into a round cake pan. Place cake pan in the frying basket and Bake for 14 minutes. Let sit for 10 minutes. Distribute crushed cheddar cheese crisps over the top and serve.

## Pineapple & Veggie Souvlaki

Servings: 4
Cooking Time: 35 Minutes
**Ingredients:**
- 1 can pineapple rings in pineapple juice
- 1 red bell pepper, stemmed and seeded
- 1/3 cup butter
- 2 tbsp apple cider vinegar
- 2 tbsp hot sauce
- 1 tbsp allspice
- 1 tsp ground nutmeg
- 16 oz feta cheese
- 1 red onion, peeled
- 8 mushrooms, quartered

**Directions:**
1. Preheat air fryer to 400°F (205°C). Whisk the butter, pineapple juice, apple vinegar, hot sauce, allspice, and nutmeg until smooth. Set aside. Slice feta cheese into 16 cubes, then the bell pepper into 16 chunks, and finally red onion into 8 wedges, separating each wedge into 2 pieces.
2. Cut pineapple ring into quarters. Place veggie cubes and feta into the butter bowl and toss to coat. Thread the veggies, tofu, and pineapple onto 8 skewers, alternating 16 pieces on each skewer. Grill for 15 minutes until golden brown and cooked. Serve warm.

## Cheddar Bean Taquitos

Servings: 4
Cooking Time: 25 Minutes
**Ingredients:**
- 1 cup refried beans
- 2 cups cheddar shreds
- ½ jalapeño pepper, minced
- ¼ chopped white onion
- 1 tsp oregano
- 15 soft corn tortillas

**Directions:**
1. Preheat air fryer at 350ºF. Spread refried beans, jalapeño pepper, white onion, oregano and cheddar shreds down the center of each corn tortilla. Roll each tortilla tightly. Place tacos, seam side down, in the frying basket, and Air Fry for 4 minutes. Serve immediately.

## Kale & Lentils With Crispy Onions

Servings: 4
Cooking Time: 40 Minutes
**Ingredients:**
- 2 cups cooked red lentils
- 1 onion, cut into rings
- ½ cup kale, steamed
- 3 garlic cloves, minced
- ½ lemon, juiced and zested
- 2 tsp cornstarch
- 1 tsp dried oregano
- Salt and pepper to taste

**Directions:**
1. Preheat air fryer to 390°F (200°C). Put the onion rings in the greased frying basket; do not overlap. Spray with oil and season with salt. Air Fry for 14-16 minutes, stirring twice until crispy and crunchy. Place the kale and lentils into a pan over medium heat and stir until heated through. Remove and add the garlic, lemon juice, cornstarch, salt, zest, oregano and black pepper. Stir well and pour in bowls. Top with the crisp onion rings and serve.

## Colorful Vegetable Medley

Servings: 4
Cooking Time: 20 Minutes
**Ingredients:**
- 1 lb green beans, chopped
- 2 carrots, cubed
- Salt and pepper to taste
- 1 zucchini, cut into chunks
- 1 red bell pepper, sliced

**Directions:**

1. Preheat air fryer to 390°F (200°C). Combine green beans, carrots, salt and pepper in a large bowl. Spray with cooking oil and transfer to the frying basket. Roast for 6 minutes.
2. Combine zucchini and red pepper in a bowl. Season to taste and spray with cooking oil; set aside. When the cooking time is up, add the zucchini and red pepper to the basket. Cook for another 6 minutes. Serve and enjoy.

## Stuffed Portobellos

Servings: 4
Cooking Time: 45 Minutes
**Ingredients:**
- 1 cup cherry tomatoes
- 2 ¼ tsp olive oil
- 3 tbsp grated mozzarella
- 1 cup chopped baby spinach
- 1 garlic clove, minced
- ¼ tsp dried oregano
- ¼ tsp dried thyme
- Salt and pepper to taste
- ¼ cup bread crumbs
- 4 portobello mushrooms, stemmed and gills removed
- 1 tbsp chopped parsley

**Directions:**
1. Preheat air fryer to 360°F (180°C). Combine tomatoes, ¼ teaspoon olive oil, and salt in a small bowl. Arrange in a single layer in the parchment-lined frying basket and Air Fry for 10 minutes. Stir and flatten the tomatoes with the back of a spoon, then Air Fry for another 6-8 minutes. Transfer the tomatoes to a medium bowl and combine with spinach, garlic, oregano, thyme, pepper, bread crumbs, and the rest of the olive oil.
2. Place the mushrooms on a work surface with the gills facing up. Spoon tomato mixture and mozzarella cheese equally into the mushroom caps and transfer the mushrooms to the frying basket. Air Fry for 8-10 minutes until the mushrooms have softened and the tops are golden. Garnish with chopped parsley and serve.

## Mushroom Bolognese Casserole

Servings: 4
Cooking Time: 20 Minutes
**Ingredients:**
- 1 cup canned diced tomatoes
- 2 garlic cloves, minced
- 1 tsp onion powder
- ¾ tsp dried basil
- ¾ tsp dried oregano
- 1 cup chopped mushrooms
- 16 oz cooked spaghetti

**Directions:**
1. Preheat air fryer to 400°F (205°C). Whisk the tomatoes and their juices, garlic, onion powder, basil, oregano, and mushrooms in a baking pan. Cover with aluminum foil and Bake for 6 minutes. Slide out the pan and add the cooked spaghetti; stir to coat. Cover with aluminum foil and Bake for 3 minutes until and bubbly. Serve and enjoy!

## Fake Shepherd´s Pie

Servings: 6
Cooking Time: 40 Minutes
**Ingredients:**
- ½ head cauliflower, cut into florets
- 1 sweet potato, diced
- 1 tbsp olive oil
- ¼ cup cheddar shreds
- 2 tbsp milk
- Salt and pepper to taste
- 2 tsp avocado oil
- 1 cup beefless grounds
- ½ onion, diced
- 2 cloves garlic, minced
- 1 carrot, diced
- ½ cup green peas
- 1 stalk celery, diced
- 2/3 cup tomato sauce
- 1 tsp chopped rosemary
- 1 tsp thyme leaves

**Directions:**
1. Place cauliflower and sweet potato in a pot of salted boiling water over medium heat and simmer for 7 minutes until fork tender. Strain and transfer to a bowl. Put in avocado oil, cheddar, milk, salt and pepper. Mash until smooth.
2. Warm olive oil in a skillet over medium-high heat and stir in beefless grounds and vegetables and stir-fry for 4 minutes until veggies are tender. Stir in tomato sauce, rosemary, thyme, salt, and black pepper. Set aside.
3. Preheat air fryer to 350°F. Spoon filling into a round cake pan lightly greased with olive oil and cover with the topping. Using the tines of a fork, run shallow lines in the top of cauliflower for a decorative touch. Place cake pan in the frying basket and Air Fry for 12 minutes. Let sit for 10 minutes before serving.

## Tortilla Pizza Margherita

Servings: 1
Cooking Time: 15 Minutes
**Ingredients:**
- 1 flour tortilla
- ¼ cup tomato sauce
- 1/3 cup grated mozzarella
- 3 basil leaves

**Directions:**
1. Preheat air fryer to 350°F (175°C). Put the tortilla in the greased basket and pour the sauce in the center. Spread across the whole tortilla. Sprinkle with cheese and Bake for 8-10 minutes or until crisp. Remove carefully and top with basil leaves. Serve hot.

## Lentil Fritters

Servings: 9
Cooking Time: 12 Minutes
**Ingredients:**
- 1 cup cooked red lentils
- 1 cup riced cauliflower
- ½ medium zucchini, shredded (about 1 cup)
- ¼ cup finely chopped onion
- ¼ teaspoon salt
- ¼ teaspoon black pepper
- ½ teaspoon garlic powder
- ¼ teaspoon paprika
- 1 large egg
- ⅓ cup quinoa flour

**Directions:**
1. Preheat the air fryer to 370°F (185°C).
2. In a large bowl, mix the lentils, cauliflower, zucchini, onion, salt, pepper, garlic powder, and paprika. Mix in the egg and flour until a thick dough forms.
3. Using a large spoon, form the dough into 9 large fritters.
4. Liberally spray the air fryer basket with olive oil. Place the fritters into the basket, leaving space around each fritter so you can flip them.
5. Cook for 6 minutes, flip, and cook another 6 minutes.
6. Remove from the air fryer and repeat with the remaining fritters. Serve warm with desired sauce and sides.

## Two-cheese Grilled Sandwiches

Servings: 2
Cooking Time: 30 Minutes
**Ingredients:**
- 4 sourdough bread slices
- 2 cheddar cheese slices
- 2 Swiss cheese slices
- 1 tbsp butter
- 2 dill pickles, sliced

**Directions:**
1. Preheat air fryer to 360°F (180°C). Smear both sides of the sourdough bread with butter and place them in the frying basket. Toast the bread for 6 minutes, flipping once.
2. Divide the cheddar cheese between 2 of the bread slices. Cover the remaining 2 bread slices with Swiss cheese slices. Bake for 10 more minutes until the cheeses have melted and lightly bubbled and the bread has golden brown. Set the cheddar-covered bread slices on a serving plate, cover with pickles, and top each with the Swiss-covered slices. Serve and enjoy!

## Roasted Vegetable Thai Green Curry

Servings: 4
Cooking Time: 16 Minutes
**Ingredients:**
- 1 (13-ounce) can coconut milk
- 3 tablespoons green curry paste
- 1 tablespoon soy sauce*
- 1 tablespoon rice wine vinegar
- 1 teaspoon sugar
- 1 teaspoon minced fresh ginger
- ½ onion, chopped
- 3 carrots, sliced
- 1 red bell pepper, chopped
- olive oil
- 10 stalks of asparagus, cut into 2-inch pieces
- 3 cups broccoli florets
- basmati rice for serving
- fresh cilantro
- crushed red pepper flakes (optional)

**Directions:**
1. Combine the coconut milk, green curry paste, soy sauce, rice wine vinegar, sugar and ginger in a medium saucepan and bring to a boil on the stovetop. Reduce the heat and simmer for 20 minutes while you cook the vegetables. Set aside.
2. Preheat the air fryer to 400°F (205°C).
3. Toss the onion, carrots, and red pepper together with a little olive oil and transfer the vegetables to the air fryer basket. Air-fry at 400°F (205°C) for 10 minutes, shaking the basket a few times during the cooking process. Add the asparagus and broccoli florets and air-fry for an additional 6 minutes, again shaking the basket for even cooking.
4. When the vegetables are cooked to your liking, toss them with the green curry sauce and serve in bowls over basmati rice. Garnish with fresh chopped cilantro and crushed red pepper flakes.

## Tofu & Spinach Lasagna

Servings: 4
Cooking Time: 30 Minutes
**Ingredients:**
- 8 oz cooked lasagne noodles
- 1 tbsp olive oil
- 2 cups crumbled tofu
- 2 cups fresh spinach
- 2 tbsp cornstarch
- 1 tsp onion powder
- Salt and pepper to taste
- 2 garlic cloves, minced
- 2 cups marinara sauce
- ½ cup shredded mozzarella

**Directions:**
1. Warm the olive oil in a large pan over medium heat. Add the tofu and spinach and stir-fry for a minute. Add the cornstarch, onion powder, salt, pepper, and garlic. Stir until the spinach wilts. Remove from heat.
2. Preheat air fryer to 390°F (200°C). Pour a thin layer of pasta sauce in a baking pan. Layer 2-3 lasagne noodles on top of the marinara sauce. Top with a little more sauce and some of the tofu mix. Add another 2-3 noodles on top, then another layer of sauce, then another layer of tofu. Finish with a layer of noodles and a final layer of sauce. Sprinkle with mozzarella cheese on top. Place the pan in the air fryer and Bake for 15 minutes or until the noodle edges are browned and the cheese is melted. Cut and serve.

## Chive Potato Pierogi

Servings: 4
Cooking Time: 55 Minutes
**Ingredients:**
- 2 boiled potatoes, mashed
- Salt and pepper to taste
- 1 tsp cumin powder
- 2 tbsp sour cream
- ¼ cup grated Parmesan
- 2 tbsp chopped chives
- 1 tbsp chopped parsley
- 1 ¼ cups flour
- ¼ tsp garlic powder
- ¾ cup Greek yogurt
- 1 egg

**Directions:**
1. Combine the mashed potatoes along with sour cream, cumin, parsley, chives, pepper, and salt and stir until slightly chunky. Mix the flour, salt, and garlic powder in a large bowl. Stir in yogurt until it comes together as a sticky dough. Knead in the bowl for about 2-3 minutes to make it smooth. Whisk the egg and 1 teaspoon of water in a small bowl. Roll out the dough on a lightly floured work surface to ¼-inch thickness. Cut out 12 circles with a cookie cutter.
2. Preheat air fryer to 350°F (175°C). Divide the potato mixture and Parmesan cheese between the dough circles. Brush the edges of them with the egg wash and fold the dough over the filling into half-moon shapes. Crimp the edges with a fork to seal. Arrange the on the greased frying basket and Air Fry for 8-10 minutes, turning the pierogies once, until the outside is golden. Serve warm.

## Spicy Vegetable And Tofu Shake Fry

Servings: 4
Cooking Time: 17 Minutes
**Ingredients:**
- 4 teaspoons canola oil, divided
- 2 tablespoons rice wine vinegar
- 1 tablespoon sriracha chili sauce
- ¼ cup soy sauce*
- ½ teaspoon toasted sesame oil
- 1 teaspoon minced garlic
- 1 tablespoon minced fresh ginger
- 8 ounces extra firm tofu
- ½ cup vegetable stock or water
- 1 tablespoon honey
- 1 tablespoon cornstarch
- ½ red onion, chopped
- 1 red or yellow bell pepper, chopped
- 1 cup green beans, cut into 2-inch lengths
- 4 ounces mushrooms, sliced
- 2 scallions, sliced
- 2 tablespoons fresh cilantro leaves
- 2 teaspoons toasted sesame seeds

**Directions:**
1. Combine 1 tablespoon of the oil, vinegar, sriracha sauce, soy sauce, sesame oil, garlic and ginger in a small bowl. Cut the tofu into bite-sized cubes and toss the tofu in with the marinade while you prepare the other vegetables. When you are ready to start cooking, remove the tofu from the marinade and set it aside. Add the water, honey and cornstarch to the marinade and bring to a simmer on the stovetop, just until the sauce thickens. Set the sauce aside.
2. Preheat the air fryer to 400°F (205°C).
3. Toss the onion, pepper, green beans and mushrooms in a bowl with a little canola oil and season with salt. Air-fry at 400°F (205°C) for 11 minutes, shaking the basket and tossing the vegetables every few minutes. When the

vegetables are cooked to your preferred doneness, remove them from the air fryer and set aside.

4. Add the tofu to the air fryer basket and air-fry at 400°F (205°C) for 6 minutes, shaking the basket a few times during the cooking process. Add the vegetables back to the basket and air-fry for another minute. Transfer the vegetables and tofu to a large bowl, add the scallions and cilantro leaves and toss with the sauce. Serve over rice with sesame seeds sprinkled on top.

## Spaghetti Squash And Kale Fritters With Pomodoro Sauce

Servings: 3
Cooking Time: 45 Minutes
**Ingredients:**
- 1½-pound spaghetti squash (about half a large or a whole small squash)
- olive oil
- ½ onion, diced
- ½ red bell pepper, diced
- 2 cloves garlic, minced
- 4 cups coarsely chopped kale
- salt and freshly ground black pepper
- 1 egg
- ⅓ cup breadcrumbs, divided*
- ⅓ cup grated Parmesan cheese
- ½ teaspoon dried rubbed sage
- pinch nutmeg
- Pomodoro Sauce:
- 2 tablespoons olive oil
- ½ onion, chopped
- 1 to 2 cloves garlic, minced
- 1 (28-ounce) can peeled tomatoes
- ¼ cup red wine
- 1 teaspoon Italian seasoning
- 2 tablespoons chopped fresh basil, plus more for garnish
- salt and freshly ground black pepper
- ½ teaspoon sugar (optional)

**Directions:**
1. Preheat the air fryer to 370°F (185°C).
2. Cut the spaghetti squash in half lengthwise and remove the seeds. Rub the inside of the squash with olive oil and season with salt and pepper. Place the squash, cut side up, into the air fryer basket and air-fry for 30 minutes, flipping the squash over halfway through the cooking process.
3. While the squash is cooking, Preheat a large sauté pan over medium heat on the stovetop. Add a little olive oil and sauté the onions for 3 minutes, until they start to soften. Add the red pepper and garlic and continue to sauté for an additional 4 minutes. Add the kale and season with salt and pepper. Cook for 2 more minutes, or until the kale is soft. Transfer the mixture to a large bowl and let it cool.
4. While the squash continues to cook, make the Pomodoro sauce. Preheat the large sauté pan again over medium heat on the stovetop. Add the olive oil and sauté the onion and garlic for 2 to 3 minutes, until the onion begins to soften. Crush the canned tomatoes with your hands and add them to the pan along with the red wine and Italian seasoning and simmer for 20 minutes. Add the basil and season to taste with salt, pepper and sugar (if using).
5. When the spaghetti squash has finished cooking, use a fork to scrape the inside flesh of the squash onto a sheet pan. Spread the squash out and let it cool.
6. Once cool, add the spaghetti squash to the kale mixture, along with the egg, breadcrumbs, Parmesan cheese, sage, nutmeg, salt and freshly ground black pepper. Stir to combine well and then divide the mixture into 6 thick portions. You can shape the portions into patties, but I prefer to keep them a little random and unique in shape. Spray or brush the fritters with olive oil.
7. Preheat the air fryer to 370°F (185°C).
8. Brush the air fryer basket with a little olive oil and transfer the fritters to the basket. Air-fry the squash and kale fritters at 370°F (185°C) for 15 minutes, flipping them over halfway through the cooking process.
9. Serve the fritters warm with the Pomodoro sauce spooned over the top or pooled on your plate. Garnish with the fresh basil leaves.

## Thyme Meatless Patties

Servings: 3
Cooking Time: 25 Minutes
**Ingredients:**
- ½ cup oat flour
- 1 tsp allspice
- ½ tsp ground thyme
- 1 tsp maple syrup
- ½ tsp liquid smoke
- 1 tsp balsamic vinegar

**Directions:**
1. Preheat air fryer to 400°F (205°C). Mix the oat flour, allspice, thyme, maple syrup, liquid smoke, balsamic vinegar, and 2 tbsp of water in a bowl. Make 6 patties out of the mixture. Place them onto a parchment paper and flatten them to ½-inch thick. Grease the patties with cooking spray. Grill for 12 minutes until crispy, turning once. Serve warm.

## Parmesan Portobello Mushroom Caps

Servings: 2
Cooking Time: 14 Minutes
**Ingredients:**
- ¼ cup flour*
- 1 egg, lightly beaten
- 1 cup seasoned breadcrumbs*
- 2 large portobello mushroom caps, stems and gills removed
- olive oil, in a spray bottle
- ½ cup tomato sauce
- ¾ cup grated mozzarella cheese
- 1 tablespoon grated Parmesan cheese
- 1 tablespoon chopped fresh basil or parsley

**Directions:**
1. Set up a dredging station with three shallow dishes. Place the flour in the first shallow dish, egg in the second dish and breadcrumbs in the last dish. Dredge the mushrooms in flour, then dip them into the egg and finally press them into the breadcrumbs to coat on all sides. Spray both sides of the coated mushrooms with olive oil.
2. Preheat the air fryer to 400°F (205°C).
3. Air-fry the mushrooms at 400°F (205°C) for 10 minutes, turning them over halfway through the cooking process.
4. Fill the underside of the mushrooms with the tomato sauce and then top the sauce with the mozzarella and Parmesan cheeses. Reset the air fryer temperature to 350°F (175°C) and air-fry for an additional 4 minutes, until the cheese has melted and is slightly browned.
5. Serve the mushrooms with pasta tossed with tomato sauce and garnish with some chopped fresh basil or parsley.

## Effortless Mac `n´ Cheese

Servings: 4
Cooking Time: 15 Minutes
**Ingredients:**
- 1 cup heavy cream
- 1 cup milk
- ½ cup mozzarella cheese
- 2 tsp grated Parmesan cheese
- 16 oz cooked elbow macaroni

**Directions:**
1. Preheat air fryer to 400°F (205°C). Whisk the heavy cream, milk, mozzarella cheese, and Parmesan cheese until smooth in a bowl. Stir in the macaroni and pour into a baking dish. Cover with foil and Bake in the air fryer for 6 minutes. Remove foil and Bake until cooked through and bubbly, 3-5 minutes. Serve warm.

## Thyme Lentil Patties

Servings: 2
Cooking Time: 35 Minutes
**Ingredients:**
- ½ cup grated American cheese
- 1 cup cooked lentils
- ¼ tsp dried thyme
- 2 eggs, beaten
- Salt and pepper to taste
- 1 cup bread crumbs

**Directions:**
1. Preheat air fryer to 350°F (175°C). Put the eggs, lentils, and cheese in a bowl and mix to combine. Stir in half the bread crumbs, thyme, salt, and pepper. Form the mixture into 2 patties and coat them in the remaining bread crumbs. Transfer to the greased frying basket. Air Fry for 14-16 minutes until brown, flipping once. Serve.

## Charred Cauliflower Tacos

Servings: 4
Cooking Time: 10 Minutes
**Ingredients:**
- 1 head cauliflower, washed and cut into florets
- 2 tablespoons avocado oil
- 2 teaspoons taco seasoning
- 1 medium avocado
- ½ teaspoon garlic powder
- ¼ teaspoon black pepper
- ¼ teaspoon salt
- 2 tablespoons chopped red onion
- 2 teaspoons fresh squeezed lime juice
- ¼ cup chopped cilantro
- Eight 6-inch corn tortillas
- ½ cup cooked corn
- ½ cup shredded purple cabbage

**Directions:**
1. Preheat the air fryer to 390°F (200°C).
2. In a large bowl, toss the cauliflower with the avocado oil and taco seasoning. Set the metal trivet inside the air fryer basket and liberally spray with olive oil.
3. Place the cauliflower onto the trivet and cook for 10 minutes, shaking every 3 minutes to allow for an even char.
4. While the cauliflower is cooking, prepare the avocado sauce. In a medium bowl, mash the avocado; then mix in the garlic powder, pepper, salt, and onion. Stir in the lime juice and cilantro; set aside.
5. Remove the cauliflower from the air fryer basket.
6. Place 1 tablespoon of avocado sauce in the middle of a tortilla, and top with corn, cabbage, and charred cauliflower. Repeat with the remaining tortillas. Serve immediately.

# Gorgeous Jalapeño Poppers

Servings: 6
Cooking Time: 25 Minutes
**Ingredients:**
- 6 center-cut bacon slices, halved
- 6 jalapeños, halved lengthwise
- 4 oz cream cheese
- ¼ cup grated Gruyere cheese
- 2 tbsp chives, chopped

**Directions:**
1. Scoop out seeds and membranes of the jalapeño halves, discard. Combine cream cheese, Gruyere cheese, and chives in a bowl. Fill the jalapeño halves with the cream cheese filling using a small spoon. Wrap each pepper with a slice of bacon and secure with a toothpick.
2. Preheat air fryer to 325°F (160°C). Put the stuffed peppers in a single layer on the greased frying basket and Bake until the peppers are tender, cheese is melted, and the bacon is brown, 11-13minutes. Serve warm and enjoy!

# Italian Stuffed Bell Peppers

Servings: 4
Cooking Time: 75 Minutes
**Ingredients:**
- 4 green and red bell peppers, tops and insides discarded
- 2 russet potatoes, scrubbed and perforated with a fork
- 2 tsp olive oil
- 2 Italian sausages, cubed
- 2 tbsp milk
- 2 tbsp yogurt
- 1 tsp olive oil
- 1 tbsp Italian seasoning
- Salt and pepper to taste
- ¼ cup canned corn kernels
- ½ cup mozzarella shreds
- 2 tsp chopped parsley
- 1 cup bechamel sauce

**Directions:**
1. Preheat air fryer at 400ºF. Rub olive oil over both potatoes and sprinkle with salt and pepper. Place them in the frying basket and Bake for 45 minutes, flipping at 30 minutes mark. Let cool onto a cutting board for 5 minutes until cool enough to handle. Scoop out cooled potato into a bowl. Discard skins.
2. Place Italian sausages in the frying basket and Air Fry for 2 minutes. Using the back of a fork, mash cooked potatoes, yogurt, milk, olive oil, Italian seasoning, salt, and pepper until smooth. Toss in cooked sausages, corn, and mozzarella cheese. Stuff bell peppers with the potato mixture. Place bell peppers in the frying basket and Bake for 10 minutes. Serve immediately sprinkled with parsley and bechamel sauce on side.

# Basic Fried Tofu

Servings: 4
Cooking Time: 17 Minutes
**Ingredients:**
- 14 ounces extra-firm tofu, drained and pressed
- 1 tablespoon sesame oil
- 2 tablespoons low-sodium soy sauce
- ¼ cup rice vinegar
- 1 tablespoon fresh grated ginger
- 1 clove garlic, minced
- 3 tablespoons cornstarch
- ¼ teaspoon black pepper
- ⅛ teaspoon salt

**Directions:**
1. Cut the tofu into 16 cubes. Set aside in a glass container with a lid.
2. In a medium bowl, mix the sesame oil, soy sauce, rice vinegar, ginger, and garlic. Pour over the tofu and secure the lid. Place in the refrigerator to marinate for an hour.
3. Preheat the air fryer to 350°F (175°C).
4. In a small bowl, mix the cornstarch, black pepper, and salt.
5. Transfer the tofu to a large bowl and discard the leftover marinade. Pour the cornstarch mixture over the tofu and toss until all the pieces are coated.
6. Liberally spray the air fryer basket with olive oil mist and set the tofu pieces inside. Allow space between the tofu so it can cook evenly. Cook in batches if necessary.
7. Cook 15 to 17 minutes, shaking the basket every 5 minutes to allow the tofu to cook evenly on all sides. When it's done cooking, the tofu will be crisped and browned on all sides.
8. Remove the tofu from the air fryer basket and serve warm.

# Falafel

Servings: 4
Cooking Time: 10 Minutes
**Ingredients:**
- 1 cup dried chickpeas
- ½ onion, chopped
- 1 clove garlic
- ¼ cup fresh parsley leaves
- 1 teaspoon salt

- ¼ teaspoon crushed red pepper flakes
- 1 teaspoon ground cumin
- ½ teaspoon ground coriander
- 1 to 2 tablespoons flour
- olive oil
- Tomato Salad
- 2 tomatoes, seeds removed and diced
- ½ cucumber, finely diced
- ¼ red onion, finely diced and rinsed with water
- 1 teaspoon red wine vinegar
- 1 tablespoon olive oil
- salt and freshly ground black pepper
- 2 tablespoons chopped fresh parsley

**Directions:**
1. Cover the chickpeas with water and let them soak overnight on the counter. Then drain the chickpeas and put them in a food processor, along with the onion, garlic, parsley, spices and 1 tablespoon of flour. Pulse in the food processor until the mixture has broken down into a coarse paste consistency. The mixture should hold together when you pinch it. Add more flour as needed, until you get this consistency.
2. Scoop portions of the mixture (about 2 tablespoons in size) and shape into balls. Place the balls on a plate and refrigerate for at least 30 minutes. You should have between 12 and 14 balls.
3. Preheat the air fryer to 380°F (195°C).
4. Spray the falafel balls with oil and place them in the air fryer. Air-fry for 10 minutes, rolling them over and spraying them with oil again halfway through the cooking time so that they cook and brown evenly.
5. Serve with pita bread, hummus, cucumbers, hot peppers, tomatoes or any other fillings you might like.

## Rainbow Quinoa Patties

Servings: 4
Cooking Time: 20 Minutes
**Ingredients:**
- 1 cup canned tri-bean blend, drained and rinsed
- 2 tbsp olive oil
- ½ tsp ground cumin
- ½ tsp garlic salt
- 1 tbsp paprika
- 1/3 cup uncooked quinoa
- 2 tbsp chopped onion
- ¼ cup shredded carrot
- 2 tbsp chopped cilantro
- 1 tsp chili powder
- ½ tsp salt
- 2 tbsp mascarpone cheese

**Directions:**
1. Place 1/3 cup of water, 1 tbsp of olive oil, cumin, and salt in a saucepan over medium heat and bring it to a boil. Remove from the heat and stir in quinoa. Let rest covered for 5 minutes.
2. Preheat air fryer at 350°F. Using the back of a fork, mash beans until smooth. Toss in cooked quinoa and the remaining ingredients. Form mixture into 4 patties. Place patties in the greased frying basket and Air Fry for 6 minutes, turning once, and brush with the remaining olive oil. Serve immediately.

## Smoked Paprika Sweet Potato Fries

Servings: 4
Cooking Time: 35 Minutes
**Ingredients:**
- 2 sweet potatoes, peeled
- 1 ½ tbsp cornstarch
- 1 tbsp canola oil
- 1 tbsp olive oil
- 1 tsp smoked paprika
- 1 tsp garlic powder
- Salt and pepper to taste
- 1 cup cocktail sauce

**Directions:**
1. Cut the potatoes lengthwise to form French fries. Put in a resealable plastic bag and add cornstarch. Seal and shake to coat the fries. Combine the canola oil, olive oil, paprika, garlic powder, salt, and pepper fries in a large bowl. Add the sweet potato fries and mix to combine.
2. Preheat air fryer to 380°F (195°C). Place fries in the greased basket and fry for 20-25 minutes, shaking the basket once until crisp. Drizzle with Cocktail sauce to serve.

## Mushroom Lasagna

Servings: 4
Cooking Time: 40 Minutes
**Ingredients:**
- 2 tbsp olive oil
- 1 zucchini, diced
- ½ cup diced mushrooms
- ¼ cup diced onion
- 1 cup marinara sauce
- 1 cup ricotta cheese
- 1/3 cup grated Parmesan
- 1 egg
- 2 tsp Italian seasoning

- 2 tbsp fresh basil, chopped
- ½ tsp thyme
- 1 tbsp red pepper flakes
- ½ tsp salt
- 5 lasagna noodle sheets
- 1 cup grated mozzarella

**Directions:**
1. Heat the oil in a skillet over medium heat. Add zucchini, mushrooms, 1 tbsp of basil, thyme, red pepper flakes and onion and cook for 4 minutes until the veggies are tender. Toss in marinara sauce, and bring it to a bowl. Then, low the heat and simmer for 3 minutes.
2. Preheat air fryer at 375ºF. Combine ricotta cheese, Parmesan cheese, egg, Italian seasoning, and salt in a bowl. Spoon ¼ of the veggie mixture into a cake pan. Add a layer of lasagna noodles on top, breaking apart noodles first to fit pan. Then, top with 1/3 of ricotta mixture and ¼ of mozzarella cheese. Repeat the layer 2 more times, finishing with mozzarella cheese on top. Cover cake pan with aluminum foil.
3. Place cake pan in the frying basket and Bake for 12 minutes. Remove the foil and cook for 3 more minutes. Let rest for 10 minutes before slicing. Serve immediately sprinkled with the remaining fresh basil.

## Cheddar-bean Flautas

Servings: 4
Cooking Time: 15 Minutes
**Ingredients:**
- 8 corn tortillas
- 1 can refried beans
- 1 cup shredded cheddar
- 1 cup guacamole

**Directions:**
1. Preheat air fryer to 390°F (200°C). Wet the tortillas with water. Spray the frying basket with oil and stack the tortillas inside. Air Fry for 1 minute. Remove to a flat surface, laying them out individually. Scoop an equal amount of beans in a line down the center of each tortilla. Top with cheddar cheese. Roll the tortilla sides over the filling and put seam-side down in the greased frying basket. Air Fry for 7 minutes or until the tortillas are golden and crispy. Serve immediately topped with guacamole.

## Vietnamese Gingered Tofu

Servings: 4
Cooking Time: 25 Minutes
**Ingredients:**
- 1 package extra-firm tofu, cubed
- 4 tsp shoyu
- 1 tsp onion powder
- ½ tsp garlic powder
- ½ tsp ginger powder
- ½ tsp turmeric powder
- Black pepper to taste
- 2 tbsp nutritional yeast
- 1 tsp dried rosemary
- 1 tsp dried dill
- 2 tsp cornstarch
- 2 tsp sunflower oil

**Directions:**
1. Sprinkle the tofu with shoyu and toss to coat. Add the onion, garlic, ginger, turmeric, and pepper. Gently toss to coat. Add the yeast, rosemary, dill, and cornstarch. Toss to coat. Dribble with the oil and toss again.
2. Preheat air fryer to 390°F (200°C). Spray the fryer basket with oil, put the tofu in the basket and Bake for 7 minutes. Remove, shake gently, and cook for another 7 minutes or until the tofu is crispy and golden. Serve warm.

## Garlicky Roasted Mushrooms

Servings: 4
Cooking Time: 30 Minutes
**Ingredients:**
- 16 garlic cloves, peeled
- 2 tsp olive oil
- 16 button mushrooms
- 2 tbsp fresh chives, snipped
- Salt and pepper to taste
- 1 tbsp white wine

**Directions:**
1. Preheat air fryer to 350°F (175°C). Coat the garlic with some olive oil in a baking pan, then Roast in the air fryer for 12 minutes. When done, take the pan out and stir in the mushrooms, salt, and pepper. Then add the remaining olive oil and white wine. Put the pan back into the fryer and Bake for 10-15 minutes until the mushrooms and garlic soften. Sprinkle with chives and serve warm.

## Vegetarian Eggplant "pizzas"

Servings: 4
Cooking Time: 25 Minutes
**Ingredients:**
- ½ cup diced baby bella mushrooms
- 3 tbsp olive oil
- ¼ cup diced onions
- ½ cup pizza sauce
- 1 eggplant, sliced

- 1 tsp salt
- 1 cup shredded mozzarella
- ¼ cup chopped oregano

**Directions:**

1. Warm 2 tsp of olive oil in a skillet over medium heat. Add in onion and mushrooms and stir-fry for 4 minutes until tender. Stir in pizza sauce. Turn the heat off.
2. Preheat air fryer to 375ºF. Brush the eggplant slices with the remaining olive oil on both sides. Lay out slices on a large plate and season with salt. Then, top with the sauce mixture and shredded mozzarella. Place the eggplant pizzas in the frying basket and Air Fry for 5 minutes. Garnish with oregano to serve.

## Meatless Kimchi Bowls

Servings: 4
Cooking Time: 20 Minutes

**Ingredients:**

- 2 cups canned chickpeas
- 1 carrot, julienned
- 6 scallions, sliced
- 1 zucchini, diced
- 2 tbsp coconut aminos
- 2 tsp sesame oil
- 1 tsp rice vinegar
- 2 tsp granulated sugar
- 1 tbsp gochujang
- ¼ tsp salt
- ½ cup kimchi
- 2 tsp roasted sesame seeds

**Directions:**

1. Preheat air fryer to 350ºF. Combine all ingredients, except for the kimchi, 2 scallions, and sesame seeds, in a baking pan. Place the pan in the frying basket and Air Fry for 6 minutes. Toss in kimchi and cook for 2 more minutes. Divide between 2 bowls and garnish with the remaining scallions and sesame seeds. Serve immediately.

# Vegetable Side Dishes Recipes

## Fried Eggplant Slices

Servings: 3
Cooking Time: 12 Minutes

**Ingredients:**

- 1½ sleeves (about 60 saltines) Saltine crackers
- ¾ cup Cornstarch
- 2 Large egg(s), well beaten
- 1 medium (about ¾ pound) Eggplant, stemmed, peeled, and cut into ¼-inch-thick rounds
- Olive oil spray

**Directions:**

1. Preheat the air fryer to 400°F (205°C). Also, position the rack in the center of the oven and heat the oven to 175°F (80°C).
2. Grind the saltines, in batches if necessary, in a food processor, pulsing the machine and rearranging the saltine pieces every few pulses. Or pulverize the saltines in a large, heavy zip-closed plastic bag with the bottom of a heavy saucepan. In either case, you want small bits of saltines, not just crumbs.
3. Set up and fill three shallow soup plates or small pie plates on your counter: one for the cornstarch, one for the beaten egg(s), and one for the pulverized saltines.
4. Set an eggplant slice in the cornstarch and turn it to coat on both sides. Use a brush to lightly remove any excess. Dip it into the beaten egg(s) and turn to coat both sides. Let any excess egg slip back into the rest, then set the slice in the saltines. Turn several times, pressing gently to coat both sides evenly but not heavily. Coat both sides of the slice with olive oil spray and set it aside. Continue dipping and coating the remaining slices.
5. Set one, two, or maybe three slices in the basket. There should be at least ½ inch between them for proper air flow. Air-fry undisturbed for 12 minutes, or until crisp and browned.
6. Use a nonstick-safe spatula to transfer the slice(s) to a large baking sheet. Slip it into the oven to keep the slices warm as you air-fry more batches, as needed, always transferring the slices to the baking sheet to stay warm.

# Street Corn

Servings: 4
Cooking Time: 10 Minutes
**Ingredients:**
- 1 tablespoon butter
- 4 ears corn
- ⅓ cup plain Greek yogurt
- 2 tablespoons Parmesan cheese
- ½ teaspoon paprika
- ½ teaspoon garlic powder
- ¼ teaspoon salt
- ¼ teaspoon black pepper
- ¼ cup finely chopped cilantro

**Directions:**
1. Preheat the air fryer to 400°F (205°C).
2. In a medium microwave-safe bowl, melt the butter in the microwave. Lightly brush the outside of the ears of corn with the melted butter.
3. Place the corn into the air fryer basket and cook for 5 minutes, flip the corn, and cook another 5 minutes.
4. Meanwhile, in a medium bowl, mix the yogurt, cheese, paprika, garlic powder, salt, and pepper. Set aside.
5. Carefully remove the corn from the air fryer and let cool 3 minutes. Brush the outside edges with the yogurt mixture and top with fresh chopped cilantro. Serve immediately.

# Roasted Broccoli And Red Bean Salad

Servings: 3
Cooking Time: 14 Minutes
**Ingredients:**
- 3 cups (about 1 pound) 1- to 1½-inch fresh broccoli florets (not frozen)
- 1½ tablespoons Olive oil spray
- 1¼ cups Canned red kidney beans, drained and rinsed
- 3 tablespoons Minced yellow or white onion
- 2 tablespoons plus 1 teaspoon Red wine vinegar
- ¾ teaspoon Dried oregano
- ¼ teaspoon Table salt
- ¼ teaspoon Ground black pepper

**Directions:**
1. Preheat the air fryer to 375°F (190°C).
2. Put the broccoli florets in a big bowl, coat them generously with olive oil spray, then toss to coat all surfaces, even down into the crannies, spraying them a couple of times more.
3. Pour the florets into the basket, spreading them into as close to one layer as you can. Air-fry for 12 minutes, tossing and rearranging the florets twice so that any touching or covered parts are eventually exposed to the air currents, until light browned but still a bit firm. (If the machine is at 360°F (180°C), you may need to add 2 minutes to the cooking time.)
4. Dump the contents of the basket onto a large cutting board. Cool for a minute or two, then chop the florets into small bits. Scrape these into a bowl and add the kidney beans, onion, vinegar, oregano, salt, and pepper. Toss well and serve warm or at room temperature.

# Spiced Pumpkin Wedges

Servings: 4
Cooking Time: 35 Minutes
**Ingredients:**
- 2 ½ cups pumpkin, cubed
- 2 tbsp olive oil
- Salt and pepper to taste
- ¼ tsp pumpkin pie spice
- 1 tbsp thyme
- ¼ cup grated Parmesan

**Directions:**
1. Preheat air fryer to 360°F (180°C). Put the cubed pumpkin with olive oil, salt, pumpkin pie spice, black pepper, and thyme in a bowl and stir until the pumpkin is well coated. Pour this mixture into the frying basket and Roast for 18-20 minutes, stirring once. Sprinkle the pumpkin with grated Parmesan. Serve and enjoy!

# Buttery Stuffed Tomatoes

Servings: 6
Cooking Time: 15 Minutes
**Ingredients:**
- 3 8-ounce round tomatoes
- ½ cup plus 1 tablespoon Plain panko bread crumbs (gluten-free, if a concern)
- 3 tablespoons (about ½ ounce) Finely grated Parmesan cheese
- 3 tablespoons Butter, melted and cooled
- 4 teaspoons Stemmed and chopped fresh parsley leaves
- 1 teaspoon Minced garlic
- ¼ teaspoon Table salt
- Up to ¼ teaspoon Red pepper flakes
- Olive oil spray

**Directions:**
1. Preheat the air fryer to 375°F (190°C).
2. Cut the tomatoes in half through their "equators" (that is, not through the stem ends). One at a time, gently squeeze the tomato halves over a trash can, using a clean finger to gently force out the seeds and most of the juice inside, working

carefully so that the tomato doesn't lose its round shape or get crushed.
3. Stir the bread crumbs, cheese, butter, parsley, garlic, salt, and red pepper flakes in a bowl until the bread crumbs are moistened and the parsley is uniform throughout the mixture. Pile this mixture into the spaces left in the tomato halves. Press gently to compact the filling. Coat the tops of the tomatoes with olive oil spray.
4. Place the tomatoes cut side up in the basket. They may touch each other. Air-fry for 15 minutes, or until the filling is lightly browned and crunchy.
5. Use nonstick-safe spatula and kitchen tongs for balance to gently transfer the stuffed tomatoes to a platter or a cutting board. Cool for a couple of minutes before serving.

## Air-fried Potato Salad

Servings: 4
Cooking Time: 15 Minutes
**Ingredients:**
- 1⅓ pounds Yellow potatoes, such as Yukon Golds, cut into ½-inch chunks
- 1 large Sweet white onion(s), such as Vidalia, chopped into ½-inch pieces
- 1 tablespoon plus 2 teaspoons Olive oil
- ¾ cup Thinly sliced celery
- 6 tablespoons Regular or low-fat mayonnaise (gluten-free, if a concern)
- 2½ tablespoons Apple cider vinegar
- 1½ teaspoons Dijon mustard (gluten-free, if a concern)
- ¾ teaspoon Table salt
- ¼ teaspoon Ground black pepper

**Directions:**
1. Preheat the air fryer to 400°F (205°C).
2. Toss the potatoes, onion(s), and oil in a large bowl until the vegetables are glistening with oil.
3. When the machine is at temperature, transfer the vegetables to the basket, spreading them out into as even a layer as you can. Air-fry for 15 minutes, tossing and rearranging the vegetables every 3 minutes so that all surfaces get exposed to the air currents, until the vegetables are tender and even browned at the edges.
4. Pour the contents of the basket into a serving bowl. Cool for at least 5 minutes or up to 30 minutes. Add the celery, mayonnaise, vinegar, mustard, salt, and pepper. Stir well to coat. The potato salad can be made in advance; cover and refrigerate for up to 4 days.

## Smashed Fried Baby Potatoes

Servings: 3
Cooking Time: 18 Minutes
**Ingredients:**
- 1½ pounds baby red or baby Yukon gold potatoes
- ¼ cup butter, melted
- 1 teaspoon olive oil
- ½ teaspoon paprika
- 1 teaspoon dried parsley
- salt and freshly ground black pepper
- 2 scallions, finely chopped

**Directions:**
1. Bring a large pot of salted water to a boil. Add the potatoes and boil for 18 minutes or until the potatoes are fork-tender.
2. Drain the potatoes and transfer them to a cutting board to cool slightly. Spray or brush the bottom of a drinking glass with a little oil. Smash or flatten the potatoes by pressing the glass down on each potato slowly. Try not to completely flatten the potato or smash it so hard that it breaks apart.
3. Combine the melted butter, olive oil, paprika, and parsley together.
4. Preheat the air fryer to 400°F (205°C).
5. Spray the bottom of the air fryer basket with oil and transfer one layer of the smashed potatoes into the basket. Brush with some of the butter mixture and season generously with salt and freshly ground black pepper.
6. Air-fry at 400°F (205°C) for 10 minutes. Carefully flip the potatoes over and air-fry for an additional 8 minutes until crispy and lightly browned.
7. Keep the potatoes warm in a 170°F (75°C) oven or tent with aluminum foil while you cook the second batch. Sprinkle minced scallions over the potatoes and serve warm.

## Veggie Fritters

Servings: 4
Cooking Time: 35 Minutes
**Ingredients:**
- ¼ cup crumbled feta cheese
- 1 grated zucchini
- ¼ cup Parmesan cheese
- 2 tbsp minced onion
- 1 tbs powder garlic
- 1 tbsp flour
- 1 tbsp cornmeal
- 1 tbsp butter, melted
- 1 egg
- 2 tsp chopped dill
- 2 tsp chopped parsley
- Salt and pepper to taste
- 1 cup bread crumbs

**Directions:**
1. Preheat air fryer at 350ºF. Squeeze grated zucchini between paper towels to remove excess moisture. In a bowl, combine all ingredients except breadcrumbs. Form mixture into 12 balls, about 2 tbsp each. In a shallow bowl, add breadcrumbs. Roll each ball in breadcrumbs, covering all sides. Place fritters on an ungreased pizza pan. Place in the frying basket and Air Fry for 11 minutes, flipping once. Serve.

## Hot Okra Wedges

Servings: 2
Cooking Time: 35 Minutes
**Ingredients:**
- 1 cup okra, sliced
- 1 cup breadcrumbs
- 2 eggs, beaten
- A pinch of black pepper
- 1 tsp crushed red peppers
- 2 tsp hot Tabasco sauce

**Directions:**
1. Preheat air fryer to 350°F (175°C). Place the eggs and Tabasco sauce in a bowl and stir thoroughly; set aside. In a separate mixing bowl, combine the breadcrumbs, crushed red peppers, and pepper. Dip the okra into the beaten eggs, then coat in the crumb mixture. Lay the okra pieces on the greased frying basket. Air Fry for 14-16 minutes, shaking the basket several times during cooking. When ready, the okra will be crispy and golden brown. Serve.

## Mushrooms

Servings: 4
Cooking Time: 12 Minutes
**Ingredients:**
- 8 ounces whole white button mushrooms
- ½ teaspoon salt
- ⅛ teaspoon pepper
- ¼ teaspoon garlic powder
- ¼ teaspoon onion powder
- 5 tablespoons potato starch
- 1 egg, beaten
- ¾ cup panko breadcrumbs
- oil for misting or cooking spray

**Directions:**
1. Place mushrooms in a large bowl. Add the salt, pepper, garlic and onion powders, and stir well to distribute seasonings.
2. Add potato starch to mushrooms and toss in bowl until well coated.
3. Dip mushrooms in beaten egg, roll in panko crumbs, and mist with oil or cooking spray.
4. Place mushrooms in air fryer basket. You can cook them all at once, and it's okay if a few are stacked.
5. Cook at 390°F (200°C) for 5minutes. Shake basket, then continue cooking for 7 more minutes, until golden brown and crispy.

## Fried Eggplant Balls

Servings: 4
Cooking Time: 40 Minutes
**Ingredients:**
- 1 medium eggplant (about 1 pound)
- olive oil
- salt and freshly ground black pepper
- 1 cup grated Parmesan cheese
- 2 cups fresh breadcrumbs
- 2 tablespoons chopped fresh parsley
- 2 tablespoons chopped fresh basil
- 1 clove garlic, minced
- 1 egg, lightly beaten
- ½ cup fine dried breadcrumbs

**Directions:**
1. Preheat the air fryer to 400°F (205°C).
2. Quarter the eggplant by cutting it in half both lengthwise and horizontally. Make a few slashes in the flesh of the eggplant but not through the skin. Brush the cut surface of the eggplant generously with olive oil and transfer to the air fryer basket, cut side up. Air-fry for 10 minutes. Turn the eggplant quarters cut side down and air-fry for another 15 minutes or until the eggplant is soft all the way through. You may need to rotate the pieces in the air fryer so that they cook evenly. Transfer the eggplant to a cutting board to cool.
3. Place the Parmesan cheese, the fresh breadcrumbs, fresh herbs, garlic and egg in a food processor. Scoop the flesh out of the eggplant, discarding the skin and any pieces that are tough. You should have about 1 to 1½ cups of eggplant. Add the eggplant to the food processor and process everything together until smooth. Season with salt and pepper. Refrigerate the mixture for at least 30 minutes.
4. Place the dried breadcrumbs into a shallow dish or onto a plate. Scoop heaping tablespoons of the eggplant mixture into the dried breadcrumbs. Roll the dollops of eggplant in the breadcrumbs and then shape into small balls. You should have 16 to 18 eggplant balls at the end. Refrigerate until you are ready to air-fry.
5. Preheat the air fryer to 350°F (175°C).
6. Spray the eggplant balls and the air fryer basket with olive oil. Air-fry the eggplant balls for 15 minutes, rotating the balls during the cooking process to brown evenly.

## Double Cheese-broccoli Tots

Servings: 4
Cooking Time: 30 Minutes
**Ingredients:**
- 1/3 cup grated sharp cheddar cheese
- 1 cup riced broccoli
- 1 egg
- 1 oz herbed Boursin cheese
- 1 tbsp grated onion
- 1/3 cup bread crumbs
- ½ tsp salt
- ¼ tsp garlic powder

**Directions:**
1. Preheat air fryer to 375°F. Mix the riced broccoli, egg, cheddar cheese, Boursin cheese, onion, bread crumbs, salt, and garlic powder in a bowl. Form into 12 rectangular mounds. Cut a piece of parchment paper to fit the bottom of the frying basket, place the tots, and Air Fry for 9 minutes. Let chill for 5 minutes before serving.

## Sweet Potato Fries

Servings: 4
Cooking Time: 30 Minutes
**Ingredients:**
- 2 pounds sweet potatoes
- 1 teaspoon dried marjoram
- 2 teaspoons olive oil
- sea salt

**Directions:**
1. Peel and cut the potatoes into ¼-inch sticks, 4 to 5 inches long.
2. In a sealable plastic bag or bowl with lid, toss sweet potatoes with marjoram and olive oil. Rub seasonings in to coat well.
3. Pour sweet potatoes into air fryer basket and cook at 390°F (200°C) for approximately 30 minutes, until cooked through with some brown spots on edges.
4. Season to taste with sea salt.

## Green Peas With Mint

Servings: 4
Cooking Time: 5 Minutes
**Ingredients:**
- 1 cup shredded lettuce
- 1 10-ounce package frozen green peas, thawed
- 1 tablespoon fresh mint, shredded
- 1 teaspoon melted butter

**Directions:**
1. Lay the shredded lettuce in the air fryer basket.
2. Toss together the peas, mint, and melted butter and spoon over the lettuce.
3. Cook at 360°F (180°C) for 5 minutes, until peas are warm and lettuce wilts.

## Home Fries

Servings: 4
Cooking Time: 20 Minutes
**Ingredients:**
- 3 pounds potatoes, cut into 1-inch cubes
- ½ teaspoon oil
- salt and pepper

**Directions:**
1. In a large bowl, mix the potatoes and oil thoroughly.
2. Cook at 390°F (200°C) for 10 minutes and shake the basket to redistribute potatoes.
3. Cook for an additional 10 minutes, until brown and crisp.
4. Season with salt and pepper to taste.

## Sweet Potato Puffs

Servings: 18
Cooking Time: 35 Minutes
**Ingredients:**
- 3 8- to 10-ounce sweet potatoes
- 1 cup Seasoned Italian-style dried bread crumbs
- 3 tablespoons All-purpose flour
- 3 tablespoons Instant mashed potato flakes
- ¾ teaspoon Onion powder
- ¾ teaspoon Table salt
- Olive oil spray

**Directions:**
1. Preheat the air fryer to 350°F (175°C).
2. Prick the sweet potatoes in four or five different places with the tines of a flatware fork (not in a line but all around the sweet potatoes).
3. When the machine is at temperature, set the sweet potatoes in the basket with as much air space between them as possible. Air-fry undisturbed for 20 minutes.
4. Use kitchen tongs to transfer the sweet potatoes to a wire rack. (They will still be firm; they are only partially cooked.) Cool for 10 to 15 minutes. Meanwhile, increase the machine's temperature to 400°F (205°C). Spread the bread crumbs on a dinner plate.
5. Peel the sweet potatoes. Shred them through the large holes of a box grater into a large bowl. Stir in the flour, potato flakes, onion powder, and salt until well combined.

6. Scoop up 2 tablespoons of the sweet potato mixture. Form it into a small puff, a cylinder about like a Tater Tot. Set this cylinder in the bread crumbs. Gently roll it around to coat on all sides, even the ends. Set aside on a cutting board and continue making more puffs: 11 more for a small batch, 17 more for a medium batch, or 23 more for a large batch.

7. Generously coat the puffs with olive oil spray on all sides. Set the puffs in the basket with as much air space between them as possible. They should not be touching, but even a fraction of an inch will work well. Air-fry undisturbed for 15 minutes, or until lightly browned and crunchy.

8. Gently turn the contents of the basket out onto a wire rack. Cool the puffs for a couple of minutes before serving.

## Basic Corn On The Cob

Servings: 4
Cooking Time: 15 Minutes
**Ingredients:**
- 3 ears of corn, shucked and halved
- 2 tbsp butter, melted
- Salt and pepper to taste
- 1 tsp minced garlic
- 1 tsp paprika

**Directions:**
1. Preheat air fryer at 400°F. Toss all ingredients in a bowl. Place corn in the frying basket and Bake for 7 minutes, turning once. Serve immediately.

## Gorgonzola Stuffed Mushrooms

Servings: 2
Cooking Time: 15 Minutes
**Ingredients:**
- 12 white button mushroom caps
- 2 tbsp diced white button mushroom stems
- ¼ cup Gorgonzola cheese, crumbled
- 1 tsp olive oil
- 1 green onion, chopped
- 2 tbsp bread crumbs

**Directions:**
1. Preheat air fryer to 350°F. Rub around the top of each mushroom cap with olive oil. Mix the mushroom stems, green onion, and Gorgonzola cheese in a bowl.
2. Distribute and press mixture into the cups of mushrooms, then sprinkle bread crumbs on top. Place stuffed mushrooms in the frying basket and Bake for 5-7 minutes. Serve right away.

## Rosemary New Potatoes

Servings: 4
Cooking Time: 6 Minutes
**Ingredients:**
- 3 large red potatoes (enough to make 3 cups sliced)
- ¼ teaspoon ground rosemary
- ¼ teaspoon ground thyme
- ⅛ teaspoon salt
- ⅛ teaspoon ground black pepper
- 2 teaspoons extra-light olive oil

**Directions:**
1. Preheat air fryer to 330°F (165°C).
2. Place potatoes in large bowl and sprinkle with rosemary, thyme, salt, and pepper.
3. Stir with a spoon to distribute seasonings evenly.
4. Add oil to potatoes and stir again to coat well.
5. Cook at 330°F (165°C) for 4minutes. Stir and break apart any that have stuck together.
6. Cook an additional 2 minutes or until fork-tender.

## Hawaiian Brown Rice

Servings: 4
Cooking Time: 12 Minutes
**Ingredients:**
- ¼ pound ground sausage
- 1 teaspoon butter
- ¼ cup minced onion
- ¼ cup minced bell pepper
- 2 cups cooked brown rice
- 1 8-ounce can crushed pineapple, drained

**Directions:**
1. Shape sausage into 3 or 4 thin patties. Cook at 390°F (200°C) for 6 to 8minutes or until well done. Remove from air fryer, drain, and crumble. Set aside.
2. Place butter, onion, and bell pepper in baking pan. Cook at 390°F (200°C) for 1 minute and stir. Cook 4 minutes longer or just until vegetables are tender.
3. Add sausage, rice, and pineapple to vegetables and stir together.
4. Cook at 390°F (200°C) for 2 minutes, until heated through.

## Roasted Fennel Salad

Servings: 3
Cooking Time: 20 Minutes
**Ingredients:**
- 3 cups (about ¾ pound) Trimmed fennel (see the headnote), roughly chopped
- 1½ tablespoons Olive oil
- ¼ teaspoon Table salt
- ¼ teaspoon Ground black pepper

- 1½ tablespoons White balsamic vinegar (see here)

**Directions:**
1. Preheat the air fryer to 400°F (205°C).
2. Toss the fennel, olive oil, salt, and pepper in a large bowl until the fennel is well coated in the oil.
3. When the machine is at temperature, pour the fennel into the basket, spreading it out into as close to one layer as possible. Air-fry for 20 minutes, tossing and rearranging the fennel pieces twice so that any covered or touching parts get exposed to the air currents, until golden at the edges and softened.
4. Pour the fennel into a serving bowl. Add the vinegar while hot. Toss well, then cool a couple of minutes before serving. Or serve at room temperature.

## Perfect Broccolini

Servings: 4
Cooking Time: 15 Minutes
**Ingredients:**
- 1 pound Broccolini
- Olive oil spray
- Coarse sea salt or kosher salt

**Directions:**
1. Preheat the air fryer to 375°F (195°C).
2. Place the broccolini on a cutting board. Generously coat it with olive oil spray, turning the vegetables and rearranging them before spraying a couple of times more, to make sure everything's well coated, even the flowery bits in their heads.
3. When the machine is at temperature, pile the broccolini in the basket, spreading it into as close to one layer as you can. Air-fry for 5 minutes, tossing once to get any covered or touching parts exposed to the air currents, until the leaves begin to get brown and even crisp. Watch carefully and use this visual cue to know the moment to stop the cooking.
4. Transfer the broccolini to a platter. Spread out the pieces and sprinkle them with salt to taste.

## Classic Stuffed Shells

Servings: 4
Cooking Time: 35 Minutes
**Ingredients:**
- 1 cup chopped spinach, cooked
- 1 cup shredded mozzarella
- 4 cooked jumbo shells
- 1 tsp dry oregano
- 1 cup ricotta cheese
- 1 egg, beaten
- 1 cup marinara sauce
- 1 tbsp basil leaves

**Directions:**
1. Preheat air fryer to 360°F (180°C). Place the beaten egg, oregano, ricotta, mozzarella, and chopped spinach in a bowl and mix until all the ingredients are combined. Fill the mixture into the cooked pasta shells. Spread half of the marinara sauce on a baking pan, then place the stuffed shells over the sauce. Spoon the remaining marinara sauce over the shells. Bake in the air fryer for 25 minutes or until the stuffed shells are wonderfully cooked, crispy on the outside with the spinach and cheeses inside gooey and delicious. Sprinkle with basil leaves and serve warm.

## Asparagus Wrapped In Pancetta

Servings: 4
Cooking Time: 30 Minutes
**Ingredients:**
- 20 asparagus trimmed
- Salt and pepper pepper
- 4 pancetta slices
- 1 tbsp fresh sage, chopped

**Directions:**
1. Sprinkle the asparagus with fresh sage, salt and pepper. Toss to coat. Make 4 bundles of 5 spears by wrapping the center of the bunch with one slice of pancetta.
2. Preheat air fryer to 400°F (205°C). Put the bundles in the greased frying basket and Air Fry for 8-10 minutes or until the pancetta is brown and the asparagus are starting to char on the edges. Serve immediately.

## Fried Green Tomatoes With Sriracha Mayo

Servings: 4
Cooking Time: 12 Minutes
**Ingredients:**
- 3 green tomatoes
- salt and freshly ground black pepper
- ⅓ cup all-purpose flour*
- 2 eggs
- ½ cup buttermilk
- 1 cup panko breadcrumbs*
- 1 cup cornmeal
- olive oil, in a spray bottle
- fresh thyme sprigs or chopped fresh chives
- Sriracha Mayo
- ½ cup mayonnaise
- 1 to 2 tablespoons sriracha hot sauce
- 1 tablespoon milk

**Directions:**
1. Cut the tomatoes in ¼-inch slices. Pat them dry with a clean kitchen towel and season generously with salt and pepper.
2. Set up a dredging station using three shallow dishes. Place the flour in the first shallow dish, whisk the eggs and buttermilk together in the second dish, and combine the panko breadcrumbs and cornmeal in the third dish.
3. Preheat the air fryer to 400°F (205°C).
4. Dredge the tomato slices in flour to coat on all sides. Then dip them into the egg mixture and finally press them into the breadcrumbs to coat all sides of the tomato.
5. Spray or brush the air-fryer basket with olive oil. Transfer 3 to 4 tomato slices into the basket and spray the top with olive oil. Air-fry the tomatoes at 400°F (205°C) for 8 minutes. Flip them over, spray the other side with oil and air-fry for an additional 4 minutes until golden brown.
6. While the tomatoes are cooking, make the sriracha mayo. Combine the mayonnaise, 1 tablespoon of the sriracha hot sauce and milk in a small bowl. Stir well until the mixture is smooth. Add more sriracha sauce to taste.
7. When the tomatoes are done, transfer them to a cooling rack or a platter lined with paper towels so the bottom does not get soggy. Before serving, carefully stack the all the tomatoes into air fryer and air-fry at 350°F (175°C) for 1 to 2 minutes to heat them back up.
8. Serve the fried green tomatoes hot with the sriracha mayo on the side. Season one last time with salt and freshly ground black pepper and garnish with sprigs of fresh thyme or chopped fresh chives.

## Crispy Cauliflower Puffs

Servings: 12
Cooking Time: 9 Minutes
**Ingredients:**
- 1½ cups Riced cauliflower
- 1 cup (about 4 ounces) Shredded Monterey Jack cheese
- ¾ cup Seasoned Italian-style panko bread crumbs (gluten-free, if a concern)
- 2 tablespoons plus 1 teaspoon All-purpose flour or potato starch
- 2 tablespoons plus 1 teaspoon Vegetable oil
- 1 plus 1 large yolk Large egg(s)
- ¾ teaspoon Table salt
- Vegetable oil spray

**Directions:**
1. Preheat the air fryer to 375°F (190°C).
2. Stir the riced cauliflower, cheese, bread crumbs, flour or potato starch, oil, egg(s) and egg yolk (if necessary), and salt in a large bowl to make a thick batter.
3. Using 2 tablespoons of the batter, form a compact ball between your clean, dry palms. Set it aside and continue forming more balls: 7 more for a small batch, 11 more for a medium batch, or 15 more for a large batch.
4. Generously coat the balls on all sides with vegetable oil spray. Set them in the basket with as much air space between them as possible. Air-fry undisturbed for 7 minutes, or until golden brown and crisp. If the machine is at 360°F (180°C), you may need to add 2 minutes to the cooking time.
5. Gently pour the contents of the basket onto a wire rack. Cool the puffs for 5 minutes before serving.

## Pancetta Mushroom & Onion Sautée

Servings: 4
Cooking Time: 20 Minutes
**Ingredients:**
- 16 oz white button mushrooms, stems trimmed, halved
- 1 onion, cut into half-moons
- 4 pancetta slices, diced
- 1 clove garlic, minced

**Directions:**
1. Preheat air fryer to 350°F. Add all ingredients, except for the garlic, to the frying basket and Air Fry for 8 minutes, tossing once. Stir in the garlic and cook for 1 more minute. Serve right away.

## Almond Green Beans

Servings: 4
Cooking Time: 20 Minutes
**Ingredients:**
- 2 cups green beans, trimmed
- ¼ cup slivered almonds
- 2 tbsp butter, melted
- Salt and pepper to taste
- 2 tsp lemon juice
- Lemon zest and slices

**Directions:**
1. Preheat air fryer at 375°F. Add almonds to the frying basket and Air Fry for 2 minutes, tossing once. Set aside in a small bowl. Combine the remaining ingredients, except 1 tbsp of butter, in a bowl.
2. Place green beans in the frying basket and Air Fry for 10 minutes, tossing once. Then, transfer them to a large serving dish. Scatter with the melted butter, lemon juice and roasted almonds and toss. Serve immediately garnished with lemon zest and lemon slices.

## Summer Vegetables With Balsamic Drizzle, Goat Cheese And Basil

Servings: 2
Cooking Time: 17 Minutes
**Ingredients:**
- 1 cup balsamic vinegar
- 1 zucchini, sliced
- 1 yellow squash, sliced
- 2 tablespoons olive oil
- 1 clove garlic, minced
- ½ teaspoon Italian seasoning
- salt and freshly ground black pepper
- ½ cup cherry tomatoes, halved
- 2 ounces crumbled goat cheese
- 2 tablespoons chopped fresh basil, plus more leaves for garnish

**Directions:**
1. Place the balsamic vinegar in a small saucepot on the stovetop. Bring the vinegar to a boil, lower the heat and simmer uncovered for 20 minutes, until the mixture reduces and thickens. Set aside to cool.
2. Preheat the air fryer to 390°F (200°C).
3. Combine the zucchini and yellow squash in a large bowl. Add the olive oil, minced garlic, Italian seasoning, salt and pepper and toss to coat.
4. Air-fry the vegetables at 390°F (200°C) for 10 minutes, shaking the basket several times during the cooking process. Add the cherry tomatoes and continue to air-fry for another 5 minutes. Sprinkle the goat cheese over the vegetables and air-fry for 2 more minutes.
5. Transfer the vegetables to a serving dish, drizzle with the balsamic reduction and season with freshly ground black pepper. Garnish with the fresh basil leaves.

## Simple Peppared Carrot Chips

Servings: 4
Cooking Time: 15 Minutes
**Ingredients:**
- 3 carrots, cut into coins
- 1 tbsp sesame oil
- Salt and pepper to taste

**Directions:**
1. Preheat air fryer at 375ºF. Combine all ingredients in a bowl. Place carrots in the frying basket and Roast for 10 minutes, tossing once. Serve right away.

## Roasted Baby Carrots

Servings: 6
Cooking Time: 20 Minutes
**Ingredients:**
- 1 lb baby carrots
- 2 tbsp olive oil
- ¼ cup raw honey
- ¼ tsp ground cinnamon
- ¼ tsp ground nutmeg
- ¼ cup pecans, chopped

**Directions:**
1. Preheat air fryer to 360°F (180°C). Place the baby carrots with olive oil, honey, nutmeg and cinnamon in a bowl and toss to coat. Pour into the air fryer and Roast for 6 minutes. Shake the basket, sprinkle the pecans on top, and roast for 6 minutes more. Serve and enjoy!

## Crispy Noodle Salad

Servings: 3
Cooking Time: 22 Minutes
**Ingredients:**
- 6 ounces Fresh Chinese-style stir-fry or lo mein wheat noodles
- 1½ tablespoons Cornstarch
- ¾ cup Chopped stemmed and cored red bell pepper
- 2 Medium scallion(s), trimmed and thinly sliced
- 2 teaspoons Sambal oelek or other pulpy hot red pepper sauce (see here)
- 2 teaspoons Thai sweet chili sauce or red ketchup-like chili sauce, such as Heinz
- 2 teaspoons Regular or low-sodium soy sauce or tamari sauce
- 2 teaspoons Unseasoned rice vinegar (see here)
- 1 tablespoon White or black sesame seeds

**Directions:**
1. Bring a large saucepan of water to a boil over high heat. Add the noodles and boil for 2 minutes. Drain in a colander set in the sink. Rinse several times with cold water, shaking the colander to drain the noodles very well. Spread the noodles out on a large cutting board and air-dry for 10 minutes.
2. Preheat the air fryer to 400°F (205°C).
3. Toss the noodles in a bowl with the cornstarch until well coated. Spread them out across the entire basket (although they will be touching and overlapping a bit). Air-fry for 6 minutes, then turn the solid mass of noodles over as one piece. If it cracks in half or smaller pieces, just fit these back together after turning. Continue air-frying for 6 minutes, or until golden brown and crisp.

4. As the noodles cook, stir the bell pepper, scallion(s), sambal oelek, red chili sauce, soy sauce, vinegar, and sesame seeds in a serving bowl until well combined.

5. Turn the basket of noodles out onto a cutting board and cool for a minute or two. Break the mass of noodles into individual noodles and/or small chunks and add to the dressing in the serving bowl. Toss well to serve.

## Cheesy Potato Skins

Servings: 6
Cooking Time: 54 Minutes
**Ingredients:**
- 3 6- to 8-ounce small russet potatoes
- 3 Thick-cut bacon strips, halved widthwise (gluten-free, if a concern)
- ¾ teaspoon Mild paprika
- ¼ teaspoon Garlic powder
- ¼ teaspoon Table salt
- ¼ teaspoon Ground black pepper
- ½ cup plus 1 tablespoon (a little over 2 ounces) Shredded Cheddar cheese
- 3 tablespoons Thinly sliced trimmed chives
- 6 tablespoons (a little over 1 ounce) Finely grated Parmesan cheese

**Directions:**
1. Preheat the air fryer to 375°F (190°C).
2. Prick each potato in four places with a fork (not four places in a line but four places all around the potato). Set the potatoes in the basket with as much air space between them as possible. Air-fry undisturbed for 45 minutes, or until the potatoes are tender when pricked with a fork.
3. Use kitchen tongs to gently transfer the potatoes to a wire rack. Cool for 15 minutes. Maintain the machine's temperature.
4. Lay the bacon strip halves in the basket in one layer. They may touch but should not overlap. Air-fry undisturbed for 5 minutes, until crisp. Use those same tongs to transfer the bacon pieces to the wire rack. If there's a great deal of rendered bacon fat in the basket's bottom or on a tray under the basket attachment, pour this into a bowl, cool, and discard. Don't throw it down the drain!
5. Cut the potatoes in half lengthwise (not just slit them open but actually cut in half). Use a flatware spoon to scoop the hot, soft middles into a bowl, leaving ½ inch of potato all around the inside of the spud next to the skin. Sprinkle the inside of the potato "shells" evenly with paprika, garlic powder, salt, and pepper.
6. Chop the bacon pieces into small bits. Sprinkle these along with the Cheddar and chives evenly inside the potato shells. Crumble 2 to 3 tablespoons of the soft potato insides over the filling mixture. Divide the grated Parmesan evenly over the tops of the potatoes.
7. Set the stuffed potatoes in the basket with as much air space between them as possible. Air-fry undisturbed for 4 minutes, until the cheese melts and lightly browns.
8. Use kitchen tongs to gently transfer the stuffed potato halves to a wire rack. Cool for 5 minutes before serving.

## Parmesan Asparagus

Servings: 2
Cooking Time: 5 Minutes
**Ingredients:**
- 1 bunch asparagus, stems trimmed
- 1 teaspoon olive oil
- salt and freshly ground black pepper
- ¼ cup coarsely grated Parmesan cheese
- ½ lemon

**Directions:**
1. Preheat the air fryer to 400°F (205°C).
2. Toss the asparagus with the oil and season with salt and freshly ground black pepper.
3. Transfer the asparagus to the air fryer basket and air-fry at 400°F (205°C) for 5 minutes, shaking the basket to turn the asparagus once or twice during the cooking process.
4. When the asparagus is cooked to your liking, sprinkle the asparagus generously with the Parmesan cheese and close the air fryer drawer again. Let the asparagus sit for 1 minute in the turned-off air fryer. Then, remove the asparagus, transfer it to a serving dish and finish with a grind of black pepper and a squeeze of lemon juice.

## Blistered Shishito Peppers

Servings: 2
Cooking Time: 15 Minutes
**Ingredients:**
- 20 shishito peppers
- 1 tsp sesame oil
- ½ tsp soy sauce
- ½ tsp grated ginger
- Salt to taste
- 1 tsp sesame seeds

**Directions:**
1. Preheat air fryer to 375°F. Coat the peppers with sesame oil and salt in a bowl. Transfer them to the frying basket and Air Fry for 8 minutes or until blistered and softened, shaking the basket to turn the peppers. Drizzle with soy sauce and sprinkle with ginger and sesame seeds to serve.

# Buttery Rolls

Servings: 6
Cooking Time: 14 Minutes
**Ingredients:**
- 6½ tablespoons Room-temperature whole or low-fat milk
- 3 tablespoons plus 1 teaspoon Butter, melted and cooled
- 3 tablespoons plus 1 teaspoon (or 1 medium egg, well beaten) Pasteurized egg substitute, such as Egg Beaters
- 1½ tablespoons Granulated white sugar
- 1¼ teaspoons Instant yeast
- ¼ teaspoon Table salt
- 2 cups, plus more for dusting All-purpose flour
- Vegetable oil
- Additional melted butter, for brushing

**Directions:**
1. Stir the milk, melted butter, pasteurized egg substitute (or whole egg), sugar, yeast, and salt in a medium bowl to combine. Stir in the flour just until the mixture makes a soft dough.
2. Lightly flour a clean, dry work surface. Turn the dough out onto the work surface. Knead the dough for 5 minutes to develop the gluten.
3. Lightly oil the inside of a clean medium bowl. Gather the dough into a compact ball and set it in the bowl. Turn the dough over so that its surface has oil on it all over. Cover the bowl tightly with plastic wrap and set aside in a warm, draft-free place until the dough has doubled in bulk, about 1½ hours.
4. Punch down the dough, then turn it out onto a clean, dry work surface. Divide it into 5 even balls for a small batch, 6 balls for a medium batch, or 8 balls for a large one.
5. For a small batch, lightly oil the inside of a 6-inch round cake pan and set the balls around its perimeter, separating them as much as possible.
6. For a medium batch, lightly oil the inside of a 7-inch round cake pan and set the balls in it with one ball at its center, separating them as much as possible.
7. For a large batch, lightly oil the inside of an 8-inch round cake pan and set the balls in it with one at the center, separating them as much as possible.
8. Cover with plastic wrap and set aside to rise for 30 minutes.
9. Preheat the air fryer to 350°F (175°C).
10. Uncover the pan and brush the rolls with a little melted butter, perhaps ½ teaspoon per roll. When the machine is at temperature, set the cake pan in the basket. Air-fry undisturbed for 14 minutes, or until the rolls have risen and browned.
11. Using kitchen tongs and a nonstick-safe spatula, two hot pads, or silicone baking mitts, transfer the cake pan from the basket to a wire rack. Cool the rolls in the pan for a minute or two. Turn the rolls out onto a wire rack, set them top side up again, and cool for at least another couple of minutes before serving warm.

# Corn On The Cob

Servings: 4
Cooking Time: 12 Minutes
**Ingredients:**
- 2 large ears fresh corn
- olive oil for misting
- salt (optional)

**Directions:**
1. Shuck corn, remove silks, and wash.
2. Cut or break each ear in half crosswise.
3. Spray corn with olive oil.
4. Cook at 390°F (200°C) for 12 minutes or until browned as much as you like.
5. Serve plain or with coarsely ground salt.

# Brown Rice And Goat Cheese Croquettes

Servings: 3
Cooking Time: 8 Minutes
**Ingredients:**
- ¾ cup Water
- 6 tablespoons Raw medium-grain brown rice, such as brown Arborio
- ½ cup Shredded carrot
- ¼ cup Walnut pieces
- 3 tablespoons (about 1½ ounces) Soft goat cheese
- 1 tablespoon Pasteurized egg substitute, such as Egg Beaters (gluten-free, if a concern)
- ¼ teaspoon Dried thyme
- ¼ teaspoon Table salt
- ¼ teaspoon Ground black pepper
- Olive oil spray

**Directions:**
1. Combine the water, rice, and carrots in a small saucepan set over medium-high heat. Bring to a boil, stirring occasionally. Cover, reduce the heat to very low, and simmer very slowly for 45 minutes, or until the water has been absorbed and the rice is tender. Set aside, covered, for 10 minutes.
2. Scrape the contents of the saucepan into a food processor. Cool for 10 minutes.
3. Preheat the air fryer to 400°F (205°C).
4. Put the nuts, cheese, egg substitute, thyme, salt, and pepper into the food processor. Cover and pulse to a coarse paste, stopping the machine at least once to scrape down the inside of the canister.

5. Uncover the food processor; scrape down and remove the blade. Using wet, clean hands, form the mixture into two 4-inch-diameter patties for a small batch, three 4-inch-diameter patties for a medium batch, or four 4-inch-diameter patties for a large one. Generously coat both sides of the patties with olive oil spray.

6. Set the patties in the basket with as much air space between them as possible. Air-fry undisturbed for 8 minutes, or until brown and crisp.

7. Use a nonstick-safe spatula to transfer the croquettes to a wire rack. Cool for 5 minutes before serving.

## Easy Parmesan Asparagus

Servings: 4
Cooking Time: 15 Minutes
**Ingredients:**
- 3 tsp grated Parmesan cheese
- 1 lb asparagus, trimmed
- 2 tsp olive oil
- Salt to taste
- 1 clove garlic, minced
- ½ lemon

**Directions:**
1. Preheat air fryer at 375°F. Toss the asparagus and olive oil in a bowl, place them in the frying basket, and Air Fry for 8-10 minutes, tossing once. Transfer them into a large serving dish. Sprinkle with salt, garlic, and Parmesan cheese and toss until coated. Serve immediately with a squeeze of lemon. Enjoy!

## Dijon Artichoke Hearts

Servings:4
Cooking Time: 25 Minutes
**Ingredients:**
- 1 jar artichoke hearts in water, drained
- 1 egg
- 1 tbsp Dijon mustard
- ½ cup bread crumbs
- ¼ cup flour
- 6 basil leaves

**Directions:**
1. Preheat air fryer to 350°F. Beat egg and mustard in a bowl. In another bowl, combine bread crumbs and flour. Dip artichoke hearts in egg mixture, then dredge in crumb mixture. Place artichoke hearts in the greased frying basket and Air Fry for 7-10 minutes until crispy. Serve topped with basil. Enjoy!

## Succulent Roasted Peppers

Servings:2
Cooking Time: 35 Minutes
**Ingredients:**
- 2 red bell peppers
- 2 tbsp olive oil
- Salt to taste
- 1 tsp dill, chopped

**Directions:**
1. Preheat air fryer to 400°F. Remove the tops and bottoms of the peppers. Cut along rib sections and discard the seeds. Combine the bell peppers and olive oil in a bowl. Place bell peppers in the frying basket. Roast for 24 minutes, flipping once. Transfer the roasted peppers to a small bowl and cover for 15 minutes. Then, peel and discard the skins. Sprinkle with salt and dill and serve.

## Homemade Potato Puffs

Servings: 4
Cooking Time: 15 Minutes
**Ingredients:**
- 1¾ cups Water
- 4 tablespoons (¼ cup/½ stick) Butter
- 2 cups plus 2 tablespoons Instant mashed potato flakes
- 1½ teaspoons Table salt
- ¾ teaspoon Ground black pepper
- ¼ teaspoon Mild paprika
- ¼ teaspoon Dried thyme
- 1¼ cups Seasoned Italian-style dried bread crumbs (gluten-free, if a concern)
- Olive oil spray

**Directions:**
1. Heat the water with the butter in a medium saucepan set over medium-low heat just until the butter melts. Do not bring to a boil.

2. Remove the saucepan from the heat and stir in the potato flakes, salt, pepper, paprika, and thyme until smooth. Set aside to cool for 5 minutes.

3. Preheat the air fryer to 400°F (205°C). Spread the bread crumbs on a dinner plate.

4. Scrape up 2 tablespoons of the potato flake mixture and form it into a small, oblong puff, like a little cylinder about 1½ inches long. Gently roll the puff in the bread crumbs until coated on all sides. Set it aside and continue making more, about 12 for the small batch, 18 for the medium batch, or 24 for the large.

5. Coat the potato cylinders with olive oil spray on all sides, then arrange them in the basket in one layer with some air space between them. Air-fry undisturbed for 15 minutes, or until crisp and brown.

6. Gently dump the contents of the basket onto a wire rack. Cool for 5 minutes before serving.

# Rosemary Roasted Potatoes With Lemon

Cooking Time: 12 Minutes
Servings: 4

**Ingredients:**
- 1 pound small red-skinned potatoes, halved or cut into bite-sized chunks
- 1 tablespoon olive oil
- 1 teaspoon finely chopped fresh rosemary
- ¼ teaspoon salt
- freshly ground black pepper
- 1 tablespoon lemon zest

**Directions:**
1. Preheat the air fryer to 400°F (205°C).
2. Toss the potatoes with the olive oil, rosemary, salt and freshly ground black pepper.
3. Air-fry for 12 minutes (depending on the size of the chunks), tossing the potatoes a few times throughout the cooking process.
4. As soon as the potatoes are tender to a knifepoint, toss them with the lemon zest and more salt if desired.

# Beet Fries

Servings: 3
Cooking Time: 22 Minutes

**Ingredients:**
- 3 6-ounce red beets
- Vegetable oil spray
- To taste Coarse sea salt or kosher salt

**Directions:**
1. Preheat the air fryer to 375°F (190°C).
2. Remove the stems from the beets and peel them with a knife or vegetable peeler. Slice them into ½-inch-thick circles. Lay these flat on a cutting board and slice them into ½-inch-thick sticks. Generously coat the sticks on all sides with vegetable oil spray.
3. When the machine is at temperature, drop them into the basket, shake the basket to even the sticks out into as close to one layer as possible, and air-fry for 20 minutes, tossing and rearranging the beet matchsticks every 5 minutes, or until brown and even crisp at the ends. If the machine is at 360°F (180°C), you may need to add 2 minutes to the cooking time.
4. Pour the fries into a big bowl, add the salt, toss well, and serve warm.

# Pecorino Dill Muffins

Servings: 4
Cooking Time: 25 Minutes

**Ingredients:**
- ¼ cup grated Pecorino cheese
- 1 cup flour
- 1 tsp dried dill
- ⅛ tsp salt
- ¼ tsp onion powder
- 2 tsp baking powder
- 1 egg
- ¼ cup Greek yogurt

**Directions:**
1. Preheat air fryer to 350ºF. In a bowl, combine dry the ingredients. Set aside. In another bowl, whisk the wet ingredients. Add the wet ingredients to the dry ingredients and combine until blended.
2. Transfer the batter to 6 silicone muffin cups lightly greased with olive oil. Place muffin cups in the frying basket and Bake for 12 minutes. Serve right away.

# Lemony Fried Fennel Slices

Servings: 2
Cooking Time: 15 Minutes

**Ingredients:**
- 1 tbsp minced fennel fronds
- 1 fennel bulb
- 2 tsp olive oil
- ¼ tsp salt
- 2 lemon wedges
- 1 tsp fennel seeds

**Directions:**
1. Preheat air fryer to 350ºF. Remove the fronds from the fennel bulb and reserve them. Cut the fennel into thin slices. Rub fennel chips with olive oil on both sides and sprinkle with salt and fennel seeds. Place fennel slices in the frying basket and Bake for 8 minutes. Squeeze lemon on top and scatter with chopped fronds. Serve.

# Herbed Baby Red Potato Hasselback

Servings: 4
Cooking Time: 35 Minutes

**Ingredients:**
- 6 baby red potatoes, scrubbed
- 3 tsp shredded cheddar cheese
- 1 tbsp olive oil
- 2 tbsp butter, melted
- 1 tbsp chopped thyme
- Salt and pepper to taste
- 3 tsp sour cream
- ¼ cup chopped parsley

**Directions:**

1. Preheat air fryer at 350°F. Make slices in the width of each potato about ¼-inch apart without cutting through. Rub potato slices with olive oil, both outside and in between slices. Place potatoes in the frying basket and Air Fry for 20 minutes, tossing once, brush with melted butter, and scatter with thyme. Remove them to a large serving dish. Sprinkle with salt, black pepper and top with a dollop of cheddar cheese, sour cream. Scatter with parsley to serve.

## Layered Mixed Vegetables

Servings: 4
Cooking Time: 30 Minutes
**Ingredients:**
- 1 Yukon Gold potato, sliced
- 1 eggplant, sliced
- 1 carrot, thinly sliced
- ¼ cup minced onions
- 3 garlic cloves, minced
- ¾ cup milk
- 2 tbsp cornstarch
- ½ tsp dried thyme

**Directions:**
1. Preheat air fryer to 380°F (195°C). In layers, add the potato, eggplant, carrot, onion, and garlic to a baking pan. Combine the milk, cornstarch, and thyme in a bowl, then pour this mix over the veggies. Put the pan in the air fryer and Bake for 15 minutes. The casserole should be golden on top with softened veggies. Serve immediately.

## Spicy Bean Stuffed Potatoes

Servings: 4
Cooking Time: 60 Minutes
**Ingredients:**
- 1 lb russet potatoes, scrubbed and perforated with a fork
- 1 can diced green chilies, including juice
- 1/3 cup grated Mexican cheese blend
- 1 green bell pepper, diced
- 1 yellow bell pepper, diced
- ¼ cup torn iceberg lettuce
- 2 tsp olive oil
- 2 tbsp sour cream
- ½ tsp chili powder
- 2-3 jalapeños, sliced
- 1 red bell pepper, chopped
- Salt and pepper to taste
- 1/3 cup canned black beans
- 4 grape tomatoes, sliced
- ¼ cup chopped parsley

**Directions:**
1. Preheat air fryer at 400°F. Brush olive oil over potatoes. Place them in the frying basket and Bake for 45 minutes, turning at 30 minutes mark. Let cool on a cutting board for 10 minutes until cool enough to handle. Slice each potato lengthwise and scoop out all but a ¼" layer of potato to form 4 boats.
2. Mash potato flesh, sour cream, green chilies, cheese, chili powder, jalapeños, green, yellow, and red peppers, salt, and pepper in a bowl until smooth. Fold in black beans. Divide between potato skin boats. Place potato boats in the frying basket and Bake for 2 minutes. Remove them to a serving plate. Top each boat with lettuce, tomatoes, and parsley. Sprinkle tops with salt and serve.

## Roasted Brussels Sprouts With Bacon

Cooking Time: 20 Minutes
Servings: 4
**Ingredients:**
- 4 slices thick-cut bacon, chopped (about ¼ pound)
- 1 pound Brussels sprouts, halved (or quartered if large)
- freshly ground black pepper

**Directions:**
1. Preheat the air fryer to 380°F (19°C).
2. Air-fry the bacon for 5 minutes, shaking the basket once or twice during the cooking time.
3. Add the Brussels sprouts to the basket and drizzle a little bacon fat from the bottom of the air fryer drawer into the basket. Toss the sprouts to coat with the bacon fat. Air-fry for an additional 15 minutes, or until the Brussels sprouts are tender to a knifepoint.
4. Season with freshly ground black pepper.

## Sicilian Arancini

Servings: 4
Cooking Time: 20 Minutes
**Ingredients:**
- 1/3 minced red bell pepper
- 4 tsp grated Parmesan cheese
- 1 ¼ cup cooked rice
- 1 egg
- 3 tbsp plain flour
- 1/3 cup finely grated carrots
- 2 tbsp minced fresh parsley
- 2 tsp olive oil

**Directions:**
1. Preheat air fryer to 380°F (195°C). Add the rice, egg, and flour to a bowl and mix well. Add the carrots, bell peppers, parsley, and Parmesan cheese and mix again. Shape into 8 fritters. Brush with olive oil and place the fritters in the frying basket. Air Fry for 8-10 minutes, turning once, until golden. Serve hot and enjoy!

## Teriyaki Tofu With Spicy Mayo

Servings: 2
Cooking Time: 35 Minutes + 1 Hour To Marinate
**Ingredients:**
- 1 scallion, chopped
- 7 oz extra-firm tofu, sliced
- 2 tbsp soy sauce
- 1 tsp toasted sesame oil
- 1 red chili, thinly sliced
- 1 tsp mirin
- 1 tsp light brown sugar
- 1 garlic clove, grated
- ½ tsp grated ginger
- 1/3 cup sesame seeds
- 1 egg
- 4 tsp mayonnaise
- 1 tbsp lime juice
- 1 tsp hot chili powder

**Directions:**
1. Squeeze most of the water from the tofu by lightly pressing the slices between two towels. Place the tofu in a baking dish. Use a whisk to mix soy sauce, sesame oil, red chili, mirin, brown sugar, garlic and ginger. Pour half of the marinade over the tofu. Using a spatula, carefully flip the tofu down and pour the other half of the marinade over. Refrigerate for 1 hour.
2. Preheat air fryer to 400°F (205°C). In a shallow plate, add sesame seeds. In another shallow plate, beat the egg. Remove the tofu from the refrigerator. Let any excess marinade drip off. Dip each piece in the egg mixture and then in the sesame seeds. Transfer to greased frying basket. Air Fry for 10 minutes, flipping once until toasted and crispy. Meanwhile, mix mayonnaise, lime juice, and hot chili powder and in a small bowl. Top with a dollop of hot chili mayo and some scallions. Serve and enjoy!

## Broccoli Au Gratin

Servings: 2
Cooking Time: 25 Minutes
**Ingredients:**
- 2 cups broccoli florets, chopped
- 6 tbsp grated Gruyère cheese
- 1 tbsp grated Pecorino cheese
- ½ tbsp olive oil
- 1 tbsp flour
- 1/3 cup milk
- ½ tsp ground coriander
- Salt and black pepper
- 2 tbsp panko bread crumbs

**Directions:**
1. Whisk the olive oil, flour, milk, coriander, salt, and pepper in a bowl. Incorporate broccoli, Gruyere cheese, panko bread crumbs, and Pecorino cheese until well combined. Pour in a greased baking dish.
2. Preheat air fryer to 330°F (165°C). Put the baking dish into the frying basket. Bake until the broccoli is crisp-tender and the top is golden, or about 12-15 minutes. Serve warm.

## Buttered Brussels Sprouts

Servings: 4
Cooking Time: 30 Minutes
**Ingredients:**
- ¼ cup grated Parmesan
- 2 tbsp butter, melted
- 1 lb Brussels sprouts
- Salt and pepper to taste

**Directions:**
1. Preheat air fryer to 330°F (165°C). Trim the bottoms of the sprouts and remove any discolored leaves. Place the sprouts in a medium bowl along with butter, salt and pepper. Toss to coat, then place them in the frying basket. Roast for 20 minutes, shaking the basket twice. When done, the sprouts should be crisp with golden-brown color. Plate the sprouts in a serving dish and toss with Parmesan cheese.

## Savory Brussels Sprouts

Servings: 4
Cooking Time: 15 Minutes
**Ingredients:**
- 1 lb Brussels sprouts, quartered
- 2 tbsp balsamic vinegar
- 1 tbsp olive oil
- 1 tbsp honey
- Salt and pepper to taste
- 1 ½ tbsp lime juice
- Parsley for sprinkling

**Directions:**
1. Preheat air fryer at 350°F. Combine all ingredients in a bowl. Transfer them to the frying basket. Air Fry for 10 minutes, tossing once. Top with lime juice and parsley.

# RECIPE INDEX

## A

Air-fried Potato Salad ............................................. 105
Almond And Sun-dried Tomato Crusted Pork Chops ......... 74
Almond Cranberry Granola ...................................... 40
Almond Green Beans ............................................. 110
Almond-crusted Fish ............................................... 60
Annie's Chocolate Chunk Hazelnut Cookies ................. 10
Apple Crisp .......................................................... 15
Apple-cinnamon-walnut Muffins ................................ 37
Aromatic Pork Tenderloin ........................................ 77
Asian Glazed Meatballs .......................................... 23
Asparagus Wrapped In Pancetta .............................. 109

## B

Baba Ghanouj ...................................................... 32
Bacon & Chicken Flatbread ..................................... 52
Baked Apple Crisp ................................................ 14
Balsamic Caprese Hasselback ................................. 93
Baltimore Crab Cakes ............................................ 66
Basic Corn On The Cob ......................................... 108
Basic Fried Tofu ................................................... 100
Bbq Back Ribs ..................................................... 89
Beef & Barley Stuffed Bell Peppers ........................... 78
Beet Chips With Guacamole .................................... 26
Beet Fries ........................................................... 115
Best-ever Roast Beef Sandwiches ............................. 24
Blackberry Bbq Glazed Country-style Ribs .................. 81
Blistered Shishito Peppers ...................................... 112
Blueberry French Toast Sticks .................................. 42
Boneless Ribeyes .................................................. 74
Breaded Parmesan Perch ........................................ 67
Broccoli Au Gratin ................................................ 117
Brown Rice And Goat Cheese Croquettes .................. 113
Brownies After Dark .............................................. 15
Buffalo Cauliflower ................................................ 31
Buffalo Wings ...................................................... 30
Buttered Brussels Sprouts ...................................... 117
Buttery Chicken Legs ............................................. 49
Buttery Rolls ....................................................... 113

Buttery Stuffed Tomatoes ...................................... 104

## C

Calzones South Of The Border ................................ 79
Canadian-inspired Waffle Poutine ............................. 32
Carrot Muffins ..................................................... 36
Carrot-oat Cake Muffins ........................................ 11
Catfish Nuggets ................................................... 68
Cauliflower "tater" Tots ........................................ 29
Charred Cauliflower Tacos ..................................... 99
Charred Shishito Peppers ...................................... 33
Cheddar Bean Taquitos ......................................... 94
Cheddar Stuffed Portobellos With Salsa .................... 90
Cheddar-bean Flautas .......................................... 102
Cheeseburger Slider Pockets .................................. 33
Cheesecake Wontons ............................................ 9
Cheesy Egg Bites ................................................. 36
Cheesy Eggplant Lasagna ..................................... 92
Cheesy Green Pitas .............................................. 25
Cheesy Mushroom-stuffed Pork Loins ....................... 83
Cheesy Potato Skins ............................................ 112
Cheesy Tuna Tower .............................................. 73
Cherry Chipotle Bbq Chicken Wings ......................... 34
Chicken & Fruit Biryani ......................................... 44
Chicken Breasts Wrapped In Bacon .......................... 47
Chicken Burgers With Blue Cheese Sauce .................. 53
Chicken Club Sandwiches ...................................... 22
Chicken Cordon Bleu Patties .................................. 48
Chicken Cutlets With Broccoli Rabe And Roasted Peppers 46
Chicken Fried Steak With Gravy .............................. 44
Chicken Gyros ..................................................... 19
Chicken Nuggets .................................................. 46
Chicken Salad With White Dressing .......................... 58
Chicken Skewers .................................................. 56
Chicken Wellington ............................................... 58
Chile Con Carne Galette ........................................ 87
Chili Cheese Dogs ................................................ 22
Chili Corn On The Cob .......................................... 30
Chinese Firecracker Shrimp .................................... 71

| | |
|---|---|
| Chive Potato Pierogi | 97 |
| Chocolate Cake | 14 |
| Chocolate Chip Banana Muffins | 40 |
| Chorizo Sausage & Cheese Balls | 40 |
| Cinnamon Tortilla Crisps | 16 |
| Cinnamon-stick Kofta Skewers | 76 |
| Citrus Pork Lettuce Wraps | 85 |
| Classic Stuffed Shells | 109 |
| Coconut Cream Roll-ups | 17 |
| Coconut Jerk Shrimp | 71 |
| Coconut Mini Tarts | 42 |
| Coconut Shrimp With Plum Sauce | 73 |
| Colorful Vegetable Medley | 94 |
| Corn On The Cob | 113 |
| Corn Tortilla Chips | 31 |
| Corned Beef Hash | 77 |
| Cornflake Chicken Nuggets | 48 |
| Country Wings | 26 |
| Crab Stuffed Salmon Roast | 69 |
| Creamy Broccoli & Mushroom Casserole | 94 |
| Creole Chicken Drumettes | 52 |
| Crispy Cauliflower Puffs | 110 |
| Crispy Chicken Tenders | 57 |
| Crispy Lamb Shoulder Chops | 84 |
| Crispy Noodle Salad | 111 |
| Crispy Sweet-and-sour Cod Fillets | 59 |
| Crispy Wontons | 35 |
| Crunchy And Buttery Cod With Ritz® Cracker Crust | 62 |
| Crunchy Falafel Balls | 24 |
| Crunchy Fried Pork Loin Chops | 87 |
| Crunchy Lobster Bites | 31 |
| Crunchy Parmesan Edamame | 26 |
| Crunchy Rice Paper Samosas | 91 |
| Curly Kale Chips With Greek Sauce | 27 |
| Curried Pickle Chips | 28 |
| Curried Sweet-and-spicy Scallops | 70 |

### D

| | |
|---|---|
| Dark Chocolate Peanut Butter S'mores | 13 |
| Date Oat Cookies | 10 |
| Dijon Artichoke Hearts | 114 |
| Dijon Thyme Burgers | 20 |
| Double Cheese-broccoli Tots | 107 |

### E

| | |
|---|---|
| Easy Asian-style Tuna | 61 |
| Easy Caprese Flatbread | 43 |
| Easy Cheese & Spinach Lasagna | 93 |
| Easy Parmesan Asparagus | 114 |
| Easy Tex-mex Chimichangas | 85 |
| Easy Turkey Meatballs | 50 |
| Effortless Mac `n´ Cheese | 99 |
| Egg & Bacon Pockets | 42 |
| Egg & Bacon Toasts | 39 |
| Egg Rolls | 90 |
| Eggless Mung Bean Tart | 41 |
| Eggplant Parmesan Subs | 23 |
| Eggs In Avocado Halves | 28 |
| Enchilada Chicken Dip | 30 |
| Enchilada Chicken Quesadillas | 51 |
| Exotic Pork Skewers | 81 |

### F

| | |
|---|---|
| Fake Shepherd´s Pie | 95 |
| Falafel | 100 |
| Family Fish Nuggets With Tartar Sauce | 69 |
| Fancy Chicken Piccata | 47 |
| Fantasy Sweet Chili Chicken Strips | 56 |
| Farmer´s Fried Chicken | 55 |
| Farmers Market Quiche | 43 |
| Feta & Shrimp Pita | 68 |
| Fiesta Chicken Plate | 50 |
| Fish Cakes | 67 |
| Fish Sticks For Grown-ups | 61 |
| Fish-in-chips | 67 |
| Fried Eggplant Balls | 106 |
| Fried Eggplant Slices | 103 |
| Fried Green Tomatoes With Sriracha Mayo | 109 |
| Fried Green Tomatoes | 29 |
| Fried Oreos | 16 |
| Fried Spam | 86 |
| Fudgy Brownie Cake | 16 |
| Fusion Tender Flank Steak | 88 |

### G

| | |
|---|---|
| Garlic-butter Lobster Tails | 71 |
| Garlicky Roasted Mushrooms | 102 |
| German-style Pork Patties | 87 |
| Giant Buttery Chocolate Chip Cookie | 11 |
| Giant Buttery Oatmeal Cookie | 18 |

Giant Oatmeal–peanut Butter Cookie ........................... 9
Gingerbread .................................................................... 15
Gluten-free Nutty Chicken Fingers ............................... 45
Gorgeous Jalapeño Poppers ........................................ 100
Gorgonzola Stuffed Mushrooms .................................. 108
Greek Chicken Wings ................................................... 55
Greek Pork Chops ......................................................... 82
Green Peas With Mint ................................................. 107
Green Strata .................................................................. 37
Grilled Cheese Sandwich .............................................. 91
Grilled Pork & Bell Pepper Salad ................................. 83
Guajillo Chile Chicken Meatballs ................................. 57

## H
Halibut Quesadillas ....................................................... 64
Harissa Chicken Wings ................................................. 55
Hashbrown Potatoes Lyonnaise ................................... 39
Hawaiian Brown Rice .................................................. 108
Herb-crusted Sole ......................................................... 60
Herbed Baby Red Potato Hasselback ......................... 115
Herby Lamb Chops ....................................................... 78
Home Fries .................................................................. 107
Homemade Pork Gyoza ................................................ 86
Homemade Potato Puffs ............................................. 114
Homemade Pretzel Bites .............................................. 35
Home-style Fish Sticks ................................................. 71
Honey Mesquite Pork Chops ........................................ 84
Honey Pecan Shrimp .................................................... 64
Horseradish Mustard Pork Chops ................................ 85
Hot Calamari Rings ....................................................... 62
Hot Nachos With Chile Salsa ....................................... 27
Hot Okra Wedges ........................................................ 106

## I
Indian Chicken Tandoori ............................................... 51
Indian Fry Bread Tacos ................................................. 76
Indian-inspired Chicken Skewers .................................. 49
Indonesian Pork Satay .................................................. 80
Inside Out Cheeseburgers ............................................ 21
Inside-out Cheeseburgers ............................................ 21
Italian Meatballs ............................................................ 79
Italian Stuffed Bell Peppers ........................................ 100
Italian-inspired Chicken Pizzadillas .............................. 54

## J
Japanese-style Turkey Meatballs ................................. 48

Jerk Turkey Meatballs ................................................... 48

## K
Kale & Lentils With Crispy Onions .............................. 94
Kale & Rice Chicken Rolls ........................................... 47
Kale Chips ...................................................................... 26
Kawaii Pork Roast ......................................................... 84
Kielbasa Sausage With Pierogies And Caramelized Onions 74
Kochukaru Pork Lettuce Cups ...................................... 82
Korean-style Fried Calamari ......................................... 69

## L
Lamb Burgers ................................................................ 19
Lamb Chops In Currant Sauce ..................................... 78
Lamb Chops ................................................................... 84
Layered Mixed Vegetables .......................................... 116
Lemon Iced Donut Balls ............................................... 11
Lemon-blueberry Morning Bread ................................. 38
Lemony Fried Fennel Slices ....................................... 115
Lentil Fritters ................................................................. 96
Lightened-up Breaded Fish Filets ................................ 62
Lime Flaming Halibut .................................................... 70
Lollipop Lamb Chops With Mint Pesto ........................ 85

## M
Magic Giant Chocolate Cookies ................................... 12
Mahi-mahi "burrito" Fillets ........................................... 65
Maple Balsamic Glazed Salmon ................................... 70
Maple-peach And Apple Oatmeal ................................ 40
Matcha Granola ............................................................. 43
Meat Loaves .................................................................. 88
Meatless Kimchi Bowls ............................................... 103
Meatloaf With Tangy Tomato Glaze ........................... 83
Mediterranean Salmon Burgers .................................... 66
Mediterranean Sea Scallops ......................................... 62
Mini Meatloaves With Pancetta ................................... 89
Minted Lamb Chops ...................................................... 90
Miso-rubbed Salmon Fillets .......................................... 59
Mojito Fish Tacos .......................................................... 72
Mom's Tuna Melt Toastie ............................................. 65
Mongolian Beef .............................................................. 75
Morning Loaded Potato Skins ...................................... 41
Moroccan-style Chicken Strips ..................................... 54
Mozzarella En Carrozza With Puttanesca Sauce ........ 27
Mushroom Bolognese Casserole .................................. 95
Mushroom Lasagna ..................................................... 101

Mushroom, Zucchini And Black Bean Burgers .................. 93
Mushrooms ................................................................. 106
Mustard Greens Chips With Curried Sauce ..................... 34
Mustard-crusted Rib-eye ................................................ 88
Mustardy Chicken Bites ................................................. 52

## N
No-guilty Spring Rolls ................................................... 30

## O
Onion Puffs .................................................................... 28
Orange Gooey Butter Cake ............................................ 13
Orange-chocolate Cake .................................................. 16
Oreo-coated Peanut Butter Cups .................................... 10

## P
Pancetta Mushroom & Onion Sautée ............................ 110
Paprika Fried Beef ......................................................... 77
Parmesan Asparagus .................................................... 112
Parmesan Crusted Chicken Cordon Bleu ...................... 57
Parmesan Portobello Mushroom Caps .......................... 99
Parsley Egg Scramble With Cottage Cheese ................. 37
Peanut Butter S'mores ................................................... 17
Pecan-crusted Tilapia .................................................... 70
Pecan-oat Filled Apples ................................................. 18
Pecorino Dill Muffins .................................................. 115
Pepper Steak ................................................................. 81
Peppered Maple Bacon Knots ....................................... 39
Peppered Steak Bites ..................................................... 86
Peppery Tilapia Roulade ................................................ 72
Perfect Broccolini ........................................................ 109
Perfect Burgers .............................................................. 19
Piña Colada Shrimp ....................................................... 63
Pineapple & Veggie Souvlaki ........................................ 94
Piri Piri Chicken Wings ................................................. 34
Pork & Beef Egg Rolls .................................................. 76
Pork Cutlets With Almond-lemon Crust ....................... 73
Pork Pot Stickers With Yum Yum Sauce ...................... 25
Pork Tenderloin With Apples & Celery ........................ 89
Premium Steakhouse Salad ........................................... 75
Pumpkin Brownies ........................................................ 17
Pumpkin Loaf ................................................................ 36

## Q
Quinoa Green Pizza ....................................................... 91

## R
Rainbow Quinoa Patties ............................................... 101
Ranch Chicken Tortillas ................................................. 58
Red Curry Flank Steak ................................................... 78
Restaurant-style Breaded Shrimp ................................... 68
Reuben Sandwiches ....................................................... 22
Rich Salmon Burgers With Broccoli Slaw .................... 72
Roasted Baby Carrots .................................................. 111
Roasted Broccoli And Red Bean Salad ....................... 104
Roasted Brussels Sprouts With Bacon ........................ 116
Roasted Fennel Salad .................................................. 108
Roasted Red Pepper Dip ................................................ 32
Roasted Vegetable Thai Green Curry ............................ 96
Rosemary New Potatoes .............................................. 108
Rosemary Roasted Potatoes With Lemon ................... 115
Russian Pierogi With Cheese Dip .................................. 28
Rustic Berry Layer Cake ................................................ 12

## S
S'mores Pockets ............................................................. 12
Santorini Steak Bowls ................................................... 82
Satay Chicken Skewers .................................................. 53
Saucy Chicken Thighs ................................................... 46
Saucy Shrimp ................................................................. 64
Sausage And Cheese Rolls ............................................. 33
Sausage And Pepper Heros ............................................ 21
Savory Brussels Sprouts .............................................. 117
Sesame Orange Chicken ................................................ 50
Shrimp Al Pesto ............................................................. 69
Shrimp ........................................................................... 63
Sicilian Arancini .......................................................... 116
Simple Buttermilk Fried Chicken .................................. 49
Simple Peppared Carrot Chips ..................................... 111
Simple Salsa Chicken Thighs ........................................ 56
Skinny Fries ................................................................... 32
Skirt Steak With Horseradish Cream ............................. 82
Smashed Fried Baby Potatoes ..................................... 105
Smoked Paprika Sweet Potato Fries ............................ 101
Smoked Salmon Croissant Sandwich ............................ 36
Southwest Gluten-free Turkey Meatloaf ....................... 53
Spaghetti Squash And Kale Fritters With Pomodoro Sauce 98
Spiced Apple Roll-ups ................................................... 38
Spiced Mexican Stir-fried Chicken ................................ 51
Spiced Pumpkin Wedges ............................................. 104
Spicy Bean Stuffed Potatoes ........................................ 116

| Recipe | Page |
|---|---|
| Spicy Black Bean Turkey Burgers With Cumin-avocado Spread | 44 |
| Spicy Vegetable And Tofu Shake Fry | 97 |
| Spinach & Turkey Meatballs | 51 |
| Spinach And Feta Stuffed Chicken Breasts | 54 |
| Spring Vegetable Omelet | 38 |
| Sticky Drumsticks | 47 |
| Strawberry Donut Bites | 18 |
| Street Corn | 104 |
| Struffoli | 14 |
| Stuffed Cabbage Rolls | 88 |
| Stuffed Pork Chops | 79 |
| Stuffed Portobellos | 95 |
| Stuffed Shrimp | 60 |
| Succulent Roasted Peppers | 114 |
| Summer Vegetables With Balsamic Drizzle, Goat Cheese And Basil | 111 |
| Suwon Pork Meatballs | 89 |
| Sweet & Spicy Swordfish Kebabs | 60 |
| Sweet And Salty Snack Mix | 34 |
| Sweet Corn Bread | 91 |
| Sweet Potato Fries | 107 |
| Sweet Potato Puffs | 107 |

## T

| Recipe | Page |
|---|---|
| Teriyaki Chicken Bites | 54 |
| Teriyaki Salmon | 68 |
| Teriyaki Tofu With Spicy Mayo | 117 |
| Tex-mex Fish Tacos | 61 |
| Tex-mex Potatoes With Avocado Dressing | 92 |
| Thai Chicken Drumsticks | 52 |
| Thanksgiving Turkey Sandwiches | 20 |
| The Best Oysters Rockefeller | 66 |
| Thyme Lentil Patties | 99 |
| Thyme Meatless Patties | 98 |
| Tofu & Spinach Lasagna | 97 |
| Tonkatsu | 80 |
| Tortilla Crusted Chicken Breast | 56 |
| Tortilla Pizza Margherita | 96 |
| Traditional Moo Shu Pork Lettuce Wraps | 80 |
| Tri-color Frittata | 42 |
| Tuna Nuggets In Hoisin Sauce | 72 |
| Tuna Patties With Dill Sauce | 63 |
| Two-cheese Grilled Sandwiches | 96 |

## V

| Recipe | Page |
|---|---|
| Vegetable Couscous | 92 |
| Vegetarian Eggplant "pizzas" | 102 |
| Vegetarian Quinoa Cups | 41 |
| Veggie Fritters | 105 |
| Vietnamese Gingered Tofu | 102 |
| Viking Toast | 41 |

## W

| Recipe | Page |
|---|---|
| Walnut Pancake | 37 |
| White Chocolate Cranberry Blondies | 11 |
| White Wheat Walnut Bread | 39 |

## Y

| Recipe | Page |
|---|---|
| Yummy Maple-mustard Chicken Kabobs | 45 |
| Yummy Salmon Burgers With Salsa Rosa | 65 |

Printed in Great Britain
by Amazon